MINORITY INFLUENCE

Nelson-Hall Series in Psychology
Stephen Worchel, *Consulting Editor*

MINORITY INFLUENCE

Edited by

SERGE MOSCOVICI
Ecole des Hautes Etudes en Sciences Sociales, Paris

ANGELICA MUCCHI-FAINA
University of Perugia

ANNE MAASS
University of Padova

NELSON-HALL PUBLISHERS/CHICAGO

Library of Congress Cataloging-in-Publication Data

Minority influence / edited by Serge Moscovici, Angelica Mucchi-Faina.
  Anne Maass.
       p.   cm.
  Includes bibliographical references and index.
  ISBN 0-8304-1281-6
  1. Social conflict.   2. Minorities—Psychology.   3. Influence (Psychology)
  4. Social interaction.   5. Power (Social sciences)
  I. Moscovici, Serge.   II. Mucchi Faina, Angelica.   III. Maass, Anne.
  HM136.M56   1994   94–15802
                                                                              CIP

Manufactured in the United States of America

10   9   8   7   6   5   4   3   2   1

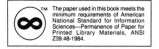

The paper used in this book meets the minimum requirements of American National Standard for Information Sciences—Permanence of Paper for Printed Library Materials, ANSI Z39.48-1984.

CONTENTS

INTRODUCTION

Research on social influence in its most recent and active forms should be considered as a converging of different interests and methods. The new developments stem from the endeavor of distinguishing between conformity and innovation, between the influence of established majorities and the influence of active dissenting minorities. There can be no doubt that over the whole range of research illustrated by the wonderful and popular book *The Social Animal* being social is equalled with conforming more or less to group pressures and norms. Those who stand aside are termed deviant, and therefore, asocial. Here is the root of the difficulty for those who are in the minority, whatever you call them. At the outset, judging by their status or by their lack of credibility, they do not seem to have many possibilities of exerting in their turn an influence on the values and ideas of the majority, in other words, of altering the composition of the group and the representation of what is social and what is not. Yet the reverse has often been seen to happen in religious or political movements, fashion, science, and culture in general. To stress the point sharply, most innovations are proposed and propagated by small groups which have to adapt them to and share them with large numbers of people. This is an exceptionally complex process to analyze whether from the social or psychological points of view. But the problem posed by Gibbon—how can a handful of weak, dispersed Christians have converted the Roman empire?—is posed again and again on a large scale in everyday life.

It was to approach this problem at least from a social-psychological perspective that research on minority influence started. It can be traced back to the late sixties when Moscovici and his collaborators presented their seminal work on the persuasive power of active minorities to a social-psychological audience accustomed to envisage the majority as the only reasonable agent of social influence. Since then, the field has undergone a number of important changes. Initially, the provocative idea that minorities can—under specified conditions—exert influence despite their powerless position was met with enthusiasm by few and with suspicion or lack of interest by many researchers. Indeed, minority influence research had maintained its minority position outside of mainstream social psychology for a long time. Publications appeared, for the most part, in Europe, whereas articles in mainstream American journals were extremely rare. With few notable exceptions (especially Charlan Nemeth and, later on, Russell Clark III) interest in minority influence among American colleagues was virtually nonexistent and even among European colleagues limited to few laboratories. Still during the seventies, textbooks in social psychology dedicated very little, if any, space to minority influence theory.

During the last decade, this tendency has clearly reversed—as illustrated, among others, by this volume. An increasing number of American social psychologists have become interested in this area of research and have made important contributions. Regular workshops on minority influence research, for the most part sponsored by the European Association of Experimental Social Psychology (held in Geneva 1985, in Perugia 1989, and in Valencia 1990), have seen a steadily increasing number of American participants and publications in American journals on this topic have clearly increased over the last decade. At the same time, minority influence— originally limited to few laboratories—has become a topic of investigation in a wide range of European universities, and textbooks cover minority influence just as any other area of psychological inquiry. In other words, the area has gained recognition on both sides of the Atlantic ocean. This volume is, indeed, the first collection of minority influence research in which there is an almost perfect balance between the two continents with half of the chapters being written by American authors and the other half representing a broad range of European countries (France, Switzerland, Italy, Spain, and Germany).

Hand in hand with the increasing interest in and recognition of minority influence, a diversification occurred both in terms of theory and research paradigms. Whereas earlier research was mostly concerned with demonstrating the persuasive power of minorities and with testing the predictions of Moscovici's (1976, 1980) theory, research and theorizing on minority influence have recently been extended in various directions either by theoretical refinement or by investigating the interplay with neighboring theories. On the one hand, recent minority influence research has stressed new aspects of the minority's persuasive power that had either not been recognized or had played a secondary role in earlier studies. The most notable example of such theoretical refinement is Nemeth's (1986) model focusing on the minority's capacity to induce divergent thinking (see Nemeth's contribution to this volume, Chapter 1). On the other hand, increasing research effort has been dedicated to investigating intersections with neighboring fields and to integrating minority influence theory with related theories such as social identity theory (see studies on ingroup-outgroup categorization by Clark and Maass, 1988a, 1988b; Martin, 1988a, 1988b, 1988c; Mugny, Perez, Kaiser, and Papastamou, 1984; Perez and Mugny, 1985, 1987), social comparison theory (see Gorenflo and Crano, 1989), and group polarization (Clark, 1988). The present volume includes two examples of such theoretical integrations, one by Crano investigating the interplay between minority influence and social comparison, the other by Clark investigating the intersection between minority influence and group polarization. Both these chapters illustrate the value of such integrative efforts suggesting that the investigation of the interplay of minority influence with neighboring theories constitutes, indeed, a very promising route.

At the same time, minority influence researchers have started to investigate systematically the conditions under which minorities will or will not be influential, thereby delimitating with greater precision the applicability of minority influence theory. It is worthwhile noting that, contrary to many other fields of research, the identification of such delimitations in this case are by no means a function of failures to obtain the predicted minority influence effects but rather are the result of precise theoretical considerations. For example, Worchel is arguing convincingly in his contribution to this volume (see Chapter 5) that the influence process has to be conceptualized as embedded in a larger group context. Since groups are evolving over time, the chances of a minority to be influential will vary according to the current stage of the group's development. Along the same line, Mucchi-Faina (Chapter 6), Maass and Volpato (Chapter 7), and Trost and Kenrick (Chapter 8) argue that minorities will produce very different, and at times, opposing effects depending on the conditions under which the influence attempt takes place.

Not surprisingly, this theoretical diversification of the past decade was accompanied by a diversification and refinement of experimental paradigms and measurement. Outcome measures had to be increasingly sensitive to different facets of minority influence including hidden, indirect, and at times even unconscious changes and variations in thought processes (e.g., divergent vs. convergent thinking). Consequently, experimental paradigms and measures were developed that were increasingly able to tap the multiple subtle effects of minority influence. Two excellent examples of such techniques are included in this book. The first is the spectrometer method that had proven to be a useful tool of minority influence research since the very beginning of the field and that had subsequently undergone a number of refinements. The chapter by Personnaz and Personnaz (Chapter 9) provides the first complete overview of studies using this paradigm and discusses the rationale and the advantages of this procedure. The other example is a creative technique that has recently been developed by Perez, Mugny, and their collaborators (see Brandstaetter et al., 1991; Butera, Kaiser, and Roux, Chapter 10) in which latent and indirect changes are assessed in such a subtle way that subjects are almost certainly unaware of what is being measured. Finally, Petrillo (Chapter 11) underlines the heuristic value of investigating the influence of real–life minorities through historical methods, content analyses, etc., and encourages the use of field studies as an important, complementary technique to traditional experiments.

Organization of This Volume

Contributions to this volume are grouped into three sections, representing theoretical developments, identification of delimitations, and methodological issues. The first section is dedicated to theoretical developments that represent either refinements of the original theory (Nemeth, see Chapter 1), integrations with neighboring theories (Crano, Chapter 2; and Clark, Chapter 3), or mathematical models (Witte, Chapter 4).

Nemeth's chapter offers a creative extension of minority influence theory by moving away from a narrow definition of influence as "prevailing" towards a definition that includes how minority dissent affects the ways in which we think about an issue. A series of studies are presented which provide compelling evidence for the minority's ability to stimulate better recall of information, divergent strategies for problem solving, greater originality, and the detection of correct solutions that otherwise would have gone undetected. These findings are then applied to a broader range of settings including contributions made by minority dissent in groups, organizations, and societies with the resulting argument of why we should "welcome and not fear the voices of dissent."

The chapter by Crano analyzes the role of social comparison processes in minority influence and provides an integrative model, called the "context/ comparison model." Crano argues that social comparison processes are fundamental in social influence and that the reliance on minority or majority sources as potential comparison partners will depend on task characteristics. In particular, when tasks are perceived as objective people are hypothesized to be more susceptible to dissimilar others (e.g., outgroup sources) whereas the opposite is predicted for tasks perceived to be subjective. Here ingroup sources provide a better source of social comparison and, consequently, will be more influential than outgroup sources. The results of different studies reported in this chapter are clearly supportive of the "context/comparison model" and suggest that our understanding of minority and majority influence may profit greatly by a careful investigation of social comparison g_eprocesses involved. More generally, this chapter suggests that related theories and their interplay with minority influence may constitute a rich source for future development.

A similar pattern emerges from Clark's chapter relating minority influence to group polarization. Although these fields have developed at different times and perfectly independently of each other, there are some striking parallels between minority influence and group polarization, suggesting that in both cases opinion shifts depend, in part, upon the population's initial inclination on a given issue. More importantly, Clark argues that the processes underlying group polarization (namely, persuasive arguments and social comparison processes) may play an important (though not exhaustive) role in minority influence as well. Thus, although the two areas are idiosyncratic in many ways, they also share some important psychological processes. Clark's chapter suggests that greater attention to the link between these two areas of inquiry and to their commonalities may, indeed, advance our knowledge of both social influence phenomena.

In contrast to the previous chapters, Witte's chapter is embedded in the tradition of mathematical models describing psychological phenomena. Closely following the example of previous models (Latané and Wolf, 1981; Tanford and Penrod, 1984; Witte, 1987), this author presents an extended formal model of social influence in which new parameters are included in order to account for research findings derived from both sociological and psychological research (such as the "Zeitgeist effect," the cohesion effect) that cannot easily be accounted for by previous models.

The second group of contributions are those that identify delimitations of minority influence and that define the conditions that facilitate or impede a wide variety of minority effects. The first chapter of the section is Worchel's (Chapter 5) in which he argues that the persuasive power of minorities can only be understood within the larger context of group development. The basic assumption is that groups evolve over time in a predictable manner and that the potential impact of the minority will depend, to a large extent, on the current stage of group development. Worchel provides compelling experimental evidence that minorities are, indeed, considerably more influential in later stages of group development but are likely to be rejected at earlier stages when group identification and cohesion are essential to the group's survival. Beyond the specific findings, this chapter makes the provocative point that the time has come to look at social influence in a more dynamic way and to extend the time frame under which influence phenomena are studied beyond the specific influence setting.

The following three chapters are all concerned with distinguishing and predicting the different types of influence a minority is able to exert. During the last decade, minority influence research has identified a wide variety of changes a minority is able to induce in the influence target, varying not only in the extent to which they are public vs. private, direct vs. indirect, but also as to what is being changed (attitudes, thought processes) and in which direction these changes occur (toward the minority position, away from the minority position, or independent of or orthogonal to the minority position).

Mucchi-Faina (Chapter 6) investigates the diverse types of influence a minority is able to exert either through a process of assimilation (conversion or modeling) or through a process of differentiation from the influence source (boomerang effects, divergence, or opinion shifts). For each of these reactions, Mucchi-Faina identifies the respective facilitating or impeding conditions and discusses those explanations that appear most promising in face of the existing empirical evidence to date. Most importantly, Mucchi-Faina proposes an integrative model in which the different reactions to a minority's influence attempt are conceptualized as the interactive function of affective (feeling) and cognitive elements (different modalities of information processing).

Maass and Volpato's contribution (Chapter 7) follows a similar route by asking when people's opinions will converge toward the minority and when their thoughts will diverge, leading to the discovery of new solutions that are not those proposed by the minority but that would have gone undetected without the influence of the minority. In other words, this chapter tries to identify the conditions under which conversion is likely to occur (see Moscovici's theory) and those under which divergence is likely to occur (see Nemeth's theory). The results of the research program reported here suggest that the minority is most likely to induce divergent thought processes in settings that foster creativity when personal relevance is high and in people who enjoy effortful cognitive endeavors, suggesting that Moscovici's and Nemeth's versions of minority influence theory have specific realms of applicability.

Trost and Kenrick (Chapter 8) investigate in detail the striking effects of ego-involvement and personal relevance on people's reactions to minorities. Whereas past minority influence research was almost exclusively concerned with issues of limited personal relevance to the subjects, Trost and Kenrick analyze the persuasive power of minorities on highly involving issues. With reference to research on persuasion and attitude change, these authors argue that the personal relevance of the issue under consideration will not only enhance the motivation to engage in effortful cognitive processing but will also bias thought production so that people generate more unfavorable and fewer favorable thoughts about a counter-attitudinal minority message. Their findings do, in fact, provide strong evidence that the impact of a minority on a recipient's private attitudes reverses when the issue is of high personal relevance resulting in rejection rather that acceptance of the minority position. These findings are not only interesting from an applied point of view but also suggest that ego-involvement may be a critical determinant of minority influence and, as such, ought to be incorporated into minority influence theory.

The last group of studies is concerned with methodological issues and offers, in part, innovative and sophisticated strategies for how to assess the multiple facets of minority influence. Personnaz and Personnaz (Chapter 9) present a very subtle measure of indirect and even unconscious changes in perception attributable to the presence of a minority, namely, the spectrometer method. These authors have utilized (and refined) this sophisticated technique over the years. In the current chapter, they explain the rationale and the potential of this paradigm and provide the first general review of studies using the spectrometer method.

Perez et al.'s contribution (Chapter 10) draws a theoretical distinction between consensus and uniformity and introduces highly sophisticated methods (in particular the ''cheese'' perceptual paradigm) able to identify the critical factors (norms, stimulus type, etc.) that favor one or the other influence modes. Beyond its methodological contribution, this chapter illustrates the complementary relation that exists between minority and majority influence, both of which are able to induce conversion but under different circumstances and following a different psycho-social dynamic.

In the last chapter addressing methodological issues, Petrillo (Chapter 11) argues in favor of field studies which continue to be surprisingly rare in minority influence research. On one side, this chapter presents a number of arguments supporting the importance of field studies as a complementary means of theory testing as well as hypothesis generation. On the other side, this contribution provides the first summary of field studies related to minority influence theory. The conclusions of this chapter are encouraging in two ways: Not only do many of the historical observations on real-life minorities converge with laboratory findings, but they often go beyond experimental research by suggesting a dynamic group process that evolves over time and is, in part, quite consistent with Worchel's model of group development.

Taken together, these chapters provide a rich and, we believe, largely representative overview of the major developments that have occurred in the area of minority influence in the past decade and that have helped to overcome its initial status as a provocative but not entirely respectable form of social science. Beyond illustrating the current state of the art, many contributions of this volume also contain more or less explicit suggestions for a wide range of future developments which, we hope, will be able to advance this lively field of research both methodologically and conceptually.

PART ONE
Theoretical Advancement

CHAPTER ONE

THE VALUE OF MINORITY DISSENT

Charlan Jeanne Nemeth

"...learn to welcome and not to fear the voices of dissent"—Sen. J. Fulbright (1964)

In this book on minority influence, we have the opportunity to reflect on the influence exerted by this "minority" research area. Prior to the late 1960s, the study of influence in social psychology was dominated by considerations of conformity and independence. In part due to the influential work of Asch (1956) and his imaginative paradigms, scores of studies investigated why individuals (or a minority of individuals) agreed with the majority view even when that view was in error (see Allen, 1965). The ability to resist such influence pressure and to state one's own authentic (and correct) views was an important research topic, one which we termed independence. However, we rarely studied the effects of that independence— the impact of that independently differing view on the majority's judgments.

In the late 1960s, Faucheux and Moscovici (1967) and Moscovici, Lage, and Naffrechoux (1969) demonstrated that impact. In the latter study, when a minority of two individuals in a group of six consistently judged blue stimuli to be "green," nearly 9 percent of the majority's responses were also "green." In addition, most individuals changed their categorization of "blue-green" stimuli such that the more "blue" stimuli were categorized as "green." Here, we had a situation in which the minority of individuals did not simply say "yes" or "no" to a system of answers; they repeatedly maintained an opposing view and had significant influence on the majority's judgments.

Our Impact

Over the past twenty years, we have seen the impact of these studies and the theories that have ensued (Moscovici and Faucheux, 1972; Moscovici and Nemeth, 1974; Moscovici, 1976; Mugny, 1982). We have seen how the minority, though underestimated and even derided, can influence the majority. Scores of studies have been stimulated by that work (see Maass and Clark, 1984). Further, the field that once was dominated by considerations of influence as that stemming from the majority or from those holding high status or power has now come to appreciate the impact of those low in power, status, or numbers (see Chaiken and Stangor, 1987; Levine and Russo, 1987).

To further illustrate this point, a cursory look at the indexes of several prominent social psychology textbooks reveals a significant change in the way the topic of influence is treated. Texts by those of us in the field of minority influence have understandably given considerable treatment to the topics of "minority" or "minority influence." My own textbook (Nemeth, 1974) devoted a full thirty-two-page chapter to the topic (Moscovici and Nemeth, 1974). Moscovici's text (Moscovici, 1984, 1988) devoted thirty-eight pages specifically to minority influence (Doms and Moscovici, 1988) and drew on that work in three other chapters (Paicheler and Moscovici, 1988; Abric, 1988; Nemeth, 1988).

Perhaps more significant, textbooks by researchers in other fields have come to include the topics of "minority" and "minority influence." The Wrightsman (and subsequently Deaux and Wrightsman) text had no entry for the topic of minority influence in the first edition (1972). In the 1984 edition, there were two pages and in 1988 there were four pages on it. David Myer's textbook devoted four pages in 1987 and eleven pages in 1990 to this topic. Hewstone et al.'s text devoted sixteen pages to the topic. And there is currently in press a special issue of the *British Journal of Social Psychology* devoted entirely to minority influence (Nemeth, 1994). Thus, the influence of this work has been obvious and, increasingly, researchers in the traditional areas of attitude change and persuasion have come to utilize this research in their own work.

A Change in Perspective

Part of the reason for such interest is that the work on minority influence has forced us to look more broadly at how "sources" persuade and how "targets" of persuasion form and change attitudes. For example, the work on minority influence has questioned the emphasis on liking and status as the vehicles of influence. Many theories had concentrated on the power of credibility (Hovland et al., 1953) and its components, for example, attractiveness, similarity, and expertise (Petty and Cacioppo, 1981) or on "techniques" such as flattery or ingratiation (Carnegie, 1952; Jones, 1964; Jones and Wortman, 1973). The work on minority influence did not emphasize liking or expertise. We repeatedly found that minorities were believed to be in error and they were disliked; they were especially disliked when they maintained their position (Nemeth and Wachtler, 1983; Nemeth and Brilmayer, 1987). Yet, such consistency and its attendant dislike not only did not lessen the minority's influence but it was found to be essential for persuading others to the minority position (Moscovici et al., 1969; Nemeth et al., 1974). Further, compromise and the liking engendered by such compromise was found to be ineffective for private change to the minority position (Nemeth and Brilmayer, 1987).

Other studies on minority influence forced us to look at the multiple ways in which influence can be exerted. In particular, this research pointed to the important distinction between public/direct change and private/latent influence. Many studies show little or no public movement to the minority position. However, private judgments, judgments on indirect measures or on related issues (Maass and Clark, 1984; Mugny, 1982; Nemeth and Wachtler, 1983) have been significantly influenced by the minority. To illustrate, Perez and Mugny (1986), found that Ss may not have moved toward the minority's position on the issue of abortion but showed significant influence on the related issue of birth control.

An Extended Definition of Influence

Still another manifestation of influence is a change in the way the "targets" of influence think about the issue in response to persuasion attempts. This has been the focus of my own work over the past fifteen years and was stimulated by the recognition, very early in this research area, that minority influence was much broader (and deeper) than direct movement to the proposed position. As stated previously, we sometimes found no direct movement to the minority position and yet, we found substantial private movement to that position. Furthermore, we noticed that even when majority individuals resisted the minority position, they often spoke about the issue differently (Nemeth and Wachtler, 1974).

These observations took on additional meaning during the early and mid-1970s when I, and a number of other researchers, (Davis et al., 1975; Nemeth, 1977; Saks, 1977) investigated the issues raised by Supreme Court decisions permitting a reduction in size of the jury (Johnson v. Louisiana, 1970) and non-unanimity of their verdicts (Apodaca et al. v. Oregon, 1970). While much of our focus was on "verdicts" (i.e., who "prevailed") it

5

became clear that this did not address the central issue confronting us—that is, how do we improve the quality of decision making? How do we increase the likelihood that all the facts will be taken into account, that alternative explanations of those facts will be considered and debated, that there will be robust conflict as the jurors attempt to "piece together the puzzle of historical truth" (see generally Nemeth, 1977; 1981).

It was this interest on the detection of "truth" that led to a focus on the *process* of decision making and the role of influence, especially minority influence, in that process. For example, we found that the requirement of unanimity fostered "robust conflict" rather than "polite and academic conversation" and resulted in perceptions that justice had been served. Furthermore, these processes were especially evident in groups where minority voices persisted, where the number of their comments was approximately the same as the number of comments expressed by the majority, where the minority maintained its position, especially in the categories of giving information and giving opinions (Nemeth, 1977).

The Movement to "Divergent Thought"

The work on jury decision making and its emphasis on process—coupled with observations over years of research on how minorities swayed discussion and judgments—led to what was initially a "hunch." We considered that minority dissent, even when it did not influence movement to its position, might stimulate cognitive activity such that the "detection of truth" might be served.

Part of this "hunch" came from a review of the available literature on how majorities and minorities exercise influence. Several differences were noted. People exposed to a disagreeing majority experience much more stress than those exposed to a disagreeing minority. People start with the assumption that the majority is correct and that the minority is incorrect; they assume that "truth" lies in numbers. Furthermore, they are motivated to assume that. Believing that the majority is correct permits movement to that position (or maintenance of a majority position) and with it the resulting sense of acceptance and the avoidance of the dislike that is engendered by holding a minority position.

Another part of this "hunch" came from the experimental evidence showing an inverted U-shaped relationship between stress and performance (Yerkes and Dodson, 1908). Thus, we hypothesized that a small amount of stress (perhaps that caused by a disagreeing minority) could stimulate cognitive activity and motivation and result in improved performance. A great deal of stress (perhaps that caused by a disagreeing majority) could lead to increased cognitive activity and motivation but would result in a

Figure 1.1: Sample stimulus used in Nemeth and Wachtler (1983), Creative problem solving as a result of majority versus minority influence, *European Journal of Social Psychology,* 13: 45–55.

Standard   Comparison

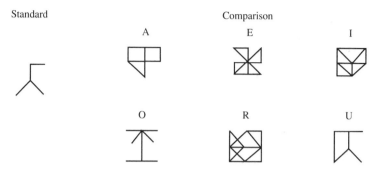

narrow focus of attention (Easterbrook, 1959) and poorer performance. Furthermore, we predicted where this focus might be. Given the motivated assumption to believe that the majority was correct, this focus engendered by the majority might be a very specific one; Ss might view the issue from the position posed by the majority.

The initial study (Nemeth, 1976; Nemeth and Wachtler, 1983) had Ss in groups of six view a standard figure and six comparison figures. They were asked to name all the comparison figures that contained the standard. One was easy to detect; the other five were difficult. Under instructions to be correct, Ss tended to name only the one that was "easy" (e.g., "U" in figure 1.1). Depending on the experimental condition, either four individuals (the majority "source" condition) or two individuals (the minority "source" condition) noticed the figure embedded in two comparison figures (e.g., "E and U" in figure 1.1). Again, depending on the condition, this judgment of "E" was either correct or incorrect. In our example, "E" is correct; it could be made to be incorrect by removing one line.

The results demonstrated the differential effects of majorities and minorities. With regard to the usual definition of "direct influence," which would involve the following of the source's judgment, majorities exercised more direct influence than minorities. Using the example, Ss were more likely to say "E and U" if a majority expressed that judgment than if a minority expressed it. However, the minority source exerted a different kind of influence. Subjects exposed to the minority judgment of "E and U" were likely to detect the standard figure in "novel" comparison figures; that is, those not suggested by the minority. Furthermore, they were correct. To illustrate, the novel comparison figures in figure 1.1 are A, I, O, and R. Subjects exposed to a minority view that "E and U" contained the standard detected it in "I and R" which are correct. They tended not to "guess" that it was contained in "A and O" which are incorrect. Furthermore, these findings held regardless of the correctness of the "source."

The results of this first study were consistent with the hypothesis that Ss exposed to a majority view tend to follow that view. By contrast, Ss exposed to the minority view did not tend to follow the minority view; however, they were able to detect novel correct solutions. We speculated that Ss exposed to the minority view were stimulated to look at the issue from multiple perspectives, one of which was that posed by the minority. They scrutinized all the comparison figures. In the process, they were able to detect truths that otherwise would have gone undetected.

This speculation was tested in a study which was designed to track "process," the ways in which people solved the problem, in order to test the hypothesis that minority views stimulate divergent thought (multiple perspectives) while majority views stimulate convergent thought from the perspective they pose (Nemeth and Kwan, 1987).

In this study, Ss in groups of four were shown a letter string (e.g., tNOWap) and were asked to name the first three letter word they noticed. Under brief exposures, Ss said "NOW," the word formed by capital letters in forward sequencing. After three such slides, they were given feedback such that one person (minority condition) or three persons (majority condition) noticed the word formed by the backward sequencing of these capital letters. Thus, feedback in the minority condition might be "won, now, now, now" whereas, in the majority condition, it would be "won, won, won, now."

After such feedback, Ss were shown a series of ten slides, each composed of a letter string. They were given fifteen seconds for each slide to write down all the words they could form from that set of letters. The results showed that Ss exposed to the minority view found more words than did those exposed to the majority view or those exposed to no dissent (the control group). The latter two conditions did not differ significantly.

To analyze the thought processes culminating in this performance, it is important to recognize that people can form their words using a forward sequencing of the letters (e.g., tow, no, nap), a backward sequencing (e.g., ant, on, pan), or a mixed sequencing (e.g., not, ton, wan). The results showed that Ss in the majority condition found more words using a backward sequencing than did control Ss but this appeared to be at the expense of finding words using the forward or mixed sequencing. Thus their performance was comparable to the control. By contrast, Ss in the minority condition utilized all three strategies in the service of significantly better performance.

The preceding study lent credence to the assumption that majorities stimulated convergent thought from the perspective they posed. Subjects exposed to the majority view that focussed on backward sequencing utilized that strategy significantly more often; however, this was at the expense of other strategies. Subjects exposed to a minority view that focussed on backward sequencing utilized all available strategies, one of which was the perspective held by the minority. As a result, they showed significantly better performance than either Ss exposed to the majority view or those exposed to no dissent (control Ss).

Still another study demonstrated the enhanced quality of cognitive processes as a result of exposure to minority views (Nemeth, Mayseless, Sherman, and Brown, 1990). Subjects in groups of four heard a tape recorded list of fourteen words consisting of four words from the category of "fruits" and two words each from the categories of "birds," "clothing," "transportation," "tools," and "furniture." In addition, the four "fruit" words were the first two and the last two words in the list. One such list was: "apple, peas, shoes, pliers, couch, hawk, bike, coat, lamp, hammer, dove, car, grapes, cherry."

Subjects were asked to name the first category of word they noticed. Due to primacy, recency and frequency, Ss wrote down "fruits." After three such lists, Ss were given feedback. They were told that one person (minority condition) or three persons (majority condition) first noticed "birds." Thus, the feedback would be "birds, fruits, fruits, fruits" or "birds, birds, birds, fruits" in the minority and majority conditions, respectively. This feedback was given for list one only or for all three lists.

After such feedback, Ss heard a tape recorded list of forty-two words. These were the same words heard on the three lists of fourteen words but were now presented in random order. Subjects were asked to write down all the words they could remember. When feedback was given for one list only, no differences were observed between the majority and minority conditions nor between these experimental conditions and a control. When feedback was given consistently over the three trials, however, there were significant differences. Subjects exposed to the minority view of "birds" recalled significantly more words than did Ss in the control condition and the latter recalled significantly more words than Ss exposed to the majority view of "birds." Thus, when feedback was consistent over three trials, the minority view stimulated significantly better recall and the majority view stimulated significantly poorer recall than evidenced by control Ss.

Some interesting differences emerged with a second dependent variable as well. After hearing the list of forty-two words (which were the same as those on which disagreement was based), Ss listened to a totally new list of thirty words. These words represented new categories as well (e.g., gems, occupations). The results showed, again, that Ss in the minority condition recalled significantly more words. On this second dependent variable, however, it was a main effect. Whether the feedback was once or three times, the minority view stimulated significantly better recall than the majority view.

Moving to Creativity

The stimulation of better recall, multiple strategies in the service of performance, and the detection of correct novel solutions all argue for the positive contributions of exposure to minority views. However, the stimulation of divergent thought raises another possibility as well. This possibility is that influence processes and, in particular, minority dissent, might stimulate creativity.

To test the possibility that minority views would stimulate originality of thought while majority views might stimulate conventionality of thought, we (Nemeth and Kwan, 1985) exposed individuals to a confederate who consistently judged blue stimuli to be "green." In the majority condition, Ss were informed that this constituted a "majority judgment." They were shown evidence that approximately 80% of individuals judged these stimuli to be "green" while 20 percent judged them to be "blue." In the minority condition, they were informed that this was a "minority" judgment, namely that approximately 80 percent of people judged them to be "green" while 20 percent judged them as "blue."

After this session, individuals were asked to give word associations to the words "blue" and "green." Each individual gave seven associations to each word. Using the "norms" developed by J. J. Jenkins (Postman and Keppel, 1970) for associations to different words, we were able to score our S's associations in terms of their conventionality or originality, that is, in terms of the statistical likelihood of these associations. To illustrate, a common association to "blue" might be "green" or "sky." An "original" or statistically infrequent association might be "jeans" or "jazz."

Our data show that Ss exposed to the "minority" dissent gave more original (uncommon) associations to "blue" and to "green" than did Ss in

Table 1.1*

	Majority	Minority	Control
Uniqueness of first association	9.97$_a$	8.98$_a$	11.66$_a$
Uniqueness of associations 2–7	6.35$_a$	2.97$_b$	4.26$_c$
Uniqueness of 1–7	7.15$_a$	3.85$_b$	6.00$_a$

*Subscripts in common indicate that the means are not different at the .07 level.

Source: Adapted from Nemeth, C. and J. Kwan$_i$ (1985), Originality of word associations as a function of majority vs. minority influence, *Social Psychology Quarterly*, 48, 277–82.

the majority condition or the control. Furthermore, there is some evidence that Ss exposed to the "majority" dissent thought in even more conventional terms than control Ss. While the differences between the majority condition and the control condition are not significant over all seven associations, there is a significant difference if you remove the first association, which tends to be highly conventional. Then, Ss in the majority condition had significantly more conventional associations than even the control Ss.

Some General Conclusions and Exaggerated Applications

This line of work has proven to be very gratifying for us. From an intellectual standpoint, the work on minority influence has stimulated us as researchers to reconsider old truisms—for example, the relationship between status and influence or between liking and influence. It has caused us to recognize that strength can lie in being underestimated. It has forced us to consider influence in broader and more subtle terms. Thus, influence may be manifested by thinking about the issue in different ways. It is not only when the source "prevails," that is, when the target succumbs to the position espoused by the source, that influence has been exerted.

In addition, we find that minority dissent appears to provide practical benefits. Our research shows that exposure to minority dissent stimulates us to take in more information, to think about that information in more divergent ways, to perform better, to think more creatively, and to detect correct solutions that otherwise would have gone undetected. Thus, it provides positive contributions to the quality of performance and, by implication, decision making.

We have long recognized that minority views provide some benefits. For example, the minority view may be true or hold a partial truth. Our research, however, shows that the positive contributions made by minority dissent do not depend on the truth or falsity of the espoused position. Whether correct or incorrect, they stimulated the detection of correct solutions (Nemeth and Wachtler, 1983). We have also recognized the usefulness of minority dissent for thwarting the "strain toward uniformity" that has characterized many poor decisions (Janis, 1982). In documenting the defective decision making that is caused by "concurrence seeking," Janis has recommended mechanisms to permit the expression of differing views (e.g., the leader refraining from voicing his or her own position) or to foster dissent (e.g., designating an individual as a "devil's advocate"). Such mechanisms are aimed at thwarting the rush to judgment characterized by concurrence seeking and the assumption of unanimity.

The present research argues, however, that minority views do more than retard the negative consequences of concurrence seeking. They actually stimulate the individual to think—and, importantly, to think in more divergent ways than he or she would do if alone. The consequence of this increased divergent cognitive activity is that performance and the detection of correct solutions is facilitated. Furthermore, there is evidence from the recent ingenious work of the Italian social psychologists (see Volpato et al., 1990; Mucchi-Faina et al., 1991) that these findings will translate to the realm of attitude change.

As one considers the larger societal issues raised by this line of work, we must first remember that people are unable or unwilling to recognize the contributions made by minority dissent. The minority is initially ridiculed and derided and influence rarely takes the form of moving to their position; rather, it is characterized by a change in the ways one thinks about the issue. In addition, people often view minority dissent as an obstacle to moving forward. Dissent fosters conflict. Minority views create stress, anger, and irritation, feelings that people are motivated to reduce. Thus, it is understandable that people would tend to underestimate the contribution made by persistent minority views and, in fact, fear their message. Yet, minority views do appear to aid problem solving and decision-making processes mainly by stimulating divergent thought about the issue. Perhaps as we learn to value the contributions made by some forms of conflict and, in particular, by the open airing and confrontation of authentically differing views, we will learn to heed Fulbright's (1964) advice about welcoming and not fearing the voices of dissent and where we "dare to think about unthinkable things because when things become unthinkable, thinking stops and action becomes mindless."

References

Abric, J-C. (1988). La creativite des groupes. In S. Moscovici (Ed.), *Psychologie sociale*. Paris: Presses Universitaires de France.

Allen, V. L. (1965). Situational factors in conformity. In L. Berkowitz (Ed.), *Advances in Experimental Social Psychology*, pp. 133–175. New York: Academic Press.

Apodaca, Cooper, and Madden v. Oregon, 92 U.S. 1928, 1972.

Asch, S. E. (1956). Studies on independence and conformity: A minority of one against a unanimous majority. *Psychological Monographs, 70* (416).

Carnegie, D. (1952). *How to Win Friends and Influence People*. New York: Simon and Schuster.

Chaiken S., and Stangor, C. (1987). Attitudes and attitude change. *Annual Review of Psychology,* 38, 575–630.

Davis, J. H., Kerr, N. L., Atkin, R. S., Holt, R., and Meek, D. (1975). The decision processes of 6- and 12-person mock juries assigned unanimous and two-thirds majority rules. *Journal of Personality and Social Psychology,* 32, 1–14.

Deaux, K., and Wrightsman, X. (1984). *Social Psychology in the Eighties.* Belmont, CA: Wadsworth.

Doms, M., and Moscovici, S. (1988). Innovation et influence des minorites. In S. Moscovici (Ed.), *Psychologie Sociale.* Paris: Presses Universitaires de France.

Easterbrook, J. A. (1959). The effect of emotion on the utilization and the organization of behavior. *Psychological Review,* 66, 183–201.

Faucheux, C. and Moscovici, S. (1967). Le style du commortement d'une minorite et san influence sur les responses d'une majorité. *Bulletin du C.E.R.P.,* 16, 337–360.

Fulbright, J. (1964). Speech to the United States Senate, March 27, 1964.

Hewstone, M., Stroebe, W., Codol, J. P., and Stephenson, G. (Eds.). (1988). *Introduction to Social Psychology.* Oxford: Basil Blackwell.

Hovland, C. I., Janis, I. L., and Kelley, H. H. (1953). *Communication and persuasion: Psychological studies of opinion change.* New Haven, CT: Yale University Press.

Janis, I. L. (1982). *Groupthink.* 2nd ed. Boston: Houghton Mifflin.

Johnson *v.* Louisiana, 92 U.S. 1935, 1972.

Jones, E. E. (1964). *Ingratiation: A Social Psychological Analysis.* New York: Appleton-Century-Crofts.

Jones, E. E., and Wortman, C. (1973). *Ingratiation: An Attributional Approach.* Morristown, NJ: General Learning Press.

Levine, J. L., and Russo, E. (1987). Majority and minority influence. In C. Hendrick (Ed.), *Review of Personality and Social Psychology,* vol. 8. Beverly Hills, CA: Sage.

Maass, A., and Clark, R. D., III. (1984). The hidden impact of minorities: Fourteen years of minority influence research. *Psychological Bulletin,* 95, 428–450.

McGrath, J. (1984). *Groups: Interaction and Performance.* Englewood Cliffs, NJ: Prentice-Hall.

Moscovici, S. (1976). *Social Influence and Social Change.* London: Academic Press.

Moscovici, S. (1984). *Psychologie Sociale.* Paris: Presses Universitaires de France.

Moscovici, S. (1988). *Psychologie Sociale,* 2d ed. Paris: Presses Universitaires de France.

Moscovici, S. and Faucheux, C. (1972). Social influence conformity bias and the study of active minorities. In L. Berkowitz (Ed.), *Advances in Experimental Social Psychology,* vol. 6, pp. 150–202. New York: Academic Press.

Moscovici, S., Lage, E., and Naffrechoux, M. (1969). Influence of a consistent minority on the responses of a majority in a color perception task. *Sociometry,* 32, 365–380.

Moscovici, S., and Nemeth, C. (1974). Social influence II: Minority influence. In C. Nemeth (Ed.), *Social Psychology: Classic and Contemporary Integrations.* Chicago: Rand-McNally.

Mucchi-Faina, A., Maass, A., and Volpato, C. (1991). Social influence: The case of originality. *European Journal of Social Psychology,* 21, 183–197.

Mugny, G. (1982). *The Power of Minorities*. New York: Academic Press.

Myers, D.G. (1983). *Social Psychology*. New York: McGraw-Hill.

Myers, D.G. (1987). *Social Psychology*, 2d ed. New York: McGraw-Hill.

Nemeth, C. (1974). *Social Psychology: Classic and Contemporary Integrations*. Chicago: Rand-McNally.

Nemeth, C. (1976, July). A comparison between conformity and minority influence. Paper presented to the International Congress on Psychology, Paris, France.

Nemeth, C. (1977). Interactions between jurors as a function of majority vs. unanimity decision rules. *Journal of Applied Social Psychology,*7,38–56.

Nemeth, C. (1981). Jury trials: Psychology and law. In L. Berkowitz (Ed.), *Advances in Experimental Social Psychology*, vol. 14, pp. 309–367. New York: Academic Press.

Nemeth, C. (1986). Differential contributions of majority and minority influence. *Psychological Review,*93,23–32.

Nemeth, C., (1988). Processus de groupe et jurys: Les etats-unis et la france. In S. Moscovici (Ed.), *Psychologie Sociale*. Paris: Presses Universitaires de France.

Nemeth, C. (Ed.). (1994). "Minority Influence." Special Issue. *British Journal of Social Psychology*.

Nemeth, C., and Brilmayer, A. (1987). Negotiation vs. influence. *European Journal of Social Psychology,*17,45–56.

Nemeth, C., and Kwan, J. (1985). Originality of word associations as a function of majority vs. minority influence. *Social Psychology Quarterly,*48,277–282.

Nemeth, C., and Kwan, J. (1987). Minority influence, divergent thinking and detection of correct solutions. *Journal of Applied Social Psychology,*17,786–797.

Nemeth, C., Mayseless, O., Sherman, J., and Brown, Y. (1990). Improving recall by exposure to consistent dissent. *Journal of Personality and Social Psychology,*58,429–437.

Nemeth, C. and Staw, B. (1990). The tradeoffs of social control and innovation within groups and organizations. In L. Berkowitz (Ed.), *Advances in Experimental Social Psychology*, vol. 22, pp. 175–210. New York: Academic Press.

Nemeth, C., Swedlund, M., and Kanki, B. (1974). Patterning of the minority's responses and their influence on the majority. *European Journal of Social Psychology,*6,437–439.

Nemeth, C., and Wachtler, J. (1974). Creating perceptions of consistency and confidence: A necessary condition for minority influence. *Sociometry,*37,529–540.

Nemeth, C., and Wachtler, J. (1983). Creative problem solving as a result of majority versus minority influence. *European Journal of Social Psychology,* 13,45–55.

Osborn, A.F. (1953). *Applied Imagination*. New York: Scribner's.

Paicheler, G., and Moscovici, S. (1988). Suivisme et conversion. In S. Moscovici (Ed.), *Psychologie Sociale*. Paris: Presses Universitaires de France.

Perez, J., and Mugny, G. (1986). Induction experimentale d'une influence minoritaire indirecte. *Cahiers de Psychologie Sociale*, 32, 15–24.

Petty, R. E., and Cacioppo, J. T. (1981). *Attitudes and Persuasion: Classic and Contemporary Approaches*. Dubuque, IA: C. Brown.

Postman, L., and Keppel, G. (1970). *Norms of Word Association.* New York: Academic Press.

Saks, M. J. (1977). *Jury Verdicts.* Lexington, MA: Heath.

Volpato, C, Maass, A., Mucchi-Faina, A., and Vitti, E. (1990). Minority influence and social categorization. *European Journal of Social Psychology,*20,119–132.

Wrightsman, L. S. (1972). *Social Psychology in the Seventies.* Belmont, CA: Wadsworth.

Yerkes, R. M., and Dodson, J. D. (1908). The relation of strength of stimulus to rapidity of habit formation. *Journal of Comparative Neurology of Psychology,* 18,459–482.

CHAPTER TWO

CONTEXT, COMPARISON, AND CHANGE: METHODOLOGICAL AND THEORETICAL CONTRIBUTIONS TO A THEORY OF MINORITY (AND MAJORITY) INFLUENCE

William D. Crano

The study of social influence is social psychology's most intense and long-standing preoccupation. Research on social influence typically focuses on the manner in which the majority imposes its will on a minority, and the effects of such an imposition on attitudes and behavior (cf. Brewer and Crano, 1994; Crano, 1970, 1975; Levine, 1980; Levine and Russo, 1987). Much research of this type is designed in a way that renders the influence source impervious to change pressures, while the target is placed in a position of subservience, powerlessness, and dependency. Moscovici and his colleagues have challenged the definition of social influence implicit in designs of this variety, arguing that they have had a constraining influence on the way influence is conceptualized and investigated (cf. Moscovici, 1976, 1980; Moscovici and Mugny, 1987). It is clear, they maintain, that it is not always the majority that influences the minority. Available throughout our history are impressive examples of powerless minorities that have succeeded in converting the majority to their way of thinking. Galileo, Darwin, Christ, Freud, Marx, Einstein, all minority voices at one point, had profound effects on their worlds and ours, even though they were in no position to put pressure on anyone to listen to them.

From the standard perspective which views conformity as a response to social pressure, it is difficult to explain how these men could have had the impact they did. Is something wrong with the classical influence model? Moscovici answered this question affirmatively, and in a series of penetrating observations and studies criticized the standard approach, highlighted its empirical and logical shortcomings, and proposed a model that not only admitted to the possibility that the minority could influence the majority, but laid out the conditions under which this was most likely to occur (cf. Moscovici, 1985).

To Moscovici, the classical conformity model assumed an asymmetric relationship in which minority group members could be the targets, but never the sources of influence, and the majority could be the source, but never the influence target. The standard operating procedures of the conformity laboratory did not afford the minority the opportunity to persuade the majority of anything. As we can observe from even a cursory review of history, this is not the way the world works—at least, not always. To counter the standard orientation, Moscovici proposed a "symmetric" view, in which minority and majority groups each had the power to confront and influence one another. Further, and more controversially, he insisted that the psychological processes mobilized in response to influence differ as a function of the (majority or minority) status of the influence source, as do the behavioral outcomes that ensue as a consequence of such processes.

Majority influence, Moscovici argues, depends on social pressure. It stimulates a process of social comparison through which people ascertain where they are in relation to the "party line." The pressure of the majority is such that people change their public behavior so as to approximate the majority position without really thinking deeply about the issue at hand. The change of public behavior forestalls conflict, since the individual appears to be in harmony with the majority norm. However, this process typically does not focus attention on the implications of the counter-attitudinal arguments, and as such, seldom results in lasting belief change. Although people outwardly comply with the majority's demands, their original beliefs are not brought into competition with the majority-inspired alternatives. Thus, when (majority) group pressure or surveillance is relaxed, behavior and expressed attitudes return to their original position.

Minorities cannot bring the same kinds of pressure to bear to promote their stance. Indeed, minorities often are outwardly rejected, for to be seen as agreeing with a stigmatized minority is not a pleasant prospect. As Mugny et al. (1984) found, agreement in some cases implies an identification with the minority, a state of affiliation that most would rather avoid. This is not to suggest that minorities cannot cause change. By its very existence, a minority transgresses group norms, thereby suggesting alternative ways of thinking. In consequence, Moscovici argues, the minority causes cognitive conflict merely by making its position known. This conflict, in turn, can provoke people to reexamine their beliefs and actions (cf. Nemeth, 1986; Nemeth and Kwan, 1987; Nemeth et al., 1990), and such reexamination may result in attitude and behavior change. Generally, the change is not immediate; some cognitive work must occur before the minority's message is accepted. When the threat of identification with the minority is removed, its position may be adopted precisely because of this processing, and the minority may thus come to exert a lasting influence on attitudes and behaviors.

The present chapter is concerned with the validity of these propositions, and with alternative possibilities inspired by a critical reexamination of prior research. The central questions issuing from this critique are the central questions with which the field as a whole must contend: Can a minority exert influence on the majority? Are the processes by which minorities and the majority exert influence the same, or fundamentally different? Can minority influence be reinterpreted in terms of differences in the (in-group and out-group) social categorization of source and target? And, in light of the lack of consensus evident in the literature: Are there contextual features that moderate minority or majority (or in-group/out-group) influence? In attempting to resolve these questions, in this chapter I will reflect upon some of the central theoretical and methodological issues that currently cloud the picture. Solution of these problems will have beneficial implications for future progress, and will contribute to the development of the alternative theoretical model to be proposed. In short, this chapter hopes to make not only a substantive, theoretical contribution, but a methodological one as well.

The Dual Process Hypothesis

Are different cognitive processes brought on line as a consequence of the majority or minority status of a source of influence? The answer to this question is as controversial as it is important. One side of the issue are the proponents of the dual process position (e.g., Clark and Maass, 1988; Maass and Clark, 1984; Maass et al., 1987; Moscovici, 1974, 1976, 1980, 1985; Moscovici, Lage, and Naffrechoux, 1969; Mugny, 1975, 1982; Nemeth, 1986; Nemeth et al., 1990), whose work suggests that special conditions are necessary before a minority can be effective. However, given these conditions (described below), different psychological processes are activated, and different patterns of behavior ensue as a result of these processes.

On the other side of the theoretical fence are those who believe that a single process can explain the persuasive impact (processes and outcomes) of minority and majority influence (e.g., Latane and Wolf, 1981; Levine, 1980, 1989; Levine and Russo, 1987; Tanford and Penrod, 1984; Wolf, 1985, 1987), or those who hold that the evidence, while not completely one–sided, does not favor the dual process explanation (e.g., Kruglanski and Mackie, 1990).

Support for both positions is available, but as Kruglanski and Mackie's review suggests, the critical tests have yet to be done. How can we decide between the two opposing positions? What constitutes acceptable proof? Let us consider the following possibility to gain an appreciation for the complexities involved. Suppose that in a standard social influence context, we find very different reactions to majority and minority sources. Consistent with much of the research of the dual process camp, we find that minority sources have little immediate impact, but they stimulate conversion effects over time, such that when removed from the setting, the (minority) source's position comes to be accepted. The majority source, on the other hand, induces immediate compliance—but when removed from the setting, its influence disappears.

Do such results support the dual-process position? Perhaps, but first, extraneous associations between source status and source attractiveness must be controlled. This qualification is crucial, for in much research that supports the dual process position, there exists the possibility that variations are caused by features associated with, but not isomorphic to, the (minority) status of the influence source. How does it work? Consider the following possibility. A minority source who espouses an unpopular position may prove very attractive to subjects who are inclined to identify with the underdog (cf. Doms and van Avermaet, 1980; Perez and Mugny, 1990). The continuing popularity of James Dean's character in *Rebel Without a Cause* or *East of Eden* provides a good example of the compelling outsider—a minority of one—whom many find exceptionally attractive. Dean's effectiveness resides not in his minority status, but in his romantic personification of the rugged individualist who, against all odds, is so convinced of his position that he will sacrifice everything for it. It may well be the attribution of tragic selflessness that lies at the core of his attractiveness and consequent persuasiveness (cf. Kelman, 1961), rather than his status as a minority (of one).

We have known for many years that a source willing to espouse a position that will cause him or her to experience personal recrimination or hardship will prove more persuasive than one who spouts the party line (cf. Eagly et al., 1978; Koeske and Crano, 1968). For example, consider a study in which General William Westmoreland, then in charge of the U.S. forces in Vietnam, was said to have stated that the U.S. press had grossly *underestimated* the number of casualties the Americans had suffered (see table 2.1). In these circumstances, Koeske and Crano (1968) found that

Table 2.1   Congruous and Incongruous Messages

Statement	Westmoreland	Carmichael
Congruous	U.S. bombing of North Vietnam has partially reduced the influx of men and military supplies to the South.	There are many documented reports of extensive police brutality in Negro neighborhoods.
Incongruous	Generally speaking, the number of U.S. casualties in the Vietnamese conflict has far exceeded that reported in the U.S. press.	Often, Negroes have not taken the initiative required to benefit from civil rights legislation.

Source: Koeske and Crano, 1968.

Westmoreland was more readily believed than when his statement was more congruous with his known position. This result is impressive in light of our results which indicated that mean credibility of these two statements was *reversed* when no source attribution was made. At the time of this research, it would have been difficult to find a person more representative of the majority than Westmoreland.

In the same study, a communication somewhat critical of black people was attributed to Stokeley Carmichael, a fiery spokesman for civil rights. When attributed to Carmichael, this message was more persuasive than one that was consistent with his standard "Black Power" speech. The persuasiveness of the arguments was reversed, however, when the source attribution was removed. At the time of the study, Carmichael could not be viewed as anything but the epitome of the minority grouper.

Clearly, it was not minority or majority status of these sources that accounted for their effectiveness, but the fact that they were voicing positions that were antagonistic to their known stands on the issues. They were going to suffer for having made these statements, but were willing to articulate them nonetheless. Is not this selflessness comparable to the minority source who is willing to champion a position, consistently, against all odds, despite ridicule and ostracism? Such persons are to be admired for their courage and steadfastness, and it may be this admiration, rather than minority status, per se, that is the basis of their effectiveness.

Of course, minority and majority sources may be differentially effective even in the absence of any extraneous source x process interactions, but this has yet to be established to the satisfaction of many social psychologists. In part, this failure may be attributed to three problems that beset previous research. Let us consider these issues.

21

Three Problems in Search of Resolution

Factorialization of Source and Target

In retrospect, it is clear that one of the chief problems with much of the earlier literature came about as a result of the failure to cross, or factorialize, the majority/minority status of the influence target with the majority/minority status of the source of influence. Often, the status of the influence source is controlled, but that of the target is not. It is *assumed* in the vast majority of studies that subjects will identify with the majority. Lacking precise control over identification, however, it is conceivable that subjects identify instead with the minority, due in part to reasons of source attractiveness discussed earlier. Such identification enhances the influence of the minority source, but as has been argued, is only tangentially related to minority status per se. The solution to this problem is conceptually (if not logistically) simple: control subjects' self-identification while simultaneously controlling the status of the source. If such control can be brought to bear, then effects attributable to source status cannot be redefined in terms of the extraneous sequelae associated with status.

Social Identity

Failing to control subjects' self-identifications opens the possibility that it is not minority/majority status per se that matters in social influence, but rather social categorization—the complementarity, or lack thereof, of the in-group or out-group status of the source and target. As such, when a minority source causes an apparent conversion reaction, we cannot know if it has occurred because (1) the source is a minority, and has stimulated the processes Moscovici hypothesizes, (2) subjects have identified with the source, who is admired for flying bravely in the face of convention (see above), (3) the source is a member of an *out-group,* vis-à-vis the subject, and under some circumstances, out-group sources are very effective (Gorenflo and Crano, 1989), or (4) because the source, a bloodied but unbowed rebel, has become a person to emulate, and is assimilated by the subject into his or her *in-group* (cf. Turner et al., 1987). Without controlling subjects' social identification, we cannot know which, if any, of these possibilities obtains. Possibilities 3 and 4 may be very troublesome for standard minority influence explanations, because they foster an alternative interpretation of minority influence based on social identity theory. This alternative would suggest that minority effects are merely the result of a confounding of the minority/majority status of subject and influence source, and are better understood in terms of the groups by which individuals define themselves.[1]

Conceptualization of the Minority (and Majority)

The third problem to be addressed has to do with the central question, What is a minority? Are minorities to be defined in terms of *number* (Doms, 1984; Latane and Wolf, 1981; Moscovici and Personnaz, 1980; Personnaz, 1981; Personnaz and Guillon, 1985), *power* (Maass, Clark, and Haberkorn, 1982; Moscovici, 1976; Mugny, 1982), *status* (e.g., Aebischer et al., 1984) or *outrageousness* of stated position (e.g., Moscovici, 1985)? Although all of these very different definitions have been employed, most researchers define the minority in numeric terms. While convenient from a methodological point of view, such numeric manipulations of minority and majority status do not seem completely faithful realizations of the conflict that Moscovici envisioned when he discussed the operation of the minority on majority opinion. Indeed, both Moscovici (1976) and Mugny (1982) have implied that considerations of number alone do not wholly capture the psychological meaning of minority status. When reading Moscovici, for example, one cannot help but be struck by his insistence on the need for conflict if the minority is to prevail. He has theorized:

> [The] resolute and consistent minority—which in contrast to other members of the group, is willing to engage in conflict—may succeed in having the consensus develop around the position it maintains.... [B]y refusing to compromise ... the minority simultaneously maintains the intensity of the conflict and testifies to its unwillingness to make concessions.... The negotiation that takes place between the majority and the minority revolves around the creation of a conflict where none existed previously. (Moscovici, 1985, p. 386)

But how is this conflict realized in research? In the modal case, subjects and confederates make a series of judgments, and are told that their estimates are like those of 12 percent, or 88 percent, of earlier subjects. This manipulation does not seem to capture the conflict encompassed in Moscovici's vision. To be sure, there is disagreement, but conflict? Moscovici was concerned with hot cognition. The 12 percent versus 88 percent manipulation seems very cold to me.

But there is more to it than this. The confrontation Moscovici envisioned seems to involve an elemental conflict between the haves and the have-nots. There is more to it than numeric imbalance, and until we expand our conceptualization of minority, we will not progress far. Aebischer et al. (1984, p. 25) put it very well when they observed, "[The] integration of minority influence and social categorization is fundamental for the understanding of political or social minorities and, hence, for the generalization from minority influence of a numerical kind to minority influence of a social kind." But, one might argue, this argument is specious—everyone knows what constitutes a minority. If this is so, then let us pose a few illustrative questions. Is the white Afrikaaner a minority? If so, is he comparable to a Sicilian "guest worker" in Belgium? Both represent numerically insignificant portions of the population—but the former has considerably more power, status, self-determination, etc. Will their successful attempts at influence be driven by the same psychological processes? It would not seem so. Consider the high status elites of Simmel (1955), by definition numeric minorities. Are elites in any way comparable to stigmatized groups such as India's untouchables? Both may be described as minorities, but they are clearly distinct. In the first instance, we have a numeric minority of high power and status; in the latter, a derogated out-group of great number.

How do we equate these "minorities"? How do we "standardize" them so that they can be compared along some common metric of "minority-ness" (cf. Crano, 1986)? And if we cannot, can we determine whether some kinds of minorities are likely to have one effect, and other kinds of minorities another (or perhaps, none)? In brief, how do we extract the features of each group that are responsible for their differential impact?

To address these issues, we must at a minimum refine our conceptualization of minority *and* majority. Clearly, majority and minority may be defined in terms of number (unquestionably the most common operationalization employed in past research), but majority and minority can also refer to social status, and it might be status, or station, that matters, rather than sheer number. We need not speculate on this matter. Both number and social status can and should be combined orthogonally in future research (e.g., Aebischer et al., 1984; Sachdev and Bourhis, 1991). If this is done, we will not only develop a more fine-grained conception of minority and majority, but a more precise understanding of the particular features of such sources that affect the success or failure of their attempts at social influence.

Prescriptions for the Future

Future research should contain treatments through which number and status are factorially combined in the operational definition of influence targets *and* sources. Although variations in number have been examined in many investigations (e.g., Arbuthnot and Wayner, 1982; Clark and Maass, 1990; Moscovici and Lage, 1976; Nemeth, Wachtler, and Endicott, 1977), none of these studies has simultaneously manipulated number and status. Status manipulations are necessary to differentiate elites from stigmatized groups.

How can we begin to determine the direct and interactive effects of status and number? A good starting point involves a two-way categorization process, in which influence sources are defined in terms of number and status, or social power. This scheme recognizes that minorities can be stigmatized, elites, or not otherwise characterized (i.e., numeric)—and the same definitional rules can be applied to majorities. Exemplars of each of these types, formed by crossing number and status, are presented in table 2.2. The outcomes of this crossing are sensible, and are well-represented in common, everyday experience. In the middle column of the table, majority/minority status is defined by the standard numeric groupings. When relying on this type of definition, we are forced as good methodologists to assume that the groups do not differ in ways other than number. In many circumstances, this assumption will not prove plausible. When status is combined with number, we create the following group types:

1. Elites, who are, by definition, positively evaluated, but numerically insignificant. Groups or individuals possessing rare but highly valued skills (e.g., brain surgeons, TV repairmen) or exalted social status (e.g., priests, judges) are examples of elites.
2. Positively evaluated majorities (variously identified as "the people," "the common man," "the silent majority," etc.), widely represented in everyday experience, are the touchstones against which minority effects most often are compared. In the absence of physical or cultural evidence to the contrary, we generally assume that people belong to this amorphous group.
3. Untouchables—numerically common but powerless and stigmatized groups also are well-represented in everyday experience (e.g., the blacks of South Africa, the Untouchables of India). For many years both groups have provided an unhappy example of stigmatized, but numerically significant, out-groups.
4. Examples of the prototypic minority grouper, a numerically rare, stigmatized outcast, are also all too easy to recall from common experience. These individuals, deviates or outcasts, are the least powerful of our four types—they are not only stigmatized, but few in number as well.

The combination of number and status complicates the issue somewhat. With this added complexity, the terms *majority* and *minority* are rendered unacceptably imprecise; as such, they should be used only when qualified. Is the added complication worthwhile? There can be little doubt of

Table 2.2   Categorization of Influence Source by Number and Status

| Number | Status of the Influence Source | | |
	High	Unknown	Low
High	Moral Majority	Numeric Majority	Untouchables
Low	Elites or Experts	Numeric Minority	Outsiders or Outcasts

this. By combining number with status, we arrive at a richer and more informative conceptualization of influence source. The recommendation to combine status and number is in accord with the call of Maass et al. (1982) for a distinction between in-group and out-group minorities, and extends their proposition in important ways (see also Volpato et al., 1990). As Maass et al. (1982) assert, the in-group or out-group property of a minority source may be critically important—but this property can and should be treated independently of the dimensions of number and status.

Furthermore, as has been argued in this chapter, it is a mistake to restrict our focus to influence *sources*. Characteristics of the *target* must affect susceptibility to influence, and probably interact with source characteristics as well. Considerable past research, however, has taken the target's majority group identification as given. As has been argued, this assumption is not free of cost. With sufficient experimental ingenuity, the influence target can be cast in the role of any of the general types formed by the factorial combination of number and status, just as can the source. By manipulating these features for both source and target, we can specify with great precision the aspects of source or target that make for greater or lesser (source) persuasiveness, greater or lesser (target) susceptibility, and the manner in which these factors interact. In brief, by following this prescription, we obtain a more fine grained picture of the operative source and target factors that mediate social influence. Research that honors these recommendations may unravel the complicated web of theory and data that characterizes this field.[2]

What Do We Know?

The methodologically grounded observations presented to this point contain a number of suggestions regarding the manner in which future research on (majority and minority) social influence might progress. In addition, the observations allow us profitably to review past research, to reflect upon what we know on the basis of accomplishments to date, and to formulate refinements that will result in a "second-generation" theoretical model that may prove more powerful and parsimonious than that currently available. This alternative model, whose test should involve designs that take advantage of the methodological suggestions provided to this point, draws primarily from Festinger's (1954) theory of social comparison, especially as modified by Goethals and Nelson (1973), Gorenflo and Crano (1989), and Olson, Ellis, and Zanna (1983). "Revised" social comparison theory suggests that attention to people's perceptions of the subjective or objective nature of the judgments they are asked to report will allow for a more precise understanding of the processes that moderate behavior in social influence contexts.

To begin the construction of this alternative model, let us begin with what we know. A review of the minority influence literature reveals four robust sets of findings. These findings are concerned with: *consistency effects, compliance vs. conversion, convergent and divergent thought,* and the *transfer, or generalization, of influence.* For present purposes, work on convergent and divergent thought will not be considered, except as it affects transfer.

Consistency

Consistency refers to the necessity for the minority to maintain an unwavering commitment to its cause when arguing its case. A minority that is inconsistent in presenting its position is almost certain to fail (Moscovici and Mugny, 1983). An impressive experimental demonstration of the necessity for minority group consistency was provided in one of the earliest studies in the field. In this experiment, Moscovici et al. (1969) brought together six individuals in an apparently simple perceptual judgment task. Subjects were to judge the colors of slides flashed onto a screen. All the slides were obviously blue. However, in one of the experimental conditions, two of the group of six subjects responded "green," consistently, on every trial. These two respondents were experimental confederates. Under these conditions, 8 percent of the naive subjects' responses were green, too. This occurred despite the fact that control subjects never said anything but blue when judging the slides.

To emphasize the importance of consistency, Moscovici et al. (1969) ran a second condition in which the two confederates responded "green" on only two-thirds of the judgment trials, and "blue" on the remainder. In this circumstance, the confederates had no influence on the judgments of the four naive subjects.

Transfer, or Generalization of Effects

Considerable research by Nemeth (1986) and others (e.g., Maass et al., 1987) suggests that under some conditions, minorities induce divergent thinking. If this is so, then it is reasonable to look for corollary aspects of minority influence that may occur as time passes. The emphasis on the passage of time is intended, because the "mulling-over" of the minority's message, a concomitant of the divergent thinking process, demands time. Accordingly, a minority's effects should be seen most clearly after some time has passed. In a comprehensive summary of time-dependent aspects of minority influence, Perez and Mugny (1990) have discussed an intriguing series of studies which suggest that the minority's message may not only have an influence (albeit a delayed one) on people's attitudes and behavior, but that this influence might generalize to other, related, issues as well. The transfer of minority influence to related realms of cognition is thought to be the result of divergent thinking.

The general form of these studies is illustrated in Perez and Mugny's (1987) study, in which Spanish high school girls read a message strongly in favor of the legalization of abortion. This position was contrary to Spanish law, and to the attitudes of the subjects as well. The message was attributed either to a speaker of minority or majority status. After reading the message, the subjects expressed their attitudes toward abortion *and* birth control. Results indicated that the pro-abortion message was most successful when source and subject were in the same (i.e., the majority) group. However, this direct influence had little indirect impact—it did not influence subjects' attitudes toward contraception. A different pattern occurred when a minority speaker was the source of the pro-abortion message. In this case, the speaker had little direct impact on attitudes toward abortion. However, the message had an indirect influence, by changing subjects' attitudes (positively) toward birth control. These results suggest that minority influence can spread beyond the boundaries of the targeted topic to other, related, issues.

Compliance versus Conversion (Direct versus Latent Influence)

Reviews of dual process theorists (cf. Moscovici, 1980, 1985; Nemeth, 1986) suggest strongly that minority respondents can affect the judgments of naive subjects. But, does this influence persist? Do subjects' responses represent genuine change, or are they merely the temporary verbal reactions of uncertain subjects to opinions or perceptions voiced by the confident minority stooge? To answer this question, and in keeping with Festinger's (1953) recommendations of many years ago, Moscovici and Personnaz (1980) extended the ''blue-green'' research paradigm (Moscovici et al., 1969) in some ingenious ways. In addition to providing judgments of the colors of slides, subjects also were required to disclose the *afterimage* they saw when the slide was taken off the screen. This measure was added because most naive subjects are not aware of the afterimages they will see after exposure to various colors. If subjects have been swayed by the minority, but are reluctant to show it, their overt, verbal responses might register no influence. However, their reported afterimages might be sensitive indicators of social influence, since most would not consciously control their reports of such images (see Personnaz and Guillon, 1985, for an extended discussion of this approach).

To test their idea, Moscovici and Personnaz (1980) exposed pairs of subjects (one of whom was a confederate) to slides that were unambiguously and invariably blue. In the first phase of the study, all subjects responded silently, noting the color they perceived on each slide presentation. After a series of silent judgments, the experimenter collected the subjects' responses, and provided information to them regarding the modal response. Half the subjects were told that 81.8 percent of a representative sample of the population perceived the slides as being blue, while the remaining 18.2 percent of the population saw the slides as green. The remaining half of the subject sample was told the opposite, that is, that 18.2 percent had judged the slides as blue, while the remaining 81.8 percent had judged them as green.

The interactive judgment task then began; (blue) slides were flashed onto the screen, and subject and confederate reported their perceptions aloud. The confederate always said green. For some subjects, the confederate's reported perception was a minority response since they had been told earlier that only 18.2 percent of the population perceived the slides as green. For the remaining subjects, who had been told that 81.8 percent of the population saw the slide as green, the confederate's was a majority response.

After a series of fifteen slides, a new response mode was introduced. In this new context, subjects were to view another set of slides, to *write* the color they saw, and indicate through the use of a color wheel the *afterimage* they perceived when the slide was extinguished. Both responses were silent and thus, private and inaccessible to the confederate.

The results of this study, and of others like it (cf. Moscovici and Personnaz, 1986; Personnaz, 1981) are extremely interesting. First, there was very little influence, majority- or minority-inspired, in the public response condition. Despite the fact that some subjects knew that more than 80 percent of a representative sample of their peers perceived the slide as being green, and their partners sided with this majority, their public responses were unaffected. Almost without exception, subjects reported the blue slide as being blue. Subjects paired with the confederate whose "green" response was consistent with the minority were equally uninfluenced *in their verbal reports* of the slides. However, when subjects responded in private, in the last phase of the experiment, some interesting deviations from this null pattern began to emerge. Again, there was little evidence of majority or minority influence on the color naming task. Nearly everyone wrote "blue" when the slides were flashed onto the screen. However, the visual afterimages subjects reported were significantly affected by the minority or majority status of the confederate with whom they had been paired.

Those involved with the majority confederate reported afterimages that tended toward the complement of blue, which is orange. This is an informative result, because it suggests that in the public response session, these subjects had reported what they had seen—they said the slides they saw were blue, and the afterimages they reported after each slide were the complement of this color.

The subjects in the minority confederate condition, however, reported afterimages that corresponded to having been exposed to *green* slides. Rather than orange, that is, the afterimages these subjects reported tended toward the red end of the spectrum, and red is the complement of *green*. Despite the fact that they continued to *report* seeing blue slides, the afterimage results suggested that they had been influenced, but because they were unwilling to acknowledge minority influence, either to the confederate or to themselves, they responded "blue" on their verbal reports. The influence of the minority was manifest on a measure subjects did not consciously monitor.

This is an extraordinary and controversial finding. Some attempts at replication have failed, or produced results that were inconsistent with the original findings (Doms and van Avermaet, 1980; Sorrentino, King, and Leo, 1980), while others have reproduced and extended the original data pattern (Moscovici and Personnaz, 1986; Personnaz, 1981; Personnaz and Guillon, 1985). The factors that mediate success or failure of the effect are not immediately obvious. However, some possibilities are suggested by an elaborated extension of Festinger's (1954) social comparison theory, and research based on this extension (Gorenflo and Crano, 1989) provides the basis for a possible integration of the paradoxical results. More importantly, this extension supplies the foundation for an alternative theoretical approach that I have termed the Context/Comparison Model. This model subsumes much prior research, and in combination with the methodological observations presented earlier, provides a framework that not only facilitates understanding of the processes of social influence, but also affords a theoretical structure that can guide the development of relevant research in the future. The model suggests a series of hypotheses that are important for developing an understanding of (majority and minority) social influence. The methodological refinements developed earlier in this chapter are essential, however, for without them, the potential contribution of the model will not be realized.

The Context/Comparison Model

Although the basis of this integrative model is social comparison theory, we need not review the theory in detail. For present purposes, it is sufficient to recall that Festinger assumed that in the absence of objective evidence, we are driven to compare our skills and attitudes with those of other people, in order to gauge our relative ability or the validity of our attitudes. Further, he hypothesized that our preferred comparison partners would be people *similar* to us on the dimension under comparison:

> One does not evaluate the correctness or incorrectness of an opinion by comparison with others whose opinions are extremely divergent from one's own. (Festinger, 1954, p. 120)

The data have not always proved kind to this aspect of Festinger's theory. Indeed, in some instances, dissimilar others are clearly preferred as comparison targets (e.g., Earle, 1986; Goethals, 1972, 1986; Goethals and Darley, 1977, 1988; Kruglanski and Mayseless, 1987; Olson, Herman, and Zanna, 1986; Suls, 1986). Such findings suggest a search for moderators of Festinger's expectation of comparison preference (cf. Crano, 1986; Crano and Brewer, 1986).

One potential moderator is concerned with the distinction between subjective preferences, or values, and objectively verifiable facts (cf. Asch, 1952; Ayer, 1952; Kaplan, 1989; Laughlin and Ellis, 1986; Mugny, 1984; Schonbar, 1945). Judgments of objective fact might arouse comparison needs that are very different from those involving subjective preferences. In social comparison research, studies by Goethals and Nelson (1973), Goethals and Darley (1977), Gorenflo and Crano (1989), and Olson, Ellis, and Zanna (1983) support this possibility. Following Kelley (1973), Olson et al. (1983) conceptualized judgments as being either subjective (involving a value) or objective (involving a belief). If a perceiver believes his or her evaluation is caused by the characteristics of the object, the judgment is defined as objective. However, if the evaluation is judged to be the outcome of the interaction of stimulus characteristics with the perceiver's own attitudes or preferences, it is defined as subjective. In discussing results of a study based on this distinction, Olson et al. (1983, pp. 433–34) observed that their data "indicate that the nature of the judgment itself affects the strength of the drive (for social comparison). Indeed, the objective-subjective dimension may have additional implications not explored. . . . For example, individuals may prefer similar others for evaluating judgments they consider to be subjective, but the similarity of referent others may be less important for evaluating objective judgments."

Some of the "additional implications" of the objective-subjective distinction were investigated by Gorenflo and Crano (1989), whose research focused on the choice of comparison partner in situations involving either objective or subjective judgments. In this investigation, the apparent similarity or dissimilarity of potential comparison partners was manipulated over a wide spectrum via the minimal groups technique (cf. Hogg and Abrams, 1990; Hogg and Turner, 1987; Tajfel, Billig, Bundy, and Flament, 1971; Tajfel and Turner, 1986). In the first of Gorenflo and Crano's two experiments, subjects were classified randomly through minimal groups procedures into "overestimator" or "underestimator" groups, and told that such people tend to differ in terms of personality characteristics and processes of judgment. They then proceeded to the central experimental task, which involved reviewing the credentials of a hypothetical college applicant and judging his suitability for the university.

Subjects received considerable information about the applicant, including his grades in high school, his standardized achievement test scores, a letter of recommendation from a teacher, a personal statement of plans and goals, and information about his job and leisure-time activities. To manipulate conceptions regarding the objective or subjective nature of the judgment task, some subjects were told that they possessed all the information the typical college admissions offer had available, and that this information was sufficient to form an objective judgment of the candidate. Accordingly, they were to base their judgments exclusively on the information presented. The remaining subjects, assigned to the subjective judgment condition, were told that the information presented them was *not* sufficient to form an objective decision about the candidate; as such, they were to fall back on their beliefs and preferences in forming their judgments.

Subjects evaluated the candidate on a number of rating scales, and wrote a detailed memorandum regarding their perceptions of his qualifications. They then were told that all members of the experimental session, over- and underestimators alike, had evaluated the same candidate, and they were given the opportunity to compare their judgments with a member of one or the other of these groups. To express their choice of comparison partner, subjects were given a 7–point scale through which they could note their preference for comparing their ratings with an overestimator and an underestimator. Analysis of these preferences revealed a strong and significant interaction effect: those who believed their judgments were subjective strongly preferred similar to dissimilar comparison partners; those who thought their judgments were objective strongly preferred dissimilar comparison partners.

Gorenflo and Crano's second study, which employed a modified mock jury methodology, replicated and extended the results of the first. Taken together, these two experiments indicate that the preference for similar or dissimilar comparison partners is affected strongly by the apparent subjective or objective nature of the required judgment. Since the required judgments differed considerably in the two studies—subjects played the role of either college admissions officers or jurists in a murder trial—the convergence of findings argues strongly for the generality of effects across issues and types of judgment. Convergent evidence from research on group decision making (e.g., Kaplan, 1989; Laughlin and Ellis, 1986) reinforces these findings. In brief, research suggests that when subjects view their judgments as subjective, they prefer to compare with like others; when judgments are thought to be objective, dissimilar comparison partners are preferred. Results that may be interpreted as consistent with this observation have been a part of our literature for many years (cf. Mills and Kimble, 1973; Sperling, 1946, as detailed in Asch, 1952; Schonbar, 1945).

Extrapolating from preferences to susceptibilities leads to interesting and potentially fruitful speculation. If subjective *preference* for one or another type of (similar or dissimilar) comparison partner implies greater *susceptibility* to such a source, then these results have the potential to speak to the issue of social influence. They suggest that people may be differentially sensitive to in-group or out-group influence as a consequence of (1) the nature of judgment task in which they are engaged, and (2) their own social identification vis-à-vis the influence source. If subjects believe the judgment they are to make is subjective (i.e., dependent upon personal attitudes or values) they are much more open to communications from people like themselves. If a person considers him- or herself to be a member of the majority, a common assumption of much research in this area, the Context/ Comparison model suggests that they would be more susceptible to majority influence. However, if the task were perceived as objective (factual), information or communications from outsiders (in this example, from representatives of the minority) should prove more influential.

These predictions are reversed if targets consider themselves members of a minority. Although considerations of judgmental subjectivity/objectivity lend some complexity to the predictive model, they are sensible, and provide a useful vehicle for reconceptualizing earlier findings.[3]

Reinterpretations based on the Context/Comparison Model

The "Blue-Green" Studies

Let us now reconsider some of the earlier empirical results in light of the Context/Comparison model, beginning with the "blue-green" controversy. The model suggests that differing subjective impressions of the *nature* of the experimental task lie at the root of the apparently paradoxical findings in this area. Consider the possibility that Moscovici and Personnaz gave subjects the impression that the color judging task was fundamentally objective.[4] In such a circumstance, subjects would be more open to influence from outsiders (in the context of this experiment, to minority sources). Even if identical instructions were used in the studies of Sorrentino et al. (an impossibility, given the language differences involved), subjects might have formed different impressions of the subjective or objective nature of the judgment task as a consequence of variations in their past histories. In North America, for example, subjects in judgment tasks are commonly told that "there are no right or wrong answers . . . just tell us what you think (or see)." This emphasis on the primacy of each individual's perceptions would lead subjects to the assumption that the task was fundamentally subjective.

In France, instructions of this type are not common; rather, the objective nature of experimental task is underscored, and subjects are urged to work hard to give valid answers to all questions. This stress on validity would foster the presumption that the judgments to be made were objective. Why would one need to work hard to generate a subjective estimate? Thus, even if the wording of the instructions was identical from study to study in this controversial area of research (and they could not have been, given the different languages, contexts, etc., that of necessity characterized the studies), the attributions subjects formed might have differed *systematically* as a consequence of different past experiences, based at least partially on cultural differences that characterize social psychological experimentation in France and North America.

If such differences obtained, then French subjects who considered themselves to be members of the majority would be more open to conversion influence from outsiders (in this particular instance, minority sources), and the data support this expectation. On the other hand, if the majority group subjects of Sorrentino et al. formed the impression that the color judging task was subjective, as hypothesized here, they would be more influenced by others like themselves, and thus (in this context) would prove resistant to minority sources of influence. This expectation, too, was confirmed. The proffered Context/Comparison model offers a reasonable and parsimonious integration of previously paradoxical findings.

Consistency

To further establish the utility of the Context/Comparison position, let us consider consistency effects, which have been widely reported in the literature on minority influence. Review of this literature indicates that consistency is necessary if a minority is to have influence. Why is this so? The Context/Comparison model suggests that consistency is critical because an unwavering stance on a position implies that the judgment under consideration is not open to debate—that it is *objective*, and hence correctly answerable in only one way. Two plus two always equals four, and one's unwavering subscription to this position suggests that this is an objective fact. This same implication may be conveyed by a consistent stance even in circumstances in which the objectivity of the issue at question is neither well-established nor immediately obvious.

This interpretation suggests that out-group consistency in attempts at influence would not matter if the influence target deemed the issue under consideration to be subjective. The perception that the judgment was fundamentally subjective would destroy the effect of out-group consistency on influence. Such a finding would cast a very different theoretical light on prior findings. It would suggest that consistency affects judgments because it alters subjects' perception of the (objective or subjective) nature of the task. Support for this Context/Comparison-based interpretation can be derived from Mugny's (1982, 1984; Papastamou and Mugny, 1985) work on flexible and rigid minorities. This research disclosed that while it is necessary for the minority to maintain an unwavering commitment to its cause when arguing its case, minorities that were rigid in fostering their position were ineffective. Mugny speculated that a minority source's rigid negotiating style would be perceived by majority targets as dogmatic. The root of dogmatic, of course, is dogma, which by Webster's definition is "a system of doctrines proclaimed by a church." In other words, dogma is a system of *subjective positions,* not *objective facts.* By adopting a rigid negotiating style, the minority sources might have rendered their messages subjective. As Gorenflo and Crano (1989) demonstrated, people seek *in-group* sources (i.e., representatives of the majority, in the case of the majority group subjects used in much past research) to validate subjective judgments. They are quite resistant to out-group influence on subjective issues. Is it this variation in preference, and consequent susceptibility, that explains the differential effectiveness of rigid and flexible minorities?

Compliance, Conversion, and Transfer

The implications of the Context/Comparison model for the issues of compliance, conversion, and transfer of influence are straightforward, testable, and organize the results of much previous research. Direct and latent influence is hypothesized to be a function of the (social) identification of source and target, and the perceived subjectivity/objectivity of the critical judgment. Crossing these two factors results in the model presented in table 2.3. The model assumes a general persuasive advantage of in-group influence sources. As shown, in-group sources are hypothesized to be the most effective influence agents in situations involving subjective judgments; conversely, out-group sources will generate resistance when subjective judgments are at issue.[5] For objective judgments, in-group sources are not expected to generate resistance, but neither will they prove efficient agents of influence; out-group sources, however, will prove especially effective in objective judgment conditions.

The predictions of table 2.3 are thought to obtain *ceteris paribus*. However, considerable research has indicated that subjects often resist acceding to, and thus identifying with, members of a minority group (cf. Mugny et al., 1984). As such, *some* of the influence effects of table 2.3, which are predicated on the basis of an unmodulated Context/Comparison model, might be attenuated (but not reversed) in *public* response contexts. An extended predictive model, based on considerations attending to the established reluctance of majority group individuals to identify overtly with representatives of minority groups is presented in table 2.4. This presentation outlines the pattern of predictions based on the Context/Comparison model as modified by the potential impact of source and target membership

Table 2.3   General Influence Predictions of the Context/Comparison Model

Source	Task	Direct	Type of Influence Latent	Transfer
In-group	Subjective	+	+	+
In-group	Objective	0	0	0
Out-group	Subjective	−	−	−
Out-group	Objective	+	+	+

Note: In this table, plus signs (+) indicate the greatest susceptibility to influence or diffusion, minus signs (−) indicate greatest resistance; 0 suggests that no particular susceptibility or resistance is likely to be encountered.

Table 2.4   Influence Predictions of the Context/Comparison Model, Modified by Considerations of Source and Target (Majority/Minority) Status

Source	Target	Task	Direct	Type of Influence Latent	Transfer
Majority	Majority	Subjective	+	+	+
Majority	Majority	Objective	0	0	0
Majority	Minority	Subjective	−	−	−
Majority	Minority	Objective	+	+	+
Minority	Majority	Subjective	−	−	−
Minority	Majority	Objective	−	+	+
Minority	Minority	Subjective	?	+	+
Minority	Minority	Objective	0	0	0

Note: In this table, plus (+) signs indicate the greatest susceptibility to influence or diffusion, minus (−) signs indicate greatest resistance, and 0 suggests that no particular susceptibility or resistance is likely to be encountered. The question mark (?) indicates that a prediction cannot be made, owing to the potential influence of extraneous factors outside the boundaries of the model.

in minority or minority groups. Examination of table 2.4 allows us to predict variations in susceptibility and resistance in different social influence contexts.

Objective Judgment Contexts

In objective task contexts, we assume that minority subjects will be susceptible to majority influence, and will display changes consistent with this influence. Majority group subjects in objective contexts, however, although more susceptible to minority sources, may refrain from exhibiting change overtly. Accordingly, we expect an attenuation of apparent (direct) influence in such contexts. This prediction is consistent with the findings of Perez and Mugny (1987, 1990).

Latent influence, or conversion, should not be affected by majority subjects' lack of enthusiasm for identifying publicly with minorities. As such, the strongest evidence for minority influence on the majority is expected in objective contexts, on measures of conversion or latent influence. Majority influence on the minority should also be evident in objective task contexts, but as noted, such effects are expected to be evident in public, or direct, circumstances, as well as on measures of latent change and transfer. Relative to their impact on the minority in objective settings, majority sources are not expected to prove overly effective in situations involving majority targets. A similar lack of influence of minority sources on minority targets is expected in objective judgment contexts.

Subjective Judgment Contexts

In subjective judgment contexts, a very different pattern of influence and susceptibility is hypothesized to emerge. In subjective circumstances, majority targets will prove most susceptible to majority influence sources, and this susceptibility will be evident in both direct *and* latent influence contexts. Minority targets will be most susceptible to minority sources; at a minimum, this susceptibility will be expressed most clearly in terms of conversion. Whether minority sources will influence minority targets in direct (subjective) influence contexts remains, as yet, unanswered. Majority targets will prove highly resistant to minority sources in subjective judgment contexts, just as minority targets will resist majority sources in these circumstances.

Transfer

In studies of the generalization of influence (cf. Mugny and Doise, 1979), or transfer, as it is termed here, the result pattern should be similar to that predicted for latent influence, or conversion. For majority targets, larger transfer effects will be induced by minority sources in objective contexts, and by majority sources in subjective contexts. Among minority targets, greater transfer will be induced by majority sources in objective contexts, and by minority sources in subjective ones. Transfer will be most strongly attenuated in subjective judgment contexts involving a lack of congruence in source/target status.

An Empirical Test

Recent research conducted on some of the issues discussed explicitly in this chapter supports the predictions derived on the basis of the Context/Comparison model. In this research (Crano, 1990), subjects were divided into minority or majority groups on the basis of a minimal groups procedure. The fine-grained number and status combinations that distinguish aspects of majority and minority group membership, which were discussed earlier in this chapter, were not employed in this research. Rather, subjects learned that their responses placed them either among 80 percent of their peers, who had answered similarly, or in a 20 percent minority. Then, in concert with an experimental confederate, who also had been designated as being a member of the majority or the minority, they answered a series of obscure factual questions derived from Pettigrew's (1958) *category width scale*. Half the sample was told the task involved objective judgment processes, and they were to strive to be as accurate as they could. The remaining subjects were told that the questions were so obscure as to be essentially subjective, and thus, they were to rely upon their best hunches and intuitions.

On the initial fifteen trials, subjects expressed their judgments individually, via computer. Immediately after each judgment, they were exposed to the confederate's judgments, which were flashed onto the computer screen. These responses were programmed so as always to be greater than the subject's. This influence tactic had the effect of driving subjects' responses in the direction of greater category width.

After the public response trials, subjects made a series of private judgments. They were not exposed to the confederate's answers, and were told that their own answers would not be broadcast to other subjects. Analysis of subjects' public and private judgments disclosed an interesting and complex pattern of results. First, minority sources were found to be more persuasive than majority sources in the public response phase of the experiment, irrespective of the social identification of the target. Furthermore, this differential influence was maintained in the private response phase.

The main effect of minority source superiority was qualified by results which demonstrated significant differences in influence as a consequence of the interaction of task subjectivity or objectivity, and the in-group or out-group status of the confederate vis-à-vis the subject. Because the majority/minority status of both subject *and* confederate had been completely crossed in the design, the effects of complementarity of social identification could be studied in addition to the more standard issue of the differential effectiveness of majority and minority sources. This analysis demonstrated that those subjects who thought the task was subjective were significantly more influenced by in-group confederates, whereas those who believed the judgment task was objective were significantly more influenced by out-group confederates. *These differences held irrespective of the subject's majority or minority status, and were found in both public and private response sessions.*

These results suggest that a dual process explanation of influence effects might be tenable, but the trigger for one or the other process might be the apparent (subjective or objective) nature of the critical judgment, not the majority or minority status of the influence source, per se. The main effect which indicated greater minority influence across both public and private response sessions can be integrated with the findings of task objectivity/ subjectivity if we postulate that this result was obtained because of the exceptionally obscure nature of the judgments required of subjects. This explanation posits that minority influence is most likely to occur on tasks that are outside the common experience of the influence targets. This observation is offered as a possibility, it has not yet been tested—but it is fully consistent with much of Nemeth's work on the effects of minority influence on judgment quality (e.g., Nemeth and Kwan, 1987; Nemeth et al., 1977; Nemeth et al., 1990). Given the preliminary nature of this research, it is not possible to answer the question of single versus dual processes in social influence. The brief description of results that has been presented here is intended primarily to stimulate further research, and to provide a model of the manner in which such research might be undertaken in the future. At a minimum, however, it provides strong evidence for the Context/Comparison model, and hopefully will stimulate further tests of its utility.

Concluding Observations

We have been hard at the study of social influence at least since the time of the great Muzafer Sherif (1936), whose work on social factors in perception stands even today as a model of creativity and good science. Over the course of more than a half-century, we have learned much about social influence and attitude change—but we also might have become

39

somewhat complacent in our thinking and in the manner in which we investigated our ideas during that time. With Moscovici's innovative work on minority influence came not only a plethora of new issues and ideas that demanded investigation and resolution, but a revitalization of interest about fundamental issues of social influence.

Research on minority influence to this point has been useful and instructive, and it is our task now to capitalize upon past contributions to further our knowledge of the processes involved in the persistence and change of beliefs. In doing so, we might discover that we must traverse paths that earlier research did not consider, and which at first glance might appear contrary to the implications of previous investigation. Far from denigrating the work of the past, these new directions in theory and method stand in homage to the earlier scientific contributions on which they are based—and from which ultimately they may depart.

The challenges facing social influence research are daunting, but their solution holds great promise for progress. At a minimum, we must develop a more refined conceptualization of what constitutes minority and majority—what are the features of these social groupings that matter. Recommendations regarding factors that might affect the power to influence—number and status—have been proposed in this chapter. They appear reasonable, but they have yet to withstand critical empirical test.

Another issue that must be addressed is the interplay between social identity theory (cf. Turner et al., 1987) and the still-evolving theory of minority/majority influence. Were the differences observed in the standard minority research of the past attributable to the majority/minority status of an influence source, or to the complementarity, or lack thereof, of the social status of source and target? The Context/Comparison model offers one means of addressing this issue, but much remains to be done, despite the useful and important progress that has been made on this front (cf. Perez and Mugny, 1990). To understand social influence, we would be well-advised to study the impact of majority and minority sources on majority and minority targets. And, we must expand our view of majority and minority status beyond considerations of number alone. In light of the present review, it is clear that designs that involve less than a full crossing of source and target are inevitably equivocal. This requirement demands a very major commitment of research energies, given the necessity for an expanded conceptualization of majority and minority, but these prices must be paid if real progress is to be made. Will we succeed? In light of the energy, persistence, and commitment of those actively involved in this area, and the growing numbers of investigators on both sides of the Atlantic whose interest in fundamental processes of social influence has been reinvigorated as a consequence of their efforts, a bright future for this fundamental, indeed, self-definitional, area of social psychology seems a good bet, if not a foregone conclusion.

Notes

Preparation of this chapter was facilitated by Grant SBR9396057 from the National Science Foundation.

1. See Aebischer et al. (1984), Sachdev and Bourhis (1991), and Volpato et al. (1990) for research which bears on this issue.

2. Because previous research has not made use of the recommended method of conceptualizing majority and minority entities, I am forced to ignore my own prescriptions on the pages that follow. Although compelled to use the generic terms "minority" and "majority," it should be understood that I am doing so in order to facilitate communication, and to make use of prior research in developing my arguments. In the future, I hope to be able to employ the more precise categorization scheme, and thereby to explore and perhaps understand the features of "minority" and "majority" groups that promote or impede their ability to influence.

3. To alleviate some of the complexity, tables 2.2 and 2.3, presented later in this chapter, outline the predictions that may be derived from a consideration of task objectivity/subjectivity and majority/minority source and target status.

4. By personal communication, Bernard Personnaz has assured me that this is so.

5. Note that for majority group subjects, in-group sources will be representatives of the majority; for minority subjects, the in-group source will be a minority representative. For out-group sources, these relationships will be reversed—minority sources will be out-group to majority subjects; majority sources will be out-group to minority subjects.

References

Aebischer, V., Hewstone, M., and Henderson, M. (1984). Minority influence and musical preference: Innovation by conversion not coercion. *European Journal of Social Psychology,* 14, 23–33.

Arbuthnot, J., and Wayner, M. (1982). Minority influence: Effects of size, conversion, and sex. *Journal of Psychology,* 111, 285–295.

Asch, S.E. (1952). *Social Psychology.* New York: Prentice-Hall.

Ayer, A. J. (1952). *Language, Truth, and Logic.* New York: Dover.

Brewer, M. B., and Crano, W. D. (1994). *Social Psychology.* Minneapolis/St. Paul, MN: West.

Clark, R. D., III, and Maass, A. (1988). Social categorization in minority influence: The case of homosexuality. *European Journal of Social Psychology,* 18, 347–364.

Clark, R. D., III, and Maass, A. (1990). The effects of majority size on minority influence. *European Journal of Social Psychology,* 20, 99–117.

Crano, W. D. (1970). Effects of sex, response order, and expertise in conformity: A dispositional approach. *Sociometry,* 33, 239–252.

Crano, W. D. (1975). Conformity behavior: A social psychological analysis. In C. N. Cofer and H. E. Fitzgerald (Eds.), *Psychology: A Programmed Modular Approach.* Homewood, IL: Irwin.

Crano, W. D. (1986). Research methodology: The interaction of substance with investigative form. In V. P. Makosky (Ed.), *The G. Stanley Hall Lecture Series,* vol. 6, pp. 5–38. Washington, DC: American Psychological Association.

Crano, W. D. (1990). Social Comparison, Social Identification, and Social Influence. Paper presented at the conference on The Roots of Persuasion, Valencia, Spain.

Crano, W. D., and Brewer, M. B. (1986). *Principles and Methods of Social Research.* Boston: Allyn and Bacon.

Doms, M. (1984). The minority influence effect: An alternative approach. In W. Doise and S. Moscovici (Eds.), *Current Issues in European Social Psychology,* vol. 1, pp. 1–33. Cambridge: The University Press.

Doms, M., and van Avermaet, E. (1980). Majority influence, minority influence, and conversion behavior: A replication. *Journal of Experimental Social Psychology,* 16, 283–292.

Earle, W. B.(1986). The social context of social comparison: Reality versus reassurance. *Personality and Social Psychology Bulletin,* 12, 159–168.

Eagly, A. H., Wood, W., and Chaiken, S. (1978). Causal inferences about communicators and their effect on opinion change. *Journal of Personality and Social Psychology,* 36, 424–435.

Festinger, L. (1953). An analysis of compliance behavior. In M. Sherif and M. O. Wilson (Eds.), *Group Relations at the Crossroads.* New York: Harper.

Festinger, L. (1954). A theory of social comparison processes. *Human Relations,* 7, 117–140.

Goethals, G. R. (1972). Consensus and modality in the attribution process: The role of similarity and information. *Journal of Personality and Social Psychology,* 21, 84–92.

Goethals, G. R. (1986). Social comparison theory: Social psychology from the lost and found. *Personality and Social Psychology Bulletin,* 12, 261–278.

Goethals, G. R., and Darley, J. M. (1977). Social comparison theory: An attributional approach. In J. M. Suls and R. L. Miller (Eds.), *Social Comparison Processes: Theoretical and Empirical Perspectives,* pp. 259–278. Washington, DC: Hemisphere.

Goethals, G. R., and Darley, J. M. (1987). Social comparison theory: Self-evaluation and group life. In B. Mullen and G. R. Goethals (Eds.), *Theories of Group Behavior,* pp. 21–47. New York: Springer-Verlag.

Goethals, G. R., and Nelson, R. E. (1973). Similarity in the influence process: The belief-value distinction. *Journal of Personality and Social Psychology,* 25, 117–122.

Gorenflo, D. W., and Crano, W. D. (1989). Judgmental subjectivity/objectivity and locus of choice in social comparison. *Journal of Personality and Social Psychology*, 57, 605–614.

Hogg, M. A., and Abrams, D. (1990). *Social Identifications*, London: Routledge.

Hogg, M. A., and Turner, J. C. (1987). Social identity and conformity: A theory of referent informational influence. In W. Doise and S. Moscovici (Eds.), *Current Issues in European Social Psychology*, vol. 2, pp. 139–182. Cambridge: The University Press.

Kaplan, M. (1989). Task, situational, and personal determinants of influence processes in group decision making. In E. J. Lawler and B. Markovsky (Eds.), *Advances in Group Processes*, vol. 6, pp. 87–105. Greenwich, CT: JAI Press.

Kelley, H. H. (1973). The processes of causal attribution. *American Psychologist*, 28, 107–128.

Kelman, H. C. (1961). Processes of opinion change. *Public Opinion Quarterly*, 25, 57–78.

Koeske, G. F., and Crano, W. D. (1968). The effect of congruous and incongruous source/statement combinations upon the judged credibility of a communication. *Journal of Experimental Social Psychology*, 4, 384–399.

Kruglanski, A. W., and Mackie, D. M. (1990). Majority and minority influence: A judgmental process analysis. In W. Stroebe and M. Hewstone (Eds.), *European Review of Social Psychology*, vol. 1. Chichester, Eng.: Wiley.

Kruglanski, A. W., and Mayseless, O. (1987). Motivational effects in the social comparison of opinions. *Journal of Personality and Social Psychology*, 53, 834–842.

Latane, B., and Wolf, S. (1981). The social impact of majorities and minorities. *Psychological Review*, 88, 438–453.

Laughlin, P. R., and Ellis, A. L. (1986). Demonstrability and social combination processes on mathematical intellective tasks. *Journal of Experimental Social Psychology*, 22, 177–189.

Levine, J. M. (1980). Reaction to opinion deviance in small groups. In P. B. Paulus (Ed.), *Psychology of Group Influence*, pp. 375–429. Hillsdale, NJ: Erlbaum.

Levine, J. M. (1989). Reaction to opinion deviance in small groups. In P. B. Paulus (Ed.), *Psychology of Group Influence*, 2nd ed., pp. 187–231. Hillsdale, NJ: Erlbaum.

Levine, J. M., and Russo, E. M. (1987). Majority and minority influence. In C. Hendrick (Ed.), *Review of Personality and Social Psychology: Group Processes*, vol. 8. Newbury Park, CA: Sage.

Maass, A., and Clark, R. D., III. (1984). Hidden impact of minorities: Fifteen years of minority influence research. *Psychological Bulletin*, 95, 428–450.

Maass, A., Clark, R. D. III, and Haberkorn, G. (1982). The effects of differential ascribed category membership and norms on minority influence. *European Journal of Social Psychology*, 12, 89–104.

Maass, A., West, S. G., and Cialdini, R. B. (1987). Minority influence and conversion. In C. Hendrick (Ed.), *Review of Personality and Social Psychology*, vol. 8. Beverly Hills, CA: Sage.

Mills, J. and Kimble, C. E. (1973). Opinion change as a function of perceived similarity of the communicator and subjectivity of the issue. *Bulletin of the Psychonomic Society*, 2, 35–36.

Moscovici, S. (1974). Social influence I: Conformity and social control. In C. Nemeth (Ed.), *Social Psychology: Classic and Contemporary Integrations*, pp. 179–216. Chicago: Rand-McNally.

Moscovici, S. (1976). *Social Influence and Social Change*. New York: Academic Press.

Moscovici, S. (1980). Toward a theory of conversion behavior. In L. Berkowitz (Ed.), *Advances in Experimental Social Psychology*, vol. 13, pp. 209–239. New York: Academic Press.

Moscovici, S. (1985). Innovation and minority influence. In G. Lindzey and E. Aronson (Eds.), *Handbook of Social Psychology*, Vol. 2, 3rd ed., pp. 347–412. New York: Random House.

Moscovici, S., and Lage, E. (1976). Studies in social influence III: Majority versus minority influence in a group. *European Journal of Social Psychology*, 6, 349–365.

Moscovici, S., Lage, E., and Naffrechoux, M. (1969). Influence of a consistent minority on the responses of a majority in a color perception task. *Sociometry*, 32, 365–380.

Moscovici, S., and Mugny, G. (1983). Minority influence. In P. B. Paulus (Ed.), *Basic Group Processes*, pp. 41–64. New York: Springer-Verlag.

Moscovici, S., and Mugny, G. (1987). *Psychologie de la Conversion*. Cousset: De Val.

Moscovici, S., and Personnaz, B. (1980). Studies in social influence V: Minority influence and conversion behavior in a perceptual task. *Journal of Experimental Social Psychology*, 16, 270–282.

Moscovici, S., and Personnaz, B. (1986). Studies on latent influence by the spectrometer method I: the impact of psychologization in the case of conversion by a minority or a majority. *European Journal of Social Psychology*, 16, 345–360.

Mugny, G. (1975). Majorite et minorite: Le niveau de leur influence. *Bulletin de Psychologie*, 28, 831–835.

Mugny, G. (1982). *The Power of Minorities*. New York: Academic Press.

Mugny, G. (1984). The influence of minorities: Ten years later. In H. Tajfel (Ed.), *The Social Dimension: European Developments in Social Psychology*, vol. 2, pp. 498–517. Cambridge: Cambridge University Press.

Mugny, G., and Doise, W. (1979). Niveaux d'analyse dans l'étude expérimentale des processus d'influence sociale. *Information sur les Sciences Sociales*, 18, 819–876.

Mugny, G., Kaiser, C., Papastamou, S., and Perez, J. A. (1984). Intergroup relations, identification, and social influence. *British Journal of Social Psychology*, 23, 317–322.

Nemeth, C. J. (1986). Differential contributions of majority and minority influence. *Psychological Review*, 93, 1–10.

Nemeth, C. J., and Kwan, J. (1987). Minority influence, divergent thinking, and detection of correct solutions. *Journal of Applied Social Psychology,* 17, 786–797.

Nemeth, C. J., Mayseless, O., Sherman, J., and Brown, Y. (1990). Exposure to dissent and recall of information. *Journal of Personality and Social Psychology,* 58, 429–437.

Nemeth, C. J., Wachtler, J., and Endicott, J. (1977). Increasing the size of the minority: Some gains and some losses. *European Journal of Social Psychology,* 7, 15–27.

Olson, J. M., Ellis, R. Z., and Zanna, M. P. (1983). Validating objective versus subjective judgments: Interest in social comparison and consistency information. *Personality and Social Psychology Bulletin,* 9, 427–436.

Olson, J. M., Herman, C. P., and Zanna, M. P. (Eds.) (1986). *Relative Deprivation and Social Comparison: The Ontario Symposium,* vol. 4. Hillsdale, NJ: Erlbaum.

Papastamou, S., and Mugny, G., (1985). Rigidity and minority influence: The influence of the social in social influence. In S. Moscovici, G. Mugny, and E. van Avermaet (Eds.), *Perspectives on Minority Influence,* pp. 113–136. Cambridge: Cambridge University Press.

Perez, J. A., and Mugny, G. (1987). Paradoxical effects of categorization in minority influence: When being an outgroup is an advantage. *European Journal of Social Psychology,* 17, 157–169.

Perez, J. A., and Mugny, G. (1990). Minority influence: Manifest discrimination and latent influence. In D. Abrams and M. Hogg (Eds.), *Social Identity Theory: Constructive and Critical Advances.* London: Harvester Wheatsheaf.

Personnaz, B. (1981). Study in social influence using the spectrometer method: Dynamics of the phenomenon of conversion and covertness in perceptual responses. *European Journal of Social Psychology,* 11, 431–438.

Personnaz, B., and Guillon, M. (1985). Conflict and Conversion. In S. Moscovici, G. Mugny, and E. van Avermaet (Eds.), *Perspectives on Minority Influence.* Cambridge: Cambridge University Press.

Pettigrew, T. F. (1958). The measurement and correlates of category width as a cognitive variable. *Journal of Personality,* 26, 532–544.

Sachdev, I., and Bourhis, R. Y. (1991). Power and status differentials in minority and majority group relations. *European Journal of Social Psychology,* 21, 1–24.

Schonbar, R. A. (1945). The interaction of observer-pairs in judging visual extent and movement: The formation of social norms in "structured" situations. *Archives of Psychology,* 41, 1–95.

Sherif, M. (1935). A study of some social factors in perception. *Archives of Psychology,* No. 187.

Simmel, G. (1955). *Conflict and the Web of Group Affiliations.* New York: Free Press.

Sorrentino, R. M., King, G., and Leo, G. (1980). The influence of the minority on perception: A note on a possible alternative explanation. *Journal of Experimental Social Psychology,* 16, 293–301.

Suls, J. (1986). Notes on the occasion of social comparison theory's thirtieth birthday. *Personality and Social Psychology Bulletin,* 12, 289–296.

Tanford, S., and Penrod, S. (1984). Social influence model: A formal integration of research on majority and minority influence processes. *Psychological Bulletin,* 95, 189–225.

Tajfel, H., Billig., M., Bundy, R. P., and Flament, C. (1971). Social categorization and intergroup behavior. *European Journal of Social Psychology,* 1, 149–177.

Tajfel, H., and Turner, J. C. (1986). The social identity theory of intergroup behavior. In W. G. Austin and S. Worchel (Eds.), *Psychology of Intergroup Relations.* Chicago: Nelson-Hall.

Turner, J. C., Hogg, M. A., Oakes, P. J., Reicher, S. D., and Wetherell, M. (1987). *Rediscovering the Social Group: A Self-Categorization Theory.* Oxford: Blackwell.

Volpato, C., Maass, A., Mucchi-Faina, A., and Vitti, E. (1990). Minority influence and social categorization. *European Journal of Social Psychology,* 20, 119–132.

Wolf, S. (1985). Manifest and latent influence of majorities and minorities. *Journal of Personality and Social Psychology,* 48, 899–908.

Wolf, S. (1987). Majority and minority influence: A social impact analysis. In M. P. Zanna, J. M. Olson, and C. P. Herman (Eds.), *The Ontario Symposium,* Vol. 5, pp. 207–235. Hillsdale, NJ: Erlbaum.

CHAPTER THREE

A FEW PARALLELS BETWEEN GROUP POLARIZATION AND MINORITY INFLUENCE

Russell D. Clark, III

The purpose of this chapter is to explore a few parallels between two large and popular bodies of literature in social psychology. One is group polarization, which refers to individuals in groups, or groups, making more extreme judgements or engaging in more extreme behaviors than do individuals responding alone. The other is minority influence, which refers to the phenomenon that a minority that consistently represents an alternative viewpoint to a majority can change the attitudes, beliefs, and opinions of that majority. Since this volume primarily deals with minority influence, I hope to be able to show that a brief discussion of group polarization can enhance our understanding of minority influence.

There are at least two factors that have impeded discussion of group polarization and minority influence. First, the two research areas flourished at different times. Research on group polarization, including the risky-shift effect, was very popular in the 1960s, peaked around 1971, and rapidly slowed by the end of the decade. Minority influence did not generate the initial level of interest in 1969 as did the first study on the risky-shift effect in 1961, but, following Moscovici's influential review article (1980), research on minority influence rapidly increased during the 1980s, and there appears, if this volume is any indication, to be no waning of interest. Thus with the heyday of each literature spanning different time periods, researchers may not be as familiar with each area as they would otherwise be.

Second, and more importantly, investigators in the two areas were perceived and thought to have come from different traditions within social psychology. Individuals who studied group polarization were seen as representing traditional (American) social psychology where the emphasis was on "how does the majority affect the individual." Persons studying minority influence saw themselves as starting a new tradition (European) where as much attention needed to be placed on "how can the individual (minority) affect the majority." Beginning with Moscovici (1980) and continuing with Maass and Clark (1984), Mugny (1982), and Nemeth (1986), a further major barrier was driven between these two traditions by the assertion that different theoretical processes were involved in conformity research than in minority influence. Simply stated, these dual process proponents argued that conformity would occur on public and not on private measures of attitude change whereas the reverse was true for minority influence. The ultimate effect, whether intended or not, was that research on minority influence could proceed along quite nicely without any attention to findings or processes underlying conformity/majority research.

This distinction between majority and minority processes was probably very beneficial at the time. It probably became the impetus for increased interest in minority influence in the United States and provided a provocative theoretical debate (Maass and Clark, 1984), which continues today. Yet, I think the time has come for a reconsideration of the necessity and fruitfulness of the extreme dichotomy between majority and minority influence. I say this with the full knowledge of my being a participant in this issue. Even though I was a player in the group polarization literature in my earlier career, my theoretical and empirical research on minority influence have strongly favored the European view of social influence. Notwithstanding, I hope to be able to show that both areas have a lot more in common than is generally found in the social psychological literature.

As I indicated, the purpose of this chapter is to explore the similarities between group polarization and minority influence. The history of the two areas has more in common than an isolated reading of the minority influence would suggest. As we have indicated elsewhere (e.g., Maass and Clark, 1984) the following commonalities exist in the two areas: (1) each phenomenon was the result of an empirical finding that did not fit with either the theoretical or empirical literature that existed at the time, (2) the bulk of studies have used the minimal group paradigm in which groups are constituted for no other reason than a one-shot experiment, (3) a "black box approach" which focuses on mean group differences rather than the intra- and interpersonal processes has dominated, (4) mediating processes tend to be ignored, (5) group difference analyses, rather than hierarchical techniques, tend to be employed, and (6) the guru of minority influence, Serge Moscovici, was, and is, a major player in the group polarization literature. The latter, alone, would warrant a discussion of minority influence and group polarization.

The chapter is organized as follows. We begin by reviewing studies that strongly indicate that both group polarization and minority influence can be predicted, in advance, by knowing the population's inclination on a given issue. This is followed by a presentation of the critical evidence favoring both a social comparison and persuasive arguments interpretation of group polarization. Then, we look at the evidence and adopt the view that both persuasive arguments and social comparison processes can occur to enhance minority influence, although neither process is necessary for minority influence to occur as is true for group polarization. *At no time do I intend to imply that processes underlying minority influence are identical to processes underlying group polarization.*

A Predictor of Group Polarization and Minority Influence

There is a substantial amount of evidence that there is an asymmetry in both group polarization and minority influence. In the group polarization literature the shifts in decisions are usually more likely to occur in one direction on an attitude continuum than in the opposite direction. Studies in which the minority has argued for either the pro or con position on the same attitudinal issue indicate that minorities that argue on one side of an issue will have more influence than minorities that advocate the opposing side. For both group polarization and minority influence the direction of the shifts or minority influence can be predicted by the direction of the individuals' initial decisions.

Group Polarization

One of the most robust findings in the group polarization literature is that the polarization occurs in the direction of the individuals' inclinations and the size of the polarization varies directly with the extremity of the initial preferences. For example, using the ten risk taking items of the Choice-Dilemmas Instrument, Teger and Pruitt (1967) found a high correlation of -0.64 between mean initial preference and mean shift toward risk. When the two items were included that produced cautious shifts (No. 5 and No. 12), the size of the correlation increased to -0.78. Similarly, Myers and Arenson (1972), using six risky items from the Choice-Dilemmas Instrument and six new cautious items, found a correlation of -0.89 between the mean initial decisions on items and shifts on the same items. In short, polarization occurs in the direction of the initial preference and the magnitude of initial preferences can reliably predict the degree of polarization.

Similar results have been found for issues of attitude and belief. Moscovici and Zavalloni (1969) found that individuals in Paris who had mildly favorable attitudes toward Charles de Gaulle expressed even more favorable attitudes after the group discussion; persons who had mildly negative attitudes toward Americans became even more negative after the group discussion. Doise (1969) showed that individuals who had negative attitudes toward their school became even more so after the group discussion. Finally, Myers and Bishop (1971) formed groups consisting of persons who either had favorable or unfavorable attitudes toward Blacks. After the group discussion, both kinds of groups became more extreme in their attitudes in the direction of their initial preferences: the prejudiced individuals became even more so and unprejudiced individuals became even more unprejudiced.

Minority Influence

There is an increasing amount of evidence that minorities that advocate one side of an attitudinal issue will have more influence than minorities that argue for the opposing side. For example, Paicheler (1976, 1979) demonstrated that minorities were very influential when they argued for women's rights, but minorities failed to exert influence when they advocated an anti–women's rights position. Maass and Clark (1983) found that the difference between public and private responses was greater when the minority opposed gay rights than when the minority favoured gay rights. In subsequent studies (Clark and Maass, 1988a, 1990), majorities became either marginally more favorable when confronted with a heterosexual minority but majorities became significantly more unfavorable when the heterosexual minority was opposing gay rights. Finally, Clark and Maass (1988b, 1990) found that minorities that argued for abortion produced significantly more positive attitudes toward abortion whereas minorities opposing abortion produced either marginally more unfavorable attitudes toward abortion (Clark and Maass, 1988b) or no attitude change (Clark and Maass, 1990).

The observed asymmetry in minority influence is not a simple pro or con bias, because some of the studies found pro minorities to be more successful (Clark and Maass, 1988b, 1990; Paicheler, 1976, 1979), whereas other studies found con minorities to exert more influence (Clark and Maass, 1988a; Maass and Clark, 1983). Rather, a close examination of these studies reveals that minorities that advocated the viewpoint representing the sample's initial predilections produced more attitude change than did minorities that argued for the viewpoint opposing the sample's initial dispositions. For example, in the Clark and Maass experiments, the initial preference in the population was against gay rights or for abortion; in Paicheler's studies, there was a slight inclination in the population for subjects to favor women's rights. In each case, when the minority argued in the direction of the sample's preference, it was successful; when the minority advocated a position that opposed the sample's preference, the minority either was not successful (Clark and Maass, 1990; Paicheler, 1976, 1979) or was less successful (Clark and Maass, 1988a, 1988b, 1990). In short, minorities that defend the majority position in the population will have more influence than minorities that argue against the majority position in the population.

In a recent experiment, Clark (1988) investigated the hypothesis that the asymmetry in minority influence could be predicted by the population's predilections on a given issue. Employing choice dilemmas from the group polarization literature to elicit subjects' initial preferences, Clark (1988) hypothesized that: (1) for risky items, where the dominant value/preference is to favor the risky alternative, a risky minority should have more influence on a cautious majority than would a cautious minority have on a risky majority; (2) for neutral items, for which subjects place as much value on the risky as cautious alternatives, the minority should show little influence whether it argues for the risky or cautious alternatives; and (3) on cautious items, where the dominant value is to favor the cautious alternative, a cautious minority should exert more influence on a risky majority than would a risky minority exert on a cautious majority.

The following procedure was used to test these hypotheses. Subjects discussed one of three risky, neutral, or cautious choice dilemmas. For each of the value categories (risk, neutral, or caution), one half of the groups consisted of a risky minority (two confederates) and a cautious majority (four subjects), and the other half consisted of a cautious minority and a risky majority. The results clearly supported the first two hypotheses and provided partial support for the third hypothesis. The results indicated that on risky items minorities that argued for risk had more influence than minorities advocating caution; on neutral items the majority was not influenced by the minority whether it advocated the risky or cautious alternative. For cautious items, a minority that went against the value of cautious and argued for the risky alternative was unable to change the majority, but, contrary to expectations, a minority that went with the value of the item and advocated caution was unable to change a risky majority.

These results, along with those obtained by Clark and Maass and by Paicheler, strongly suggest that minorities in the laboratory are usually only effective when they represent the population majority outside the laboratory— only when minorities defend a majority position in terms of the sample population can they exert influence on a majority, who hold a minority position in terms of the population. In other words, a minority is most successful when, in fact, it represents the majority! Thus, when population preferences are taken into account, minority influence and conformity may have more similarities than the literature on minority influence would suggest.

Notwithstanding the consistent empirical support for the above findings, the suggestion that minority influence is no more than a majority/conformity effect is disquieting, to say the least, and, at best, probably wrong. The laboratory evidence simply flies in the face of reality. Our recorded history of art, music, religion, sciences, political leaders, and so on, make it very clear that innovations are not brought about by a "minority representing a majority position." Rather, innovations which became the norm often have occurred because one person, or a small minority, had consistently put forth a coherent and radical view in spite of receiving indifference, insult, ridicule, ostracism, or persecution from the majority (Archer, 1968; Kuhn, 1962; Moscovici, 1976). Quite often the hearsay, deviancy, and radicalism of one generation become the norm of the next and subsequent generations. We will return to this issue later in the chapter. Until then, I will discuss the two major explanations of group polarization which I hope can aid in the understanding of minority influence.

Understanding Group Polarization

While numerous explanations for why individuals in groups or groups themselves become more polarized have been offered and thoroughly investigated, two traditional explanations of majority influence, social comparison processes and persuasive arguments have prevailed (Myers and Lamm, 1976). The evidence for each process is conclusive. Individuals are influenced by the opinions of others and by the argumentation of their views.

Social Comparison

As applied to group polarization, the theory of social comparison has three interrelated propositions. First, any given dilemma elicits from most persons the desire to be average, cautious, or risky. Second, most individuals do perceive that she or he does have the desired position. Third, during the course of the group interaction when the actual distribution of each group member's decision becomes known, those who are deviant from the desired position, particularly in the non–valued direction, will be motivated to change; the subsequent shift in opinions will depend upon the initial value evoked by the situation—e.g., for choice-dilemmas, a cautious shift for cautious items, a risky shift for risky items, or no shift at all for neutral items.

The empirical evidence supports each of these propositions of social comparison theory (see Myers and Lamm, 1976; Myers, 1982). Most people perceive that they are at least as risky, if not more so, as their peers on risk-taking items and they admire risk-taking on items that show risky shifts; most persons believe that they are at least as cautious, if not more so, as their peers on cautious items and they admire caution on items that show cautious shifts. But, more importantly in explaining choice shifts, it is the information on others' positions alone that causes shifts. Numerous studies have shown that when subjects are only allowed to exchange position information (e.g., odd ratios for choice dilemmas) with no group discussion, risky shifts occurred on risky items and cautious shifts occurred for cautious items, although the latter are smaller than the former (e.g., Myers and Bishop, 1971; Myers, 1978; Teger and Pruitt, 1967).

Persuasive Arguments

The theory of persuasive arguments also has three interrelated propositions. First, for each choice dilemma there exists a population of arguments favoring caution, risk, or neutrality, that is, proportion of risky arguments equals cautious arguments: the number and persuasiveness of the arguments may vary with each item. Second, each person who contemplates a particular dilemma will think of some sample of the population's arguments, but not all; the arguments put forth by any set of individuals will only be partially shared prior to the group discussion. Third, the sole purpose of the group discussion is to provide the vehicle whereby each person's arguments are expressed and become fully shared; since the total population of arguments favors risk, caution, or neutrality, the larger sample of arguments made available to all in discussion will result in a risky shift, cautious shift, or no shift at all. Each proposition has received strong empirical support.

Investigating the first proposition of persuasive arguments theory, Vinokur and Burnstein (1974) had subjects first indicate their recommendations to each of two cautious, two risky, and one neutral choice dilemma and they had them list all the arguments they could think of relevant to each item, indicating whether the argument favored caution or risk. The results indicated that cautious items produced a higher proportion of caution to risk arguments, risk items produced a higher proportion of risk to caution arguments, and the proportion of arguments for the neutral items was evenly balanced between cautious and risky arguments. In addition, sharing of arguments was only partial for each item; no argument was shared by more than one-third of the subjects.

Persuasive arguments theory can use the proportion of risky to cautious arguments in the population of arguments for a given item to predict the mean of the individual decisions and the magnitude of shift for that item. Vinokur (1971) has shown that the mean of the individual decision on an item and the size of the shift for the item is directly correlated with the proportion of risky to cautious arguments in the population of arguments for that item. According to the theory, the subject's initial sample of arguments will reflect the population's biases and through the discussion each subject will increase his or her sample from the total population sample, the subject's final decision will move toward the population sample.

A critical test for persuasive arguments theory is: like with social comparison theory where position information is sufficient to produce choice shifts, can arguments alone cause shifts? The answer is in the affirmative. Employing six risk taking choice dilemmas, Clark, Crockett, and Archer (1971) compared discussion groups who could give their arguments and recommendations with arguments-only groups who could discuss their arguments, but could not say what precise recommendations they favored. The results indicated that the arguments only condition produced as large a risky shift as did the full disclosure condition. Several other studies have shown that exposure to arguments alone is enough to produce significant shifts (Burnstein and Vinokur, 1973; Myers, Bach, and Schreiber, 1974).

When individuals are initially attracted to a position, they will generate more arguments favoring than opposing their initial inclination, and they will be more influenced by arguments favoring their initial bias than by arguments that counter their initial position (e.g., Myers and Lamm, 1976). For example, in situations that elicit a value of risk, the change in the direction of caution for initially risky individuals who are exposed to a norm of caution will be less than the change in the direction of risk for initially cautious subjects who are exposed to a norm of risk (Vidmar, 1970; Wallach and Mabli, 1970; Clark and Crockett, 1971; Baron, Monson, and Bason, 1973; Ebbesen and Bowers, 1974). Similarly, using a jury task where the dominant value is not to convict an innocent person, Silzer and Clark (1977) showed that fewer arguments were needed to move subjects toward innocence than toward guilt.

Given that individuals in groups generate arguments favoring a value, opinion, or attitude that they are initially attracted to and are less influenced by arguments favoring a non-valued alternative than by those arguments that favor the value, opinion, or attitude, it follows that group polarization should only occur in situations that elicit an initial value, opinion, or attitude. Fraser, Gouge, and Billig (1971) found that choice dilemmas that elicited initial individual means between 3.5 and 4.5 on a seven point scale showed no significant shift as a result of group discussion. The regular shift toward risk occurred on items with an initial mean below 3.5 and shifts toward caution were observed on items with an initial mean above 4.5.

Of particular importance to the present discussion is a provocative study which was conducted by Vinokur and Burnstein (1978). These investigators created six-member groups which discussed either one of four risky-shift choice dilemmas, one of two cautious-shift dilemmas, or a neutral dilemma. In each group there were two subgroups consisting of the opposed extremes. For each of the dilemmas three persons favored the risky alternative while the remaining three persons argued for the cautious alternative. The authors found the typical group polarization effect: significant shifts toward risk on the risky-shift items, shifts toward caution on cautious items, and no shift for the neutral item. Moreover, the results indicated differential depolarization (i.e., one subgroup shifted more toward the other subgroup than did its opposition). On risky items, the cautious subgroup depolarized more than the risky subgroup; on cautious dilemmas, the risky subgroup depolarized more than the cautious subgroup; and on the neutral item both subgroups depolarized to the same degree.

Evidence for the Role of Social Comparison and Persuasive Arguments in Minority Influence

Social comparison processes and persuasive arguments may help us reconcile the strong discrepancy between the asymmetry observed in laboratory studies of minority influence and evidence from history. Even a cursory study of history reveals that the success of many artistic, political, religious, and scientific minorities was dependent upon some degree of defection to the minority cause by members of the existing majority and/or changes in events or conditions, which can be objectively tested and verified, came to favor the minority position.

A few examples from science and political history might be helpful at this point: The scientific community was ultimately convinced by Galileo, Darwin, and Freud because the accumulation of knowledge via an objective, agreed upon criterion for assessing truth proved the superiority of their views over those existing at the time. The acceptance of their views was probably also facilitated by an increasing number of converts over time. Similarly, one of the best examples from recent history was Winston Churchill's persistent warnings about the dangers of Nazi Germany in the 1930s. After Germany's invasion of Poland, which solidified Churchill's claims, he was made first lord of the admiralty and within a year was made prime minister of Great Britain. Churchill's rise to power was also probably facilitated by attracting supporters over time as the evidence confirmed the truth of his position. In short, a majority viewpoint can be undermined and radically changed by a minority who can objectively refute the majority position and receive supporters from the majority during the process of argument refutation. The latter process of social support for the minority position involves social comparison and the process of argument refutation consists of persuasive arguments.

Social Support

Social support has proved to be a very powerful determinant in the conformity literature. In general, group influence is substantially reduced when the subject has a supporter, but group influence can be more effective when a social supporter deserts the subject (Allen, 1975). The latter finding should be of particular interest to minority influence. If group influence is particularly effective when an ally deserts the subject, lack of uniformity, and especially desertion, by a majority member(s), should influence minority influence.

A very elaborate experiment by Kiesler and Pallak (1975) investigated the effects of a single majority member's desertion to the minority position. Subjects participated in a study on human relations and were led to believe that a group discussion would be made about a human relations case involving a fifteen-year-old delinquent who had a solid history of engaging in disruptive, aggressive, and criminal behaviors. The case was written so as to incite an unsympathetic response toward the boy. After reading the case and having made their personal recommendation, subjects were given a distribution of opinions with a majority of six and a minority of two. Given the way the case was written, subjects would see themselves as belonging to the majority. Allegedly, because of a previous technical error involving a lack of complete information, subjects were asked to give their recommendations again and were presented with a distribution of group opinions. There were six conditions: (a) subjects in the "control condition" saw the same distribution as before the technical error; (b) subjects in the reactionary condition observed one member of the majority become even more negative toward the delinquent, moving further away from the minority position; (c) subjects in the minority compromise condition saw that both minority members had changed their opinions significantly in the direction of the majority position; (d) subjects in the majority compromise condition saw one of the majority members move significantly toward the minority position; (e) subjects in a mixed compromise condition saw the minority move toward the majority and a member of the majority move toward the minority; (f) subjects in the majority defector condition observed that one of the majority members had defected by entirely adopting the minority position.

After studying the distribution of response and receiving a note from one of the minority members advocating a more lenient and positive attitude toward the delinquent boy, subjects made recommendations for a third time.

The results indicated that the reactionary, minority compromise, and both majority and minority compromise conditions did not produce any changes in the majority. Members of the majority only changed their opinions when one member of the majority moved toward or defected to the minority position. Moreover, defection of one of the majority members was more detrimental to the majority opinion than was a mere compromise on the part of a majority member.

Kiesler and Pallak's (1975) demonstration that consistent minorities have more influence when they are able to produce some movement of opinion on the part of a majority member than when it is unable to produce this movement has been called a demonstration effect by Moscovici (1976). The movement of one of the majority toward the minority position begins the disarray of the majority position and points to the correctness of the minority's point of view. The defection of a majority member should only enhance the legitimacy of the minority's message or judgement and as the dislocation of the majority continues through the movement of other majority members to the minority, the minority's innovation should become the group's new norm (cf. Rogers, 1983).

We must be careful not to overgeneralize the results of Kiesler and Pallak (1975). The procedure only allowed for movement toward and defection to the minority position by a single majority member. We simply do not know if more majority defections would have had an effect. In addition, there was no control group without the minority/majority distribution of opinions. A pretest-postest control would have more clearly allowed for the occurrence of minority influence, without a demonstration effect.

Persuasive Arguments

Although all dual model explanations of minority influence (Maass and Clark, 1984; Moscovici, 1980; Mugny, 1982; Nemeth, 1986) postulate that the minority position generates either more quantitative and/or qualitative cognitive activity than does the majority position, surprisingly few studies have investigated the effects of minority argumentation. Maass and Clark (1983) exposed subjects simultaneously to majority and minority sources of influence to investigate the persuasiveness of the majority and minority arguments on private and public measures of attitude change. The results provided two findings which are strong support for a dual process model of social influence. First, although subjects recalled an equal number of majority and minority arguments, the minority triggered more favorable arguments and fewer counter-arguments than the majority. Second, the results demonstrated that cognitive activity did mediate internalization but not public compliance. The more arguments subjects could remember that favored the minority position and the fewer arguments that opposed the minority, the greater was the private acceptance of the minority position; public compliance was unrelated to the amount and direction of cognitive activity. Thus, the results provided positive support for the position, first put forth by Moscovici, that the degree and direction of cognitive activity will mediate private attitude change but not public compliance.

A major shortcoming of the Maass and Clark (1983) study is that the persuasive arguments were not directly manipulated. Only one study, to be discussed below, has done so. Yet, given that the minority triggers more favorable arguments for its position and fewer counter-arguments than the majority, we can use an information integration framework (Anderson and Graesser, 1976) to predict how members of a majority might respond to arguments presented by a minority. According to this view, each minority argument would have both a value and a weight. The minority position becomes stronger as the number, value, and weight of their arguments increase. Conversely, the majority position weakens as the number, value, and weight of their arguments decrease. Assuming the case where the weight and value of the majority's arguments are strong, the minority can weaken the majority's position by increasing the number, value, or weight of their own arguments and/or refuting the majority's arguments. If it can be shown that a majority argument is wrong, this reduces the weight of that argument to zero. Thus, the prediction from an information integration analysis is rather straightforward. The strength of the minority position should be enhanced in direct proportion to the number and strength of favorable arguments and in inverse proportion to the number and strength of counterarguments.

Twelve Angry Men

Perhaps an ideal prototype of how social comparison processes and persuasive arguments can operate in minority influence can be seen in Rose's (1956) famous play entitled *Twelve Angry Men* (also the movie starring Henry Fonda). In this play/movie, a son is accused of murdering his father. There are three strong pieces of evidence connecting him to the murder—the murderer has used a very rare switchblade knife and two eyewitnesses had testified that the son had committed the crime. The play/movie begins with the jury leaving the courtroom. Very soon a vote is taken, and eleven votes are for guilty and one is for innocence. The play/movie continues with the lone juror who systematically refutes each of the arguments against the defendant, gaining an increasing amount of social support from the majority after each argument refutation. At the end of the play/movie, the jury unanimously voted not guilty. Thus, the lone minority member was able to provide persuasive arguments that refuted the majority position and he gained social supporters in the process.

The power of persuasive arguments and social comparison are so thoroughly interwoven throughout the play that it is impossible to determine the single, let alone the mutual, effects of each process. While the audience comes away from the play totally convinced of the defendant's innocence, we cannot determine with any precision which factors produced this universal change in judgement. Do viewers change because of the persuasive arguments, because of the majority defectors, or because of both? Is one factor more important than the other or are both equally important? Moreover, can the lone dissenter who refuses to yield to the majority still be persuasive even when he does not have strong arguments favoring the defendant or gain any dissenters? These are just a few of the important questions one can raise, and they can only be answered by careful experimental research.

Recently, Clark (1990) conducted an experiment based on the *Twelve Angry Men* play to determine the impact of social support for the minority position and the minority's use of persuasive arguments to refute the majority viewpoint. All subjects were exposed to a brief summary of a case involving first degree murder. The evidence against the defendant was as follows:

A man has been stabbed to death, and his nineteen-year-old son has been accused. Both the son and father are members of some unspecified ethnic group. They are living in a poor section of a large city in an apartment whose windows are periodically shaken by a fast moving elevated train. There are three main pieces of evidence that connect the son with the crime.

1. The murder weapon is a *very rare switchblade knife*. Both the prosecutor and the defense attorney agree that it is an unusual knife. Further, the knife must be very unique because a store clerk testified that he only had one such knife in stock, and he had sold that one to the son. However, the son testified in court that he bought the knife for a friend and lost it through a hole in his pocket before the murder took place.

2. An old man, who has suffered two strokes and walks with the aid of two canes, lives in an apartment just beneath the scene of the murder. During the trial the old man testified that on the night of the murder he heard a loud argument above and heard the son shout, *"I'm going to kill you,"* and then he heard a body fall to the floor. While hearing someone running down the stairs, he hurried to the door of his own apartment, looked out and saw the son.

3. During the murder an elevated train ran past the windows of the father's apartment. In the apartment across the tracks a women lay in bed unable to sleep, looking directly toward the scene of the murder with the passing train between. At the trial *she swore that she saw the murder and identified the son as the murderer.* The prosecutor clearly demonstrated at the trial that it was

possible to look through the windows of a moving train and identify someone on the opposite side.

Subjects were run in one of four conditions. Employing a 2(persuasive arguments) × 2(jury verdict) factorial design, half of the subjects in all conditions received the evidence that the defendant was clearly not guilty, while the other half received information that the lone dissenter argued against the evidence, but the information given to the subjects was changed such that he could not refute the evidence. In half of the conditions, subjects were presented with the jury verdict after each discussion of one of the three arguments; in the other half, subjects were not presented with the jury verdict.

In the high persuasive arguments conditions, the minority jury member unequivocally refuted the evidence against the defendant either by providing new evidence or by clearly demonstrating the fallacy of each piece of evidence. The lone dissenter was able to destroy the three principle pieces of evidence in the following way: (1) the murder weapon was not unique because the minority member was able to find an identical knife in a junk shop just around the corner from the courthouse; (2) reenacting the old man's behavior with the aid of two canes, it took the minority person thirty-nine seconds, not fifteen as the old man had testified, to reach the hallway; and (3) the woman could not have clearly seen the defendant, because people do not wear glasses while trying to sleep. In the low persuasive arguments conditions, the minority consistently argued against the evidence without being able categorically to refute it. The vignettes were changed in the following way. No mention was made of there being another knife, the old man's ability to identify the defendant was questioned, but the reenactment did not take place, and the discussion on not wearing glasses to bed was emphasized less.

For half of the conditions, the jury's verdict was given to the subjects at four different times. Subjects were presented the jury verdict after the end of the summary of the evidence against the defendant and again after the jury's summary discussion of each piece of evidence. The order of the four jury verdicts were (first number voting guilty; second number voting innocent) 11:1, 5:7, 3:9, and 0:12. In the other half of the conditions, no mention was made of jury verdicts. All experimental subjects were asked four times to indicate the probability that they felt the son was guilty of murdering his father: first after the summary of evidence against the son and after the jury's discussion of each piece of evidence.

The results of the experiment clearly demonstrated that the minority had more influence when it could refute the majority's arguments than when it could not and minority influence increased as a positive function of the number of arguments that the minority could refute. Minority influence also increased in direct proportion to the number of majority members who deserted to the minority positions. In addition, the minority was most effective when it could refute the majority's arguments and gain an increasing number of converts in the process; the minority was the least effective when both argument refutation and information on jury verdicts were absent.

The results of the Clark (1990) study provide a plausible solution to the asymmetry in minority influence, which was mentioned earlier. It was pointed out that a minority was most effective when it represented the population's majority position in the laboratory. However, the present results clearly indicate that a minority can defend a population's minority viewpoint and change the majority if the minority can either refute the majority's arguments or gain defectors from the majority; both factors occurring together enhance minority influence.

Notwithstanding, we need to be very careful about overplaying the importance of a single study. Before we can have anywhere near the same degree of confidence for the role of social comparison and persuasive arguments in minority influence as we do for group polarization, we will need much more experimental research. The minority arguments in the Clark (1990) study were very strong and came probably as close as one can get to the objective end of the objective-subjective continuum for arguments (see Crano, this volume). Would similar results be obtained with more subjective arguments? How important are the number and persuasiveness of arguments and do they integrate according to an information integration framework (Anderson and Graesser, 1976)? From a social comparison framework, would information about the people who defected in the Clark (1990) study make a difference: would the social comparison effect have been stronger if the subjects were told, as readers of the play discover, that there is a positive direct relationship between the earlier deserters and their admirable personal attributes and qualities? These are just a few of the questions that are worthy of future research.

One further point needs to be mentioned. A very interesting and provocative discussion of *Twelve Angry Men* can be found in Brown (1986). In keeping with his customary and brilliant analysis of social phenomena, Brown argued that Rose's play provided a perfect case for understanding group polarization. Brown's basic point was that the trial was quite unique in that the population of relevant arguments failed to emerge during the trial, for example, the population of arguments was for innocence but this was not revealed during the trial. Thus, the first jury verdict was incorrect because it was based on a unrepresentative presentation of the population of arguments concerning the case. The lone dissenter's refusal to go along with the other eleven jurors served two purposes and explains why Brown believes *Twelve*

Angry Men to be a perfect prototype of group polarization. With the introduction of each "new," but "correct argument," according to the arguments that exist in the population, the lone dissenter gained converts. In addition, the converts possessed personal qualities that most people admire and wish to resemble. In short, according to Brown, both persuasive arguments and social comparison processes are deeply interwoven in the play.

Professor Brown's analysis of *Twelve Angry Men* is intriguing and profound. His claim that the play interweaves both persuasive arguments and social comparison processes is compelling and further points to the need to investigate and evaluate the similarities between group polarization and minority influence. Whereas I believe that both research on majority and minority sources of influence would benefit by such an endeavor, it would be incorrect to conclude, or even lean toward believing, that the processes underlying the two sources of influence are identical. I will conclude this chapter with a brief discussion of three differences between group polarization and minority influence.

Differences Between Minority Influence and Group Polarization

Our discussion of similarities between group polarization and minority influence would be amiss without mentioning a few fundamental differences between the two phenomena. I believe there are three primary differences: (1) whereas either social comparison processes or persuasive arguments is necessary for group polarization to occur, minority influence occurs in their absence; (2) individuals spend more time processing the minority message than the majority viewpoint; and (3) the nature of the change produced by majority and minority sources tends to be different. I will briefly discuss each in turn.

Either social comparison processes or persuasive arguments are necessary for individuals in groups or groups themselves to become more polarized. For example, if the differences among individuals preferences are negligible, polarization does not occur (Willems and Clark, 1971). In groups where a population of arguments on a given issue are widely shared, which precludes the introduction of new or unshared arguments, the group's final decision does not become more polarized (Vinokur and Burnstein, 1978). However, minority influence can and does occur in the absence of either process (Maass and Clark, 1984; Moscovici, 1980; Nemeth, 1986). For example, studies that have employed the simultaneous influence paradigm, where any desertion of majority members can be prevented and both the number and quality of arguments can be controlled, the minority still exerts more influence in private than does the majority (Clark and Maass, 1988a,

1988b; Clark and Maass, 1990; Maass and Clark, 1983). Similarly, in Clark's *Twelve Angry Men* study (1990) subjects were still influenced by a minority in the absence of jury information (social comparison) or the minority's ability to refute the majority arguments (persuasive arguments), although minority influence was additionally enhanced by both majority defectors and argument refutation.

The contents of this volume will repeatedly stress the view that individuals spend more time processing the minority position than the majority viewpoint. All dual models of social influence postulate that the minority message will generate either more quantitative or qualitative cognitive information processing than does the majority message. For example, whether one emphasizes that the minority causes subjects to reexamine the issue at hand (Moscovici, 1980) or causes persons to seek and generate more novel and creative solutions (Nemeth, 1986), the common assumption is that there is differential processing of information that favors the minority position.

The available evidence strongly supports this view. Nemeth (1986; see this volume) has repeatedly shown that subjects who are exposed to a minority position are motivated to seek and obtain novel and better solutions than either the majority or minority solution, but this is unlikely to occur for subjects who are exposed to a majority position. Maass and Clark (1983) found that minorities were more likely to trigger more favorable arguments and fewer counter-arguments than majorities and the amount of attitude change was mediated by this differential cognitive activity. The latter finding is particularly interesting because the minority generated different, qualitative thought processes even when both the number and the persuasiveness of the majority and minority arguments were controlled. Finally, Clark (1990) showed that subjects changed more toward the minority position when the minority could refute the majority arguments than when the minority could not—this occurred even in the absence of jury preferences—and minority influence increased with each argument refutation.

The last difference between group polarization and minority influence to be discussed is the nature of the change produced by majority and minority sources of influence. In studies comparing both sources of influence it has been repeatedly found that minority sources elicit their influence on private, indirect, or delayed measures of attitude change and the influence of majority sources shows up on public or direct measures (Maass and Clark, 1983; Nemeth, 1986). The results for the dependent measure in research on group polarization fits with this general framework. Although delayed and indirect measures are not employed, subjects in groups rarely have difficulty polarizing during the discussion, even when not required to reach a consensus, and their post-discussion decisions are as, or slightly less, polarized than the average of their original individual decisions (Myers and Lamm, 1976). Where the post-discussion decisions fall on a private-public continuum of attitude change is, perhaps, less clear, but I suspect the post-discussion decisions for studies on group polarization are not as far toward the private end of the continuum as are similar measures in minority influence research. The basis for this assertion is that minority influence researchers with the use of indirect and delayed measures [not without their own difficulty, however (Maass and Clark, 1983)] and with more careful attempts to assure subjects' confidentiality have probably employed purer measures of private attitude change on the post-discussion decisions than have researchers who have conducted research on group polarization.

Conclusion

I have tried to show that research on group polarization and minority influence has much more in common than one commonly finds in the literature on groups. Whether individuals in groups or groups polarized or whether minorities can change majorities depends, to a large extent, on the population's inclination on the issue at hand: group polarization and minority influence most readily occur when either the majority of persons in the group (group polarization paradigm) or the minority (minority influence paradigm) argues for the population's predilection on a given issue. While social comparison and persuasive arguments processes have dominated group polarization literature, the available evidence, as scant as it is, does suggest a role for these processes in understanding minority influence. Yet, there are crucial differences between group polarization and minority influence: (1) minority influence can occur in the absence of social comparison processes or persuasive arguments, whereas group polarization cannot, (2) minorities elicit more information processing than do majorities, and (3) minority influence effects tend to be more latent and subtle than majority effects. Notwithstanding these substantial differences, if more attention can be given to the similarities between group polarization and minority influence research, the minority message of this chapter will have succeeded.

References

Allen, V.L. (1975). Social support for nonconformity. In L. Berkowitz (Ed.), *Advances in Experimental Social Psychology,* vol. 8, pp. 1–43. New York: Academic Press.

Anderson, N.H., and Graesser, C.C. (1976). An information integration analysis of attitude change in group discussion. *Journal of Personality and Social Psychology,* 33, 210–222.

Archer, J. (1968). *The Unpopular Ones.* New York: Crowell–Collier.

Baron, R.S., Monson, T.G., and Bason, P.H. (1973). Conformity pressure as a determinant of risk-taking: Replication and extension. *Journal of Personality and Social Psychology,*28,406–413.

Brown, R. (1986). *Social Psychology*, 2nd ed. New York: Free Press.

Burnstein, E. and Vinokur, A. (1973). Testing two classes of theories about group induced shifts in individual choice. *Journal of Experimental Social Psychology,*9,123–127.

Clark, R.D., III. (1988). On predicting minority influence. *European Journal of Social Psychology,*18,515–526.

Clark, R. D., III, and Crockett, W. H. (1971). Subject's initial positions, exposure to varying opinions and the risky shift. *Psychonomic Science,*23,277–279.

Clark, R. D., III. (1990). Minority influence: The role of argument refutation of the majority position and social support for the minority position. *European Journal of Social Psychology,*20,489–497.

Clark, R., Crockett, H., and Archer, R. L. (1971). Risk as a value hypothesis: The relationship between perception of self, others, and the risky shift. *Journal of Personality and Social Psychology,*20,425–429.

Clark, R.D., III and Maass, A. (1988a). Social categorization in minority influence: The case of homosexuality. *European Journal of Social Psychology,*18,347–364.

Clark, R.D., III and Maass, A. (1988b). The role of social categorization and perceived source credibility in minority influence. *European Journal of Social Psychology,*18,381–394.

Clark, R.D., III, and Maass, A. (1990). The effects of majority size on minority influence. *European Journal of Social Psychology,*20,99–117.

Doise, W. (1969). Intergroup relations and polarization of individual and collective judgements. *Journal of Personality and Social Psychology,*12,136–143.

Ebbesen, E.B. and Bowers, M. (1974). The effects of proportion of risky to conservative arguments in a group discussion and choice shift. *Journal of Personality and Social Psychology,*29,316–327.

Fraser, C., Gouge, C., and Billig, M. (1971). Risky shifts, cautious shifts, and group polarization. *European Journal of Social Psychology,*1,7–30.

Kiesler, C.A., and Pallak, M.S. (1975). Minority influence: The effect of majority reactionaries and defectors, and minority and majority compromises, upon majority opinion and attraction. *European Journal of Social Psychology,*5,237–256.

Kuhn, T. (1962). *The Structure of Scientific Revolutions*. Chicago: University of Chicago Press.

Maass, A., and Clark, R. D., III. (1983). Internalization versus compliance: Differential processes underlying minority influence and conformity. *European Journal of Social Psychology,*13,197–215.

Maass, A., and Clark, R. D., III. (1984). Hidden impact of minorities: Fifteen years of minority influence research. *Psychological Bulletin,*95,428–450.

Moscovici, S. (1976). *Social Influence and Social Change*. London: Academic Press.

Moscovici, S. (1980). Toward a theory of conversion behavior. In L. Berkowitz (Ed.), *Advances in Experimental Social Psychology,* pp. 209–239. New York: Academic Press.

Moscovici, S. and Zavalloni, M. (1969). The group as a polarizer of attitudes. *Journal of Personality and Social Psychology,* 12,125–135.

Mugny, G. (1982). *The Power of Minorities.* London: Academic Press.

Myers, D.G. (1978). Polarizing effects of social comparison. *Journal of Experimental Social Psychology,* 14,554–563.

Myers, D.G. (1982). Polarizing effects of social interaction. In M. Brandstatter, J.H. Davis, and G. Stocker-Kreichgauer (Eds.), *Group Decision Making,* pp. 125–161. London: Academic Press.

Myers, D.G. and Arenson, S.J. (1972). Enhancement of dominant risk tendencies in group discussion. *Psychological Reports,* 30,275–286.

Myers, D.G., Bach, P.J., and Schreiber, F.B. (1974). Normative and informational effects of group interaction. *Sociometry,* 37,275–286.

Myers, D.G. and Bishop, G.D. (1971). The enhancement of dominant attitudes in group discussion. *Journal of Personality and Social Psychology,* 20,386–391.

Myers, D.G. and Lamm, H. (1976). The group polarization phenomenon. *Psychological Bulletin,* 83,602–627.

Nemeth, C. (1986). Differential contributions of majority and minority influence. *Psychological Review,* 93,23–32.

Paicheler, G. (1976). Norms and attitude change: I. Polarization and styles of behavior. *European Journal of Social Psychology,* 6,405–427.

Paicheler, G. (1979). Polarization of attitudes in homogeneous and heterogeneous groups. *European Journal of Social Psychology,* 9,85–96.

Rose, R. (1954). *Twelve Angry Men.* Chicago: Dramatic Pub. Co.

Silzer, R.F. and Clark, R.D., III. (1977). The effects of proportion strength and value orientation of arguments on decision-making. *European Journal of Social Psychology,* 7,451–464.

Teger, A.I. and Pruitt, D.G. (1967). Components of group risk taking. *Journal of Experimental Psychology,* 3,189–205.

Rogers, E. M. (1983). *Diffusion of Innovations,* 3d ed. New York: Free Press.

Vidmar, N. (1970). Group composition and the risky shift. *Journal of Experimental Social Psychology,* 6,153–166.

Vinokur, A. (1971). Cognitive and affective processes in influencing risk taking in groups: An expected utility approach. *Journal of Personality and Social Psychology,* 20,472–487.

Vinokur, A. and Bernstein, E. (1974). Effects of partially shared persuasive arguments on group-induced shifts: A group-problem-solving approach. *Journal of Personality and Social Psychology,* 29,305–315.

Vinokur, A. and Burnstein, E. (1978). Depolarization of attitudes in groups. *Journal of Personality and Social Psychology,* 36,872–885.

Wallach, M.A. and Mabli, J. (1970). Information versus conformity in the effects of group discussion on risk-taking. *Journal of Personality and Social Psychology,* 14,149–156.

Willems, E.P. and Clark, R.D., III. (1971). Shift toward risk and heterogeneity of groups. *Journal of Experimental Social Psychology,* 7,204–312.

CHAPTER FOUR

MINORITY INFLUENCES AND INNOVATIONS: THE SEARCH FOR AN INTEGRATED EXPLANATION OF PSYCHOLOGICAL AND SOCIOLOGICAL MODELS

Erich H. Witte

There is no doubt that research on minorities has been and still is a stimulating approach for the whole area of research on small groups. However, such research needs a theoretical foundation if it is not to be reduced to simply one more effect such as risky-shift, autokinetic phenomena, obedience or some other effect in the literature on small groups. But it is not only the absence of theoretical explanations in the area of minority influences which causes problems; it is the polymorphic shape of the explanations on the one hand and the absence of a more general model on the other which are decisive. My main intention is to discuss theoretical models from psychological and sociological psychology, and to offer an *integration of these models* as a fundamental explanation of minority influences and innovation in small group settings.

One of the most fruitful differentiations in small group research was made by Deutsch and Gerard (1955), who divided social influence into normative and informational components. Normative social influence has to do with the expectations of other people and pressure to uniformity. Informational influence depends upon the arguments in the group and reactions displayed there as a general orientation about what to do.[1] With this differentiation in mind, combined with the distinction between psychological and sociological perspectives, we have six categories: normative, informational, and normative *plus* informational in each of the psychological and sociological perspectives.

This spectrum of possible explanations is the basis for looking for theoretical concepts. I will start by reviewing psychological models.

Psychological Explanations of Minority Influences

Two excellent summaries of psychological research on minority influences exist (Maass and Clark, 1984; Moscovici, 1985), so that it is not necessary to carry out another review of empirical results. I will focus attention on more precise models, which are able to make qualitative predictions. However, I do not want to ignore more qualitative concepts, if they aid understanding of the processes underlying quantitive predictions. I will start the discussion with concepts which concentrate on the *normative* influence: the *social impact theory* (Latané and Wolf, 1981; Wolf and Latané, 1983) and the *social influence model* (Tanford and Penrod, 1984). Next I will discuss *informational* influences in the form of *social decision schemes* (Davis, 1973, 1982) and their extensions (Stasser and Davis, 1981), and the *principles of attribution* (Kelley, 1973; Kelley and Michela, 1980). Then follow two concepts of a *combined normative and informational* influence. These are the *theory of conversion behavior* (Moscovici, 1976, 1980) and the *group situation theory* (Witte, 1979, 1987, 1990).

Concepts of the Normative Influence of Small Group Minorities

For the moment it is my intention to look only at *number* of people (N) as an influence factor. For a more detailed model, see Jackson (1987). Generally, social impact (I_p) depends upon the number of sources and the number of targets. The assumed relationship is the following:

$$I_p = s \cdot N^c \text{ sources } / N^f \text{ targets}$$

$$c, f : \text{ exponents less than 1}$$

If we define the number of minority members as the sources and the number of majority members as the targets using a logarithmic transformation we get the following linear relation:

$$\log I_p = s + c \log N \text{ sources } - f \log N \text{ targets}$$

If we assume that both exponents are equal and near 0.50 (Tanford and Penrod, 1984) we get the following formula:

$$\log I_p = s + 0.5 \, (\log N_{\text{sources}} - \log N_{\text{targets}})$$

This effect implies a higher increase of impact by small minorities. If we take a majority of 10 as the base and an increasing minority from 1 to 9, social impact as the square root of values ranging from 0.1 to 0.9 could amount to: 0.32, 0.45, 0.55, 0.63, 0.71, 0.77, 0.84, 0.89, 0.95. The qualitative characteristic of this model is the reduced increase of impact with increasing size of the minority.

The social influence model, as the next concept, is a slight modification of the social impact theory, especially founded on data fitting without explanation of the psychological processes (Tanford and Penrod, 1984). They have used the *Gompertz* growth model, because the qualitative characteristics are different from the power function used in the social impact theory. The *Gompertz* curve is S-shaped, so that the influence commences with positive acceleration with increasing numbers reaches a point of inflection, and thereafter is negatively accelerated, as in the power function. Generally, the model is the following:

$$I_p = a, e^{(-k, e^{-S/T})}$$
S : number of sources
T : number of targets

But, of course, behind such a model there are some assumptions, which explain the shape of the curve. The idea is that the impact I_p is measured by a percentage; this percentage is small and distribute as a *Poisson* model with two influence factors—S and T—which are combined multiplicatively $S \cdot \frac{1}{T}$). If we want to get linear relationships, as a comparable description for all formulas, we have to use the loglogtransformation:

$$z = \ln \, (-\ln I_p)$$

ln : logarithmus naturalis

The first logarithmic transformation is necessary because I_p is a percentage, which has some anomalies if we want to have a linear relation. For this reason we sometimes use logit and probit or single logarithmic transformations. The second logarithmic transformation is the same as in social impact theory. Thus the "complicated" *Gompertz* function is the result of the measurement of impact by percentages.

Generally, both theoretical concepts are equivalent, but if the dependent variable is a percentage we need a second logarithmic transformation so that the Gompertz function will be better fitted.

Concepts of Informational Influence of Small Group Minorities

At first I intend to regard *social decision schemes* as a single complex model which allows prediction of reactions from the distribution of the individual reactions before discussion and therefore should be able to predict the influence of minorities. The idea is that the arguments during discussion influence individual reactions. The application of the model is manifold. It has been used to analyze intellectual tasks (Laughlin and Adamopoulos, 1982), mock jury decisions (Davis, 1980) and attitudinal judgments (Kerr, Davis, Meek, and Rissman, 1975). On intellectual tasks with a correct or objective solution there is one basic social combination process called *"truth supported wins"*: two correct members are necessary and sufficient for a correct group response. There is no difference in the social decision scheme whether the group has five or four members, but only in the first case do we have a minority influence. This is a *correction effect* of small group minorities using a stimulus material with *objective* solutions. Obviously, the demonstration of the *correct* response is very successful in such a case.

On the other hand, research with mock juries and attitudinal judgments—stimulus material with only *"subjective"* solutions—is best described by the social combination process called *"majority wins"*: a majority of the group members determine the group response. This influence process—called *conformity effect*—needs a (typically two-thirds) majority, if the whole group is to accept the proposed alternative. However, we are not interested in the social decision schemes per se, but in minority influences. These are best studied in the form of mock jury decisions, because this kind of problem seems to be comparable to innovations in social, technical, and scientific fields. If we look only at six person mock juries under a simple majority rule we get, after an initial distribution of four (guilty) to two (not guilty), 16 percent (Davis et al., 1977) and 15 percent (Kerr et al., 1976) of not guilty verdicts. The minority influence is a little higher with jury decision tasks than with perceptual tasks, but, generally, it is easier to shift in a not guilty direction. This leniency bias is comparable to the *zeitgeist* effect, which means that a minority is more influential under positive zeitgeist conditions (Maass and Clark, 1984). The shifts in the guilty direction under the initial distribution of two to four are 6 percent and 11 percent. This amount seems to equal the one in the perceptual task, where nobody outside the experimental influence would choose the response of the minority.

What is interesting here is the question of the number of minority members needed to produce a change in about 10 percent of the cases. In a twelve person jury the distribution of eleven to one gives an observed transition frequency of 7 percent in the direction of the minority (not guilty) and an initial distribution of ten to two gives a percentage of 12 percent. The following preshift distributions produce a greater change in the direction of the minority. In a six person jury we get 9 percent change in the minority's direction under an initial distribution of five to one (for these data see Kerr and MacCoun, 1985, table 3). There is an effective social rule helping the minority to influence the majority in the direction of acquittal (*"in dubio pro reo"*). In the usual distribution of four to two we get 58 percent change in the minority's direction. However, a preshift distribution of two to four yields only a 13 percent change to conviction. This latter amount of change is comparable to the small group minority's conformity effect in the perceptual task.

These results mean generally we have to distinguish two situations for an innovation: one is favorable to the conformity effect of the small group minority, and one is unfavorable. But even under unfavorable conditions we observe a minority influence, which is enhanced by a consistent minority of two. The social support of the zeitgeist, the favorable condition, lies between a correction effect (objective solutions) and a conformity effect (subjective solutions), if we consider the amount of influence. Obviously, the small group minority influence depends upon the *verifiability of choice* and the corresponding arguments. It is a real innovation and without help from the zeitgeist it is very hard to influence the majority in a small group situation. The conformity effect is small; in only 10 percent of the cases will the opinion of the majority be changed.

The next question is why there is such a *small* change. This might be explained by the use of information in a small group. *Firstly,* we have the arguments about the individual choice or only the choice itself as a datum for each individual in a small group. *Secondly,* we have information about the distribution of individual choices. *Thirdly,* there is the information about consistency. And *fourthly,* we sometimes have information about the social position of the group members outside the small group. The individual group member now has the problem of evaluating the difference between his own perception or choice and the perception or choice of deviating members. Small differences are eliminated by reaching a compromise, but a large (informational) deviation results in a *qualitative* difference which has to be explained.

Such an explanation is often modelled by *attributional accounts.* Generally, attribution is the basis for the convincingness of the deviating information. A first step is to ignore the difference, because it is attributed to a single minority member, if this person is consistent. Otherwise, it can always be ignored. If there is more than one member with a deviating reaction then we have high *consensus and consistency,* which reduce a personal explanation. This seems to involve a qualitative jump in the explanation, because we have to use two dimensions to explain the observed reactions. This results in an attribution on the entity (the stimulus material). The influence of the minority may be enhanced if information is available about the disadvantage of the minority. This is the *augmenting* principle (Kelley and Michela, 1980).

On the other hand, if we have information about the minority's social position then the deviation may possibly be *discounted* as irrelevant for our own perception. Discounting is possible if we know the political orientation, the economic interests, or the scientific school of the dissenters. But if we recognize their expertise the influence of the minority could increase. This kind of explanation is the basis for the acceptance of deviating information about the ''right'' reaction. It determines the weight given to the minority's standpoint in changing one's own perception or reaction. The meaning of the deviation in the small group has to be clarified before the majority members know what to do.

Generally, there is a small amount of influence, because the members of the majority themselves have been consistent in the past and because they experience a high consensus of their subgroup. If they are certain about their choice there will be no change at all. However, this conflict between two standpoints will reduce the *certainty* in the individual reaction.

At first glance, this is a mere speculation, but in an excellent article about social influence Stasser and Davis (1981) distinguished both aspects: opinion or choice change and certainty change. Their model is a dynamic description of the social influence in mock juries, but their intention is to formulate a general process model of social influence in small groups. They differentiate four individual states of group members:

S_1—guilty and certain
S_2—guilty and uncertain
S_3—not guilty and uncertain
S_4—not guilty and certain.

A real innovation comes from a minority which is certain and tries to influence the more or less certain majority.

Without going into the details of the interaction sequence model (SIS model) the assumption is that the change can be modelled by transitional probabilities which predict the distribution of individual states at time $t+1$ from the distribution at time t. These transition probabilities depend upon two parameters, a general random shift parameter a_{ij} and an informational influence parameter, which depends upon the size of the subgroup favoring a specific choice A_1; this means n_1/n, or vice versa n_2/n, if the choice A_2 is preferred. The best fitted function for the transition probabilities (favoring A_1) seems to be the following:

$$m_{ij} = a_{ij} (n_1/n)^2$$

If we use a logarithmic transformation to give the linear relation we get for the alternative A_1:

$$\log m_{ij} = a_{ij} + 2 (\log n_1 - \log n)$$

Obviously, such a model is not very different from social impact theory, if we ignore the magnitude of the exponent. However, the impact model refers to normative influence, whereas the SIS model has its basis in informational influence, although the exponent of $c = 2$ is interpreted as a normative influence (Stasser and Davis, 1981). This comparison is only valid for a *one shot* similarity; the *dynamic* character of the SIS model is more elaborate. The end result for a minority of two against a majority of four to vote not guilty gives 8 percent convictions, which is comparable with other empirical results for real "innovations." The foundation of this prediction, however, is a process model of a combined certainty and opinion change. This change might be explained by regarding the argumentation as a perceptual influence and the attributional accounts as a certainty change. Both sets of information depend upon the number of the factions as a descriptive parameter, but the assumed *psychological processes* are argumentation and attribution.

I will now describe models which clearly distinguish both kinds of influences in their approaches.

Concepts of a Combined Normative and Informational Influence

A major shortcoming of the models described so far is that they do not explicitly distinguish between informational and normative influence and their interaction. I will concentrate on two models: the *theory of conversion behavior* (Moscovici, 1980) and *group situation theory* (Witte, 1987, 1990). Both try to explain behavior in small groups. The first is a descriptive concept of the underlying normative and informational processes, the second is a more formalized approach, which is capable of yielding quantitative predictions.

I will start with the theory of conversion behavior, which uses the differentiation of majority and minority influences as one dimension and the difference between public and private reaction as the second. With these two dimensions we get a fourfold table, for the cells of which Moscovici assumes different processes. These processes themselves are modeled on assumptions given by Kelman (1958, 1961): (a) the *majority* of a small group uses power as a normative influence mechanism with the result of *compliance* without individual change, (b) the *minority* has no power and its influence mechanism is (informational) *internalization* based on *credibility*. If (c) the reaction is *public* under the inspection of the majority in the group, normative influence "power" still exists, and the individual reaction partially conforms to the majority. This is the classical conformity effect. On the contrary, if (d) the reaction is public under a minority's influence there is only a small change, because the conformity effect still exists. However, this depends upon the verifiability of the reaction. As we have seen with intellectual tasks the influence of a minority of two members is very high if their arguments are convincing. However, under the usual majority and minority influences, the majority or the minority *experimentally* deviates from an accepted reaction outside the lab, so that the individual reaction must be balanced between two conformity processes: the one outside the lab as a general orientation and the one of the small group inside. Of course, the experimentally induced deviation is not very convincing, if outside the lab nobody would choose the induced reaction. This all depends upon the stimulus material. Indeed, it is possible to find a minority influence with material of attitudinal judgments, used in the research of the choice shift effect, where a minority influences a majority more than it is influenced by the majority, and the reactions are public and private. Obviously, what is needed is a further differentiation of the stimulus material and its degree of verifiability through the physical or social reality. If there is high verifiability individual change is only elicited by influences in the group situation, because the subject individually conforms to the usual reaction. If the verifiability of choice is medium with a social preference to one side as in the choice dilemmas, we get a minority effect without cognitive changes but with certainty changes (in the direction of higher certainty) producing a more extreme answer (Witte, 1979; Witte and Arez, 1974; Witte and Lutz, 1982). This is a minority influence under conditions of public reaction without conversion.

The most provocative and stimulating expression of the conversion theory is given by Moscovici (1980) in the following sentence (p. 237): "I would be tempted to draw the conclusion at the end of this contribution that minorities are more influential than majorities in the usual sense of the term, since they produce more genuine change." This genuine change means conversion, not compliance. This is particularly likely to occur when a minority is able to find the "right" response which is convincing for the majority. But then the public individual response is not different from the private. The greater influence of the minority is artificial, because a minority has a greater chance of convincing more people than a majority. The correction effect ("truth supported wins" as a decision scheme) is not the example which Moscovici (1980, 1985) had in mind. It is more a kind of increasing creativity by arguments coming from a minority instead of a majority, because the only form of a small group minority's influence is informational. If we take the conversion theory as a basis, then all changes are founded on convincing arguments, which remain convincing whether the reaction is public or private. The idea of a face saving strategy, if one reacts publicly, is not acceptable for me as the only explanation. Perhaps, it is only the avoidance of a conflict with the majority, if one is *not certain* about the right reaction. This is the state where people have changed their opinion, but are still not certain (see above).

In general, the confrontation between compliance and conversion and the whole discussion of the socially desirable effect of minorities is one extreme position on an ideological dimension differentiating between an optimistic view of social change with a *Hegelian* touch and a pessimistic view with a Hobbesian touch. Conversion theory is social psychology's variant of the first kind of view. This might be one reason why the third kind of influence process assumed by Kelman (1958, 1961) has been neglected by Moscovici: the attractivity of the minority which produces a change by identification (Witte, 1985). Sometimes such an influence is less desirable, for example, with the development of heroin addiction (DuPont and Greene, 1973). On the other hand, compliance always means something undesirable and the whole conformity research is based on that negative evaluation (Witte, 1987). If we turn to *solidarity* research, it becomes apparent that everybody would like to enhance this kind of behavior. But where is the difference between solidarity and conformity or compliance? In my opinion the metaphysics of conversion theory constitute a clear reaction to the metaphysics of general conformity research as its counterpart. However, the hypotheses of conversion theory are the product of such a metaphysics, and their plausibility is in danger of reducing the complexity of the phenomenon. Of course, what Moscovici has in mind exists, if he distinguishes between majority and minority influences: it is the deviate who prevents committees from group-think (Janis, 1972) or enhances the intellectual level (Nemeth, 1986) and creativity (Moscovici and Lage, 1978). This is the function of an "advocatus diaboli" which is the basis of the minority influence in common sense.

If we try to enrich the conversion theory by application of the theoretical concept on which conversion theory is founded, namely the influence processes given by Kelman, then we have to introduce a process of identification with a minority which is different from compliance and conversion in an intellectual manner. It is also possible that a minority with high social power is able to produce a conformity effect, for example, the Nazis in Germany in 1933 or the leader with high position power in a small group. Thus, focusing on specific influence processes produced only by minorities or majorities reduces the complex phenomenon in an unacceptable manner. Is it impossible that a majority has convincing arguments to produce a private change (conversion behavior)? Then it is necessary to specify the conditions under which a minority produces one of the three influence processes: compliance, identification, and conversion. This depends upon the characteristics of the minority, the kind of innovation (the stimulus material) and the generalization to natural processes. In spite of the criticism of conversion theory, the inverted view in small group research has been and will be stimulating. However, it is astonishing that this theory, which offers the possibility of explaining innovations more generally than in a small group context, has never incorporated empirical research and theoretical differentiations from sociology or political science, where we have a long tradition of innovation research (e.g., Rogers and Shoemaker, 1971).

Next I will deal with a theoretical concept which attempts to explain individual behavior in a group situation—clearly divided into normative and informational influences (Witte, 1979, 1987, 1990). The idea behind the concept is to integrate classical approaches of small group research into one middle range theory, where the normative dimensions offer an orientational framework and the arguments are the informational influence. Therefore, it is not exclusively a theory of minority influences but a concept of the general group situation, which is thus able to explain the influence of small group minorities, too. It differentiates between normative and informational dimensions. The normative dimensions guide the information integration process. Both kinds of dimensions remain in a hierarchical order with the most general at the top (see table 4.1). For the normative dimensions we have a component which stems from scientific discussion of the problem of the applicability of theories to one's own behavior (Habermas, 1966). The idea is that one can use knowledge of group situation theory to change behavior within the group. This normative component affects all other conditions so that it is of highest order. This component is called *"awareness of theory (AT)"*: the degree of familiarity with the theory, e.g., knowing how social influence works. At the moment I will only differentiate between two conditions: AT = O, no familiarity, and AT = 1, familiarity. As the second normative component I will introduce an emotional element. It has to do with group cohesion and is called *"group atmosphere (GA)"*—the average measure of how much the members of a group accept each other personally and in terms of emotional regard. The following three conditions are to be differentiated: GA = 1, mutual rejection, GA = 2, low positive regard, GA = 3, high positive regard.

As the next normative component one can take the divergence of judgments (reactions, evaluations) within the group. It represents the difficulty of the initial conditions, if a subject is to be discussed. A suggestion for measuring such differences is the range, because individual differences are not taken sufficiently into account in the classic measure, the standard deviation (Moscovici and Lecuyer, 1972). This normative dimension can be defined as follows: *"Distribution of individual choices (DIC)"*—the range of the individual choices before the group discussion. The range is divided into three conditions: DIC = 1, identical individual choices, DIC = 2, medium range, DIC = 3, extreme range.

A further point that controls behavior in the group situation is the stimulus material, as I have discussed above. It can be material for which there is a (objective) solution that will be accepted by everyone, once one person has found it. This is the basis of the correction effect. On the other hand, there is material in whose case it is only roughly clear what one is to do, for example, choice dilemma items (subjective solution). Finally, there is material where a specific orientation within a spread is missing, for example, the autokinetic effect. Dependent on the type of task set, the group interaction will be different and, of course, so will the influence of minorities. If small group minorities have the possibility of coming back to a general orientation determined by a physical or social reality—as in the case of the correction effect or as is clearly demonstrable in the risky-shift effect—then the influence will be extraordinary. I will define this normative component as follows: *verifiability of choice (VC)*—the possibility of finding a solution to a task according to social or objective points of view. Again a difference is made between three conditions: VC = 1, little verifiability, VC = 2, medium verifiability, VC = 3, high verifiability.

Finally, there is an additional component, which arises when people negotiate within a group bound by decisions. We shall define this normative component as follows: *"Commitment to a constituency (CC)"*—the degree of obligation felt by the negotiators to their initially given position. Here, too, three states are to be distinguished: CC = 1, no obligation, CC = 2, medium obligation, CC = 3, deep obligation.

The last normative dimension is a residual category, which includes normative influences not yet considered. The variable can be defined as follows: *"Uniformity pressure" (UP)*—the degree of experienced compulsion to consider super-individual values, for example, the group standard of the social value (s. below). A continuous variation is assumed here, because several variables may be involved. A certain reference to a further differentiation can be taken from social impact theory (Witte, 1990).

These normative dimensions offer an *orientational framework* in a group situation. This framework guides the information integration process about how to use reactions and arguments for one's own reaction. In general, we also have a hierarchical order of these *informational components*, which depends upon their generalizability. The most general information about how to behave is the social value (SV) or the objective standard (OS). The social value (SV) is the behavior standard of the reference group in a specific stimulus-reaction situation, for example, to be risky or cautious in specific social dilemmas. The objective standard (OS) is the behavior standard according to objective criteria, for example, the length of a line or the solution of an anagram.

The next informational component describes the *"group standard"* *(GS)*—the behavior standard in the specific group, usually the weighted mean of the individual choices before discussion: different weights may be given to the members according to their status. Because of this, a high status leader as a minority is able to influence the other members in form of a compliance effect.

The third informational component is the *"argumentation"* *(AR)* in the group—the concrete argumentation in the specific group, usually the weighted mean of the arguments on the reaction scale: different weights may be given by independent observers, according to their convincingness. (There is one study from the area of minority influence which fits the model: Clark, 1990.)

The last informational component is the *"individual value"* *(IV)*—a term introduced in order to take into account those components of the information processing and reaction that are specific to the individual member (e.g., intelligence, knowledge, independence). Like "uniformity pressure" (UP), it is a kind of residual category.

The assumption now is that we get a linear information integration of the following form:

$$Y = aSV + b(GS - SV) + c\{AR - [aSV + b(GS - SV)]\}$$

Y : forecast of individual behavior in a group situation
a, b, c : weights with $a + b + c = 1$

The weights change with the group situation. A proposed complex combination of normative and informational components is given in table 4.1.

If we now want to reconstruct as an illustration of the theory's usefulness the classical studies on minority influences used in Tanford and

Table 4.1   Model of Individual Choice Behavior in Group Situations

	"if...,	then..., "
Awareness of theory	AT = 0	go to GA
	AT = 1	$\hat{Y}$ = AR
Group atmosphere	GA = 1	no social interaction
	GA = 2	go to DIC
	GA = 3	$\hat{Y}$ = GS
Distribution of individual choices	DIC = 1	$\hat{Y}$ = GS
	DIC = 2	go to VC
	DIC = 3	group falls apart
Verifiability of choices	VC = 3	$\hat{Y}$ = SV
	VC = 2	go to CC
	VC = 1	$\hat{Y}$ = (GS + AR)/2
Commitment to a constituency	CC = 1	$\hat{Y}$ = (SV + GS + AR)/3
		= SV+1/2(GS–SV)+1/3{AR–(SV+1/2(GS–SV))}
	CC = 2	$\hat{Y}$ = $(SV_1 - GS_1 + AR_1 + SV_2 + GS_2 + AR_2)/6$
	CC = 3	$\hat{Y}$ = $1/2\ DEMAND_1 + 1/2\ DEMAND_2$
Uniformity pressure	UP varies continuously	The higher UP, the less variance has to be explained by the residual category IV (individual value).

Source: Witte, 1987, p. 1.

Penrod (1984) with a percentage of change, then we get about 10 percent individual changes in a group with six people where two are a consistent minority. Since the stimulus material used has a high verifiability of choice the prediction is no change at all in the direction of the deviating minority. This would be the case if the minority were not confederates. Under the specific condition with the help of confederates we now have to assume that the naive subject's certainty of the right reaction has been modified; this means that the verifiability of choice (VC) has changed from high to medium. In this case the group standard has an influence corresponding to the following formula:

$$Y = SV + 1/2\ (GS - SV)$$

Y : the expected percentage of change

SV : the general orientation as an individual, the right reaction R

GS : the mean of the different reactions in the group with a majority who shows "correct" (R) reactions and a minority who shows "wrong" (W) reactions

In a six-person group we get:

GS = 2/3 R + 1/3 W

Thus, the prediction is:

Y = R + 1/2 (2/3R + 1/3W − R) = 0.83 R + 0.17 W

Obviously, this percentage of wrong reactions seems to be overestimated. One plausible explanation is that the minority has not changed the certainty from high to medium for all subjects. Fortunately, Moscovici and Faucheux (1972) reported on a sample of people who give more than two wrong reactions. They call them "influenced subjects." This sample of subjects, we may assume, has reached the state of medium verifiability. For these subjects the prediction should be correct. Their percentage of change is 18.4 and 19.3 in two experiments. This seems to be an acceptable prediction. For all subjects together the easiest assumption is that only half of them have changed their certainty, with a consequent reduction of the weight from ½ to ¼. We then get 8.5 percent wrong reactions. This is a first approximation of the weight's reduction.

Obviously, the theory has to be completed if we want to predict minority influences. We then have a modification of the normative components through informational processes. This is a feedback loop which has been neglected in the theory. But because it has been the fundamental basis of the SIS shift model, with its differentiation into a certainty change as a normative shift according to the group situation theory (VC) and an opinion change as an informational shift found on the reaction scale after the information integration process, and because this model arrived at some promising predictions this feedback is very plausible. Furthermore, there are two other experiments in which the subjects who have to answer immediately after the consistent minority showed a percentage of change which was somewhat higher than usual: 14 percent and 12.5 percent (Doms, 1984).

It is now interesting to use stimulus material which has a medium verifiability (VC = 2) and with which we get natural minorities before discussion. This idea was followed by Nemeth (1982). She used four personal injury cases and discussion of the amount of money thought to be proper for compensation. There were two sub-groups asked individually. The majority preferred as a mean x_1 = \$212,288 and the minority preferred

$x_2 = \$116,088$. In a six person group, which discussed one case, there were four members of the majority and two of the minority. The assumption is that we have a normal experimental situation with medium verifiability and—as an assumption—without any new arguments during discussion, so that we can eliminate the influence of the argumentation on changes in reaction. The prediction is:

$Y = SV + 1/2(GS - SV)$
$SV = 212,288$ the mean of the majority as a general orientation
$GS = 4/6\ (212,288) + 2/6\ (116,088) = 178,419$
$Y = 195,353$

A mean of $Y_{emp} = 189,677$ was empirically observed. As a first approximation to predict the global processes of the minority's social influence this result seems acceptable. Under this condition, with natural minorities and medium verifiability, we have a normal information integration process.

I will now concentrate on some special effects which have been observed during the research on minority influences: (a) the zeitgeist effect, and (b) the cohesion effect. My intention is to give an explanation which is consistent with group situation theory.

First, we have the *zeitgeist effect*; a minority is very influential under positive zeitgeist conditions. The idea of group situation theory is that a positive zeitgeist means a social value (SV) which is in favor of the position of the minority. Under these conditions for a six-person group with two members against the four member majority and stimulus material with medium verifiability we get:

$Y = SV + 1/2\ (GS - SV)$
$GS = 2/3\ W + 1/3\ R$
$AR = SV + 1/2\ (GS - SV)$ so that the argumentation has no influence
$Y = R + 1/2\ (2/3W + 1/3R - R)$
$\quad = 0.67\ R + 0.33\ W$

This prediction measured on a nominal scale means that the influence of the minority inverted the percentages of the reaction alternatives before discussion. The influence of a minority against a zeitgeist is minimal and can be predicted in the following way:

$GS = 2/3\ W + 1/3\ R$ and $SV = W$ then
$Y = W + 1/2\ (2/3W + 1/3R - W)$
$\quad = 0.83\ W + 0.17\ R$

But this percentage is reached under the assumption of no further change resulting from argumentation. This seems to be unrealistic because the general convincingness of arguments in favor of the zeitgeist—measured by independent observers—is high, and arguments of a minority against a general orientation are seldom very convincing. Thus, the given prediction is only valid for optimal conditions, if the minority is able to find convincing arguments and the stimulus material is of medium verifiability. This is probably the condition which Nemeth (1986) had in mind when she assumed that small group minorities stimulate divergent thinking.

The next point is the *cohesive effect* (Wolf, 1979, 1985). It was generally observed that the more cohesive the group the more individuals changed in the direction of the minority position. The explanation of this effect's consistency with group situation theory is as follows: Under a group atmosphere of high positive regard (GA = 3) the group tries to find a compromise among the individual standpoints:

$$Y = GS$$
$$GS = 2/3 \ W + 1/3 \ R$$
$$Y = 0.67 \ W + 0.33 \ R$$

The influence of the minority is equivalent to its size.

In general, group situation theory is able to predict the minority influences quantitatively and qualitatively in an acceptable manner. Conversion theory concentrates only on the difference between minority and majority influences without specifying the whole complex of differences and similarities between the normative and informational components involved in this difference. Finally, the argumentation of a small group minority with more fundamental deviating choices being on a higher intellectual level is a point which is acceptable, because small groups tend to group-think. This is the function of the classical "advocatus diaboli." But it is self-evident that the positive view of minority influences depends upon several normative and informational conditions.

Sociological Explanations of Minority Influences

Sociological research on minority influences and innovation has a long tradition (Tards, 1903; Ogburn, 1922) and has culminated in comprehensive overviews by Rogers and Shoemaker (1971) and Rogers (1983). A first integration of different hypotheses had been given by Rogers (1962). Unfortunately, the different traditions of research and scientific discussion have led to a nearly complete ignorance of these sociological studies and theories in psychology. This is especially astonishing in view of the fact that the whole phenomenon is seen as sociological in nature (Moscovici, 1976). However, major reviews of this research on small group minorities deplore the static explanations and the absence of field research (Maass and Clark, 1984), but the fact is that there are many studies and theories in sociology and political science which have precisely this content. It is impossible to present this research in systematical detail and I will therefore concentrate on three classical examples with a close connection to social psychology and which combine natural observation and theoretical modeling:

a. The classical study by Coleman, Katz, and Menzel (1966) on the adoption of a new antibiotic among physicians, where the explanation is based on number of people as in social impact theory, a more *normative* aspect.
b. The study by Fliegel and Kivlin (1966), where the diffusion of innovations depended on the ascribed characteristics of the innovations, a more *informational* aspect.
c. The study by Mohr (1969) on the determinants of innovation in organizations, where the explanation is based on the ideology of the leader and the resources available for innovation: this involves concentration on informational (ideology) *and* normative (resources) influence.

With these three studies of natural innovations we have a parallel spectrum to the psychological approaches, so that it is possible to compare the studies and explanations more systematically.

A Concept of Normative Influence

In a study of adoption by doctors of a new antibiotic (Coleman et al., 1966) the process of innovation has been observed. I focus my attention here on these physicians with low social participation. The idea is that there is a constant flow of information about the innovation and no additional influence through direct contacts. Under this assumption, the *number* of new adopters per time unit—as the normative influence—is proportional only to those who have not yet adopted:

$$\frac{dy}{dt} = ß (n - y)$$

n : percentage of possible adopters: 100%
y : percentage of adopters
ß : rate of change per time unit

We then get the following curve:

$$y(t) = n(1 - e^{-ßt})$$

83

As the empirical result we get the following function:

$$y(t) = 1 - e^{-0.11t}$$

This whole explanation is based on time and number or, in this case, percentage. If we eliminate time, setting $t = 1$, we get a percentage of $y = 0.10$. This is what has been observed in the lab under condition of high verifiability (VC $= 3$) of the majority's position which means a real innovation. In this case, it seems to be necessary to diffuse the information that some other colleagues use the drug. It is not necessary to have a contact in a small group. It seems to be enough that some people deviate to reduce the certainty, which leads to a change in behavior of a small percentage. It is not clear whether number of people only is a normative or also informational influence. It is both, I suspect. In spite of this small amount of change, which at first glance seems to be a negligible experimental effect in psychological research, within about seven months there was a majority using the new antibiotic. In three years, 98 percent of the physicians were using the drug, although the first change was only of the order of 10 percent. By and large, the results found by Moscovici, Lage and Naffrechoux (1969) are not an artificial effect of the lab as an inversion of the Asch studies, but the amount of the effect has a natural counterpart.

If we look for a theoretical similarity between sociological and psychological models then we have to find the linear function between the dependent and independent variable:

$$1 - y = e^{-0.11t}$$
$$\ln(-\ln(1-y)) = 0.11 + t$$

This is what Tanford and Penrod (1984) used in order to describe the relation between number and percent of change. Here *time* is the influence factor, but the law is the same. However, as a result of looking only at variables on the surface, the psychological processes are not isolated. Yet the amount of change in different areas is an informative result. Obviously, small groups are not the only mechanism to produce innovation but advertising campaigns are also effective instruments. Usually, natural innovations need the mass media to become known and diffused in the population. The small group setting with a consistent minority is the maximization of social influence exerted by a minority. But the amount of change is not different from advertising or other indirect contacts. To reach an equal amount of social influence we do not need small group minorities, but it is possible to use them if they are able to be consistent and convincing.

A Concept of Informational Influence

It has been observed that some inventions become innovations in a short time, whereas others need a longer period, and still others never become innovations at all. There must be some characteristics of the inventions themselves which facilitate the innovation process, and others which hinder it. To determine these characteristics was the main intention of the study by Fliegel and Kivlin (1966). The field of innovation was farming practices. The authors found four different characteristics which have a significant partial correlation with the degree of adoption, that is, a correlation which is independent of influences of all other factors. These characteristics are: (a) a stepwise test of the innovation, (b) the initial costs, which means because of the positive correlation that higher costs do not hinder the innovation, (c) the utility of the innovation, which is self-evident, and (d) the compatibility with the main farming practices.

We have to look at experimental research with these characteristics of natural innovation in mind. At first an innovation is facilitated if there is an incremental strategy of adoption. This means for the experimental studies that the influence of minorities will be different if the reaction alternative is continuous or discrete. Generally, the verifiability of choice is reduced if there are several alternatives of reaction. Under these conditions the influence of a minority is easier to exercise perhaps a global concept for innovation. Secondly, there seems to be something like an assumption that what is expensive must be good, so that the level of investment in the innovation is, perhaps, assumed to be a general indication of its usefulness. This aspect has not been varied systematically in the experimental studies. Surely, it is an important point of natural innovations to know why to change. For this reason the third characteristic, the utility of the innovation, is an important point, too. The stimulus material of the experimental studies, however, is seldom complex enough to see the individual importance of an innovation for the person in question. A small group minority is perhaps more influential if it is possible to argue in favor of the utility of an innovation for each majority member. Thus, the content of the stimulus material is important for the modeling of natural innovations in the lab. The fourth point also has to do with the importance of the innovation for other actions in the same context and their necessary harmonization as an indirect effect of the change. Of course, these aspects of indirect effects must also be controlled in experimental studies, if they are to be effective simulations of natural innovations.

This small study of the perception of the characteristics of innovations stimulated experimental research to think more about the stimulus material used in small group minority influence studies. The kind of innovation used

85

is fundamentally determined by the informational influences which depend on the content. The convincingness of the arguments depends upon the perception of the aspects which are seen as relevant. The influence of small group minorities, as described in the theory of conversion behavior, depends upon the creative production of a new view with convincing arguments. For this reason the perception of the majority, the argumentation of the minority, and the amount and kind of change have to be examined more systematically. There might be a change in perception and evaluation without a behavior change. The growth of awareness of an innovation does not produce the same amount of adoption (Rogers and Shoemaker, 1971). On the other hand a change on the more conative side is not necessarily caused by a cognitive change, as was found in the choice shift research (Witte and Lutz, 1982). The scientific question is not whether minorities are more influential than' majorities, but under what conditions and in which way. There are circumstances where minorities should become more influential and the development of an optimal strategy is sometimes needed. In this case the perception of an innnovation is the basis for finding convincing arguments. Testing different forms of argumentation will be a further tool of research on informational influence.

A Concept of Combined Normative and Informational Influences

The study I now wish to describe dealt with the number of innovations introduced by organizations in a period of five years (Mohr, 1969). The data are from ninety-three public health departments. Without going into the details of this study, its main intention is to find the interdependence of normative and informational influences which determine the number of innovative strategies proposed by a single department. The informational aspect is the leader's ideology to innovate. This person is the one who becomes familiar with the innovations and informs colleagues. If the leader has a positive ideology the information diffusion is accelerated, compared with the result of a negative ideology. Additionally, the leaders of the departments were only able to introduce programs which could be financed. Therefore, their ideology is limited by the resources available for them. These resources—money and personnel—are the milieu in which leaders have to operate. This milieu is an indicator of the normative influence. If we further assume that both indicators are not able to compensate each other, their relation being multiplicative, we get the following model:

$$y = k \cdot ID^s \cdot RE^t \text{ or in a linear transformation}$$
$$\log y = \log k + s \cdot \log ID + t \cdot \log RE$$
where y : number of innovations

ID : ideology of the leader
RE : resources of the department
s, t : exponents which are less than 1
k : constant

The result of such a model is that some innovations are introduced because of their persuasive power and some because of the money available to be spent. If an expectation of innovation exists, then a bureaucracy has to spend its money on various measures, partially independently of their persuasive power. This is a pessimistic view of innovation, but everyone knows examples of such innovations. Such a normative influence seems to be experimentally realized by the instruction not to give objective answers but original ones (Moscovici and Lage, 1978). In both cases we have to measure the quality of the innovations, because change per se need not be better than no change. On the other hand, a well informed and open minded leader of a department is able to introduce new programs by convincing other people.

It is now my intention to find a kind of reformulation of this model, which is comparable to group situation theory where the normative context determines the weight of the informational components. Mohr (1969) found that the regression coefficient of number of innovations on ideology is 0.06 for departments with $100,000 and less, whereas the same coefficient is 0.28 for departments with more than $100,000. This means that the resources, interpreted as the normative context, modify the weight of the informational influence:

$$s = f(RE)$$
$$y = k\ ID^{a\ RE\ +\ b}$$
$$\log y = \log k + (a\ RE + b)\log ID$$

The result is the logarithmic transformation. The group situation theory avoids these logarithmic transformations because it uses parameters which have a direct linear relationship. However, in this model by Mohr we do have a parallel to the group situation theory, where the weighting parameter of the informational influence (ID) is modified by the normative component (RE). This way of combining both kinds of influence seems to be promising.

Discussion and a Step toward an Integrative Model

The problem is not that a minority's influence could be different from a majority's. On the contrary, it is the problem of the kind of conditions under which this happens. To solve this problem the theory of conversion behavior, as the central protagonist of this inverted conformity research, has virtually nothing to say.

The main consequence of the above discussion is the differentiation of small group minority influences and innovations. The first situation is easily described as the influence of a minority in a specific small group on the members of the majority of this group. One such influence has been called a *correction effect*, where a minority of two is able to change the majority totally because the solution presented is very convincing or objectively determined. Here the minority follows the general orientation and the minority influence is perfect, if there are at least two minority members. This minority influence, however, is no innovation. On the contrary, it is an increasing conformity. In a situation, where we have more diffuse stimulus material, but a social value guiding the individual responses as in the choice shift research, we get a minority influence, because the change of the small group minority, as the most extreme members of the group, is less than the majority's, that is, the shift compared to the arithmetic mean. This, of course, is also no innovation, because the shift is in the direction of a social value.

Then we have a small group minority who tries to influence the majority of the small group in the direction which is against the *general* social orientation *and* that of the small group majority. The members of the majority are individually certain that they have chosen the right reaction. This involves stimulus material with *high verifiability*, and the reaction of the minority is experimentally induced. These are the experiments using the paradigm of the inverted Asch studies. The result is a *simulated innovation*. The possibility of discussing this stimulus material is very much reduced, so that a real innovation with a changed "world view" is impossible. The blue-green response is at best changed during the experiment, but not for a longer period, although the individual reactions might be changed directly after contact with the confederate (Moscovici and Personnaz, 1986).[2]

Another condition of a minority influence exists if a small group minority changes the majority in a direction away from the general social orientation and the stimulus material has *medium verifiability*. We then get the full amount of influence produced by the small group minority. Under these circumstances the majority members are not certain about their reaction and accept in a predictable amount the view of the consistent minority. The result is an innovation if this influence of the small group remains stable.

A third small group minority influence exists and this also is an innovation. This is the introduction of a new alternative, which is really new and not against an existing orientation. This is the case if there is a *low verifiability* of choice and the only points of orientation are the small group standard and the argumentation.

The next normative component that has been found to be important is the *social support* given by other people outside the lab (number), as it was shown in the study by Coleman et al. (1966). Perhaps this variable is the behavioral side of verifiability, because the more people have changed, the less the verifiability of the old reaction. The verifiability is only the state at a point in time, and the changing number is its dynamic counterpart.

A further normative component is constituted by the resources for the transformation of an invention into an innovation. This variable has never been used in experimental research on innovations, because we have mostly inverted conformity studies with the classical stimuli or other constants without consequences outside the lab. The relative cost of the innovation should be a variable to be introduced in future.

Apart from the normative components, Fliegel and Kivlin (1966) have given some attributes of innovation which facilitate their adoption. These attributes could be arguments in the small group discussion. Thus, the kind of argumentation is an informational component which has to be taken into account. An argument which stresses the stepwise introduction of an innovation and, of course, its utility, combined with nearness of the new actions to the old ones might be more influential in converting the majority than an argument which overlooks these aspects. Therefore, the amount of a minority's influence depends upon the arguments chosen. The argumentation is especially important, because it is the basis of conversion behavior. Certainly, the nature of arguments must also be studied more systematically in the future. Of course, this will only be possible if the stimulus material is complex enough, contrary to the perceptual tasks used in several studies (but see Clark, 1990).

The general result of the discussion from a psychological and sociological viewpoint is the introduction of new variables into a more complex theory of small group minority influence as an innovation: verifiability of choice of the old behavior and the kind of argumentation which is convincing enough to produce conversion behavior. Furthermore, it was possible to explain the quantitative amount of a minority's influence in different social conditions. Usually, the amount is small but not neglectable as was predicted by the group situation theory. This theory was the framework to discuss other qualitative and quantitative concepts because it differentiates normative and informational aspects and uses both as predictors of the influence processes. Its theoretical tradition is also founded on sociological and psychological ideas so that it seems to be able to reintegrate the two different approaches under the perspective of a small group influence. The results are promising.

Notes

I would like to thank Angelica Mucchi-Faina and Anne Maass for their helpful comments on an earlier draft. There also exists a much longer version of this manuscript which could be ordered from the author.

1. All elements which inform the subject, *what* to do, measured on the reactive scale as the crucial behavior to be changed, are *informational* components. They are concentrated on the concrete reaction (judgment, evaluation).

All elements which guide the subject on *how* to behave in a specific group setting are called *normative* influences. Both aspects are partially independent, because the same reaction could be used in different group situations, while the same group situation could be used for divergent reactions. The normative components determine the group situation and the informational components determine the behavioral side. Both together lead to a model of social influence.

2. A fundamental discussion and a detailed critique of this experiment is given in the longer version of this article.

References

Ajzen, I., and Fishbein, M. (1980). *Understanding Attitudes and Predicting Behavior.* Englewood Cliffs, NJ: Prentice-Hall.

Clark, R. D. (1990). Minority influence: The role of argument refutation of the majority position and social support for the minority position. *European Journal of Social Psychology*,20,489–497.

Coleman, J. S., Katz, E., and Menzel, H. (1966). *Medical Innovation: A Diffusion Study.* New York: Bobbs-Merrill.

Davis, J. H. (1973). Group decision and social interaction: A theory of social decision schemes. *Psychology Review*,80,97–125.

Davis, J. H. (1980). Group decision and procedural justice. In M. Fishbein (Ed.), *Progress in Social Psychology*, vol. 1. Hillsdale, NJ: Erlbaum.

Davis, J. H. (1982). Social interaction as a combinational process in group decision. In H. Brandstätter, J. H. Davis and G. Stocker-Kreichgauer (Eds.), *Group Decision Making.* London: Academic Press.

Davis, J. H., Bray, R. M., and Holt, R. W. (1977). The empirical study of social decision processes in juries: A critical review. In J. Tapp and F. Levine (Eds.), *Law, Justice, and the Individual in Society: Psychological and Legal Issues.* New York: Holt, Rinehart and Winston.

Deutsch, M., and Gerard, H. (1955). A study of normative and informational social influence on individual judgment. *Journal of Abnormal and Social Psychology*, 51,629–636.

Doms, M. (1984). The minority influence effect: An alternative approach. In S. Moscovici and W. Doise (Eds.), *Current Issues in European Social Psychology.* Cambridge: University Press.

Dupont, R. L., and Greene, M. H. (1973). The dynamics of a heroin addiction epidemic. *Science*,181,716–722.

Fisher, R. A. (1951). *The Design of Experiments*. Edinburgh: Oliver and Boyd.

Fliegel, C. F., and Kivlin, J. E. (1966). Attributes of innovations as factors in diffusion. *American Journal of Sociology*,72,235–248.

French, J. R. P., and Raven, B. (1983). The bases of social power. In D. Cartwright and A. Zander (Eds.), *Group Dynamics*. New York: Harper and Row.

Habermas, J. (1966). *Zur Lo gik der Sozialwissenschaften* (Concerning the Logic of Social Sciences). Frankfurt am Main: Suhrkamp.

Hamilton, D. L., and Bishop, G. D. (1976). Attitudinal and behavioral effects of initial integration of white suburban neighborhoods. *Journal of Social Issues*, 32,47–56.

Jackson, J. M. (1987). Social impact theory: A social forces model of influence. In B. Mullen and G. R. Goethals (Eds.), *Theories of Group Behavior*. New York: Springer.

Janis, I. L. (1972). *Victims of Groupthink*. Boston: Houghton Mifflin.

Kelley, H. H. (1973). The process of causal attribution. *American Psychologist*,28, 107–128.

Kelley, H. H., and Michela, J. L. (1980). Attribution theory and research. *Annual Review of Psychology*,31,457–501.

Kelman, H. C. (1958). Compliance, identification and internalization: Three processes of attitude change. *Journal of Conflict Resolution*,2,51–60.

Kelman, H. C. (1961). Processes of opinion change. *Public Opinion Quarterly*,25, 57–78.

Kerr, N. L., Davis, J. H., Meek, D., and Rissman, A. G. (1975). Group position as a function of member attitudes: Choice shift effects from the perspective of social decision scheme theory. *Journal of Personality and Social Psychology*, 35,574–593.

Kerr, N. L., Atkin, R., Stasser, G., Meek, D., Holt, R., Davis, J. H. (1976). Guilt beyond a reasonable doubt: Effects of concept definition and assigned decision rule on the judgments of mock jurors. *Journal of Personality and Social Psychology*,34,282–294.

Kerr, N. L., and MacCoun, R. J. (1985). The effects of jury size and polling method on the process and product of jury deliberation. *Journal of Personality and Social Psychology*,48,349–363.

Latané, B., and Wolf, S. (1981). The social impact of majorities and minorities. *Psychological Review*,88,438–453.

Laughlin, P. R., and Adamopoulos, J. (1982). Social decision schemes on intellective tasks. In H. Brandstätter, J. H. Davis and G. Stocker-Kreichgauer (Eds.), *Group Decision Making*. London: Academic Press.

Lortie-Lussier, M. (1987). Minority influence and idiosyncrasy credit: A new comparison of the Moscovici and Hollander theories of innovation. *European Journal of Social Psychology*,17,431–446.

Maass, A., and Clark, R. D. (1984). Hidden impact of minorities: Fifteen years of minority influence research. *Psychology Bulletin*,95,428–450.

Mohr, L. B. (1969). Determinants of innovations in organizations. *American Political Science Review*,8,111–126.

Moscovici, S. (1976). *Social Influence and Social Change*. London: Academic Press.

Moscovici, S., (1980). Toward a theory of conversion behavior. *Advances in Experimental Social Psychology*,13,209–239.

Moscovici, S. (1985). Social influence and conformity. In G. Lindzey and E. Aronson (Eds.), *Handbook of Social Psychology*, vol. 2. New York: Random House.

Moscovici, S., and Faucheux, C. (1972). Social influence, conformity bias, and the study of active minorities. *Advances in Experimental Social Psychology*,6, 149–202.

Moscovici, S., and Lage, E. (1978). Studies in social influence IV. Minority influence in a context of original judgments. *European Journal of Social Psychology*,8,349–365.

Moscovici, S., Lage, E., and Naffrechoux, M. (1969). Influence of a consistent minority on the responses of a majority in a color perception task. *Sociometry*, 32,365–379.

Moscovici, S., and Lecuyer, R. (1972). Studies in group decision. I. Social space, patterns of communication and group consensus. *European Journal of Social Psychology*,2,221–244.

Moscovici, S., and Mugny, G. (1983). Minority influence. In P. B. Paulus (Ed.), *Basic Group Processes*. New York: Springer.

Moscovici, S., and Personnaz, B. (1986). Studies on latent influence by the spectrometer method I: The impact of psychologization in the case of conversion by a minority or a majority. *European Journal of Social Psychology*,16, 345–360.

Nemeth, C. (1982). Stability of faction position and influence. In H. Brandstätter, J. H. Davis and G. Stocker-Kreichgauer (Eds.), *Group Decision Making*. London: Academic Press.

Nemeth, C. (1986). Differential contributions of majority and minority influence. *Psychological Review*,93,23–32.

Ogburn, W. F. (1922). *Social Change*. New York: Allen and Unwin.

Papastamou, S. (1986). Psychologization and processes of minority and majority influence. *European Journal of Social Psychology*,16,165–180.

Raven, B. H., and Rubin, J. Z. (1983). *Social Psychology*. New York: Wily.

Rogers, E. M. (1962). *Diffusion of Innovations*. New York: Free Press. (3rd ed., 1983).

Rogers, E. M., and Shoemaker, F. F. (1971). *Communication of Innovations*. New York: Free Press.

Stasser, G., and Davis, J. H. (1981). Group decision making and social influence: A social interaction sequence model. *Psychological Review*,88,523–551.

Steiner, I. D. (1986). Paradigms and group. *Advances in Experimental Social Psychology*,20,251–289.

Tanford, S., and Penrod, S. (1984). Social influence model: A formal integration of research on majority and minority influence processes. *Psychological Bulletin*, 95,189–225.

Tarde, G. (1903). *The laws of imitation*. New York: Holt.

Witte, E. H. (1979). *Das Verhalten in Gruppensituationen: Ein theoretisches Konzept* (The behavior in group situations: A theoretical concept). Göttingen: Hogrefe.

Witte, E. H. (1985). Theorien zur sozialen Macht (Theories of social power). In D. Frey and M. Irle (Eds.), *Theorien der Sozialpsychologie*, vol. 2. Bern: Huber.

Witte, E. H. (1987). Behavior in group situations: An integrative model. *European Journal of Social Psychology*,17,403–429.

Witte, E. H. (1987a). Die Idee einer einheitlichen Wissenschaftslehre für die Sozialpsychologie (The idea of an integrated methodology for Social Psychology). *Zeitschrift für Sozialpsychologie*,18,76–87.

Witte, E. H. (1990). Social influence: A Discussion and integration of recent models into a general group situation theory. *European Journal of Social Psychology*, 20,3–27.

Witte, E. H., and Arez, A. (1974). The cognitive structure of Choice Dilemma Decisions. *European Journal of Social Psychology*,4,313–328.

Witte, E. H., and Lutz, D. H. (1982). Choice shift as a cognitive change? In H. Brandstätter, J. H. Davis and G. Stocker-Kreichgauer (Eds.), *Group Decision Making*. London: Academic Press.

Witte, E. H., and Politzky, E. (1976). Tarifverhandlungen: Ein theoretisches Konzept und seine empirische Prüfung. *Kölner Zeitschrift für Soziologie und Sozialpsychologie*,28,140–151.

Wolf, S. (1979). Behavioral style and group cohesiveness as sources of minority influence. *European Journal of Social Psychology*,9,381–395.

Wolf, S. (1985). Manifest and latent influence of majorities and minorities. *Journal of Personality and Social Psychology*,48,899–908.

Wolf, S., and Latané, B. (1983). Majority and minority influence on restaurant preferences. *Journal of Personality and Social Psychology*,45,282–292.

PART TWO

*Delimitations of
Minority Influence*

CHAPTER FIVE

MINORITY INFLUENCE IN THE GROUP CONTEXT: HOW GROUP FACTORS AFFECT WHEN THE MINORITY WILL BE INFLUENTIAL

Stephen Worchel,
Michele Grossman, and
Dawna Coutant

Two rather distinct waves have pounded the shore of social influence research. The first, which may be aptly named Power of the Majority, was set into motion by Solomon Asch in the late 1940s. Asch (1951) found that a unanimous majority exercised considerable influence over the judgments and perceptions of a lone minority. To the surprise of many, Asch found that a majority could influence a lone subject even when the majority's opinion was obviously wrong. Researchers rushed to the laboratory to duplicate and extend Asch's findings. With few exceptions (Kelman, 1958; Ross, Bierbrauer and Hoffman, 1976), the research on conformity was largely atheoretical, focusing on the conditions under which conformity occurred (Worchel, Cooper and Goethals, 1991). The research examined situational, personal, and task factors. Possibly because of the lack of theory explicating the process, the volume of research on conformity diminished and by the mid 1970s the journals were almost devoid of studies on conformity.

Just as the interest in conformity was waning, a second wave, which can be considered the Power of the Minority, rolled onto the social influence beach. This wave had its beginning in research by Moscovici (Moscovici,

97

Lage, and Naffrechoux, 1969) and Nemeth (Nemeth and Wachtler, 1974) showing that a consistent and unyielding minority could exercise considerable influence on the perceptions and opinions of the majority. This finding created the same surprise and excitement as Asch's findings on the power of the majority. The research mission of those who followed the minority influence wave, however, was very different from that embraced by conformity researchers. The emphasis of minority influence research has been on explicating the individual and internal processes. Group and contextual factors affecting minority influence have largely been ignored.

The work on minority influence has introduced some intriguing points. On the issue of style, numerous investigators found that the influential minority must be consistent, clear, confident, and unyielding (Nemeth, 1986; Mugny and Papastamou, 1980). More recently the focus has been on the cognitive effects of a minority. Research suggests that the strongest effect is latent and on private thoughts (Nemeth and Staw, 1989). There is also the intriguing suggestion that minorities stimulate heightened cognitive effort leading to creative and divergent thought processes (Nemeth, 1986).

The curious aspect of much of the work on minority influence is that it rarely considers the context in which influence occurs, such as the situation, task, personal factors, or the interactive nature of the minority and the group. This is not only curious because the concept ''minority'' implies a group and situational context, but it is also unusual because research on conformity (or majority influence) was almost fixated on these contextual features. In fact, one of the yet unsolved mysteries of minority influence concerns how to define a minority. On one hand, a ''minority'' may be determined by characterics that make the person statistically unusual in a larger population, for example, a black in the United States. Another way to define a minority involves reference to a status differential, or a state of powerlessness, for example, a black in South Africa. The minority may also be determined by the numerical representation in the immediate group of concern, for example, one woman in a group with four men. Finally, a minority may be identified by virtue of expressing an unusual attitude or perception. Regardless of the method of definition, the definition of a minority must be based on characteristics of the *group*.

It would be loathsome to suggest that the work on minority influence forsake its fruitful focus on style and process issues. It is suggested here that by incorporating these group contextual and dynamic factors into the research and theory, greater richness could be added to the understanding of the minority influence process. In addition, more attention to the role of the minority in the group could develop a more complete picture of the interpersonal dynamics in groups.

Our interest in minority influence comes from a concern with the group characteristics that affect social influence in general. A variety of processes have been placed under the heading of "group dynamics." These include social influence (conformity and minority influence), group decision-making (groupthink, group polarization), and group performance (social loafing and social facilitation). Studies examining these effects suggest that they occur in the context of a "group." Yet an examination of the groups used in much of the research shows that these groups are shallow imitations at best. The prevailing opinion (Shaw, 1981; Forsyth, 1983) is that the minimal conditions that define a group are (1) members are motivated to join the group, (2) the group endures for a reasonable period of time (has a history and a future), (3) members have a common goal, (4) the group has a clear boundary separating it from outgroups, and (5) the group has a rudimentary structure. The groups used in much of the research bring together strangers who have no past or future interaction, no boundary, no common purpose, and no sense of identity. These "groups" are not groups but aggregates and it remains a testable hypothesis to determine the different dynamics of groups and aggregates.

The Development of a Group

With this background in mind, a major challenge is to examine social dynamics including minority influence in real groups, groups that are defined by clear boundaries, a history and a future, and a sense among members that they belong together. Looking at groups in this context, one quickly realizes that groups are not static entities that remain the same over time. Groups develop, change structure and members, and adjust to temporal and situational demands. Similarly, members' feelings about their own part in the group likely change. Group members may feel more involved, more accepted, and more concerned about the group at some times more than at other times. It is reasonable to assume that these changes in the nature of the group affect the dynamics of social interaction and individual cognition and perception. Therefore, it is critical to understand the development and changes that occur in a group over time in order to completely understand group dynamics.

Our first goal in this research program was to investigate whether or not groups develop in orderly and predictable ways. If such a process could be identified, a model of group development could be related to social dynamics that take place within the group. There have been a few previous attempts to describe group development. Most of the early work was undertaken in the 1950s and 1960s by investigators associated with T groups. Tuckman and his colleagues (Tuckman and Jansen, 1977) reviewed fifty studies from this era and concluded that groups do indeed develop in rather predictable ways. Tuckman labeled the development stages as forming, storming, norming, performing, and adjourning. This work offers some interesting insight into groups, but the sample groups were limited to therapy, T groups, and small laboratory groups, and this provokes some question about the generalizability of the model. More recently, Moreland and Levine (1982; 1988) offered a stage model to describe the process through which members go after joining a group. Their work is very provocative, but because its focus is on the individual member, it is less helpful for predicting group dynamics.

At the other extreme is the work of sociologists and political scientists describing the process of revolution. The aim of revolution is the overthrow of the group in power (Paynton and Blackey, 1971). This is not the place to review this interesting body of literature, but one relevant point is worth noting. The process of revolution seems to involve identifiable stages, some of which are very similar to those noted by Tuckman in small groups.

Although this early work is very stimulating, it has some serious limitations. First of all, the range of groups involved is restricted; therefore, the resulting models may lack generalizability. Second, the work is descriptive and does not incorporate research on group dynamics or social influence. There is not an attempt to explain the observed behavior or to offer predictions about the relationship between stage of development and interpersonal or intergroup behavior. However, the work is very promising in suggesting that groups do encounter identifiable stages as they develop.

In an effort to build on and refine the previous research, extensive archival research was undertaken. Our aim was to develop a model showing how groups form and develop and relate this model to intragroup and intergroup behavior. Because of the interest in group formation, it was necessary to identify the potential members of a group before they joined together as a group and to describe the conditions that caused them to form a new group. Therefore, we focused on situations where new groups formed from existing groups. The typical condition was that some members of a parent group broke away and formed a new independent group. Unlike revolutions where the aim is to destroy the group in power, the formation of a new independent group rarely involves the destruction of the parent group. In fact, as we will show, the existence of the old parent group is often important for defining the boundaries of the new group.

The archival research and the model are described in some detail by Worchel, Coutant-Sassic, and Grossman (1992). Basically, the archival research involved identifying situations where a new group was formed and existed for a period of time. Groups that were examined ranged from large social movements, such as the Civil Rights movement and the women's movement in the United States, to new political parties in the United States,

Israel, and Poland, to small social and religious groups in local communities. Newspapers, magazines, books, and internal group documents were examined, and interviews were conducted with group members, whenever possible. Investigators collected data on the situation that existed before the group formed, the conditions that led to the formation of the new group, and intrapersonal, interpersonal, and intergroup behaviors that occurred during the group's existence. Notice was taken as to whether the group had ceased to exist, continued at a different level of activity, merged into another group, or was still functioning at the last available report.

The information collected through archival searches was supplemented with previously published models of group development (e.g., Baker, 1983; Bales and Strodtbeck, 1951; Bennis and Shepard, 1956; Goodman, 1981; Hopper, 1950; Tuckman, 1965). The data were wonderfully rich in a descriptive sense, but vague, impressionistic, and possibly biased when viewed from an empirical research approach. Yet, a number of points became clear. First, groups do develop through rather identifiable stages. These stages are characterized by the group's focus or concern. Paynton and Blackey (1971) state that, "Nothing in the course of revolutions is inevitable, but much is likely (p. 235)." The same statement characterizes group development. Not all groups exhibit all the stages, and the length of time of the stages differ from group to group, but most groups exhibit the stages in the same order. A second point is that the nature of group development is continuous and cyclical. Many groups go through the cycle of developmental stages several times during their existence. Numerous groups that were studied served as the foundation for the development of new groups, much like a star shooting off meteors. Finally, the membership of many groups is constantly changing, with new members entering and old members leaving the group. This point is especially important when studying minority influence, because these new members often introduce minority viewpoints to the group.

Having made these points, let's turn to the model of group development that was proposed. This model is described in Worchel et al, (1992), therefore only the highlights will be presented here.

A Model of Group Development

Period of Discontent

The stage for the formation of a new group is set when many individuals become discontent or disenchanted with their existing group. Members feel that the group is stagnating and not meeting their personal needs. Members often become apathetic, failing to attend meetings or voting of group issues. They feel helpless and hopeless. Interestingly, these feelings often arise after a group has been successful in achieving its stated goals. Here, members question what is to happen next in the group. In some cases, the alienation is seen in senseless violence, such as vandalism.

Precipitating Event

Some clearly identifiable event occurs that brings the individuals together and characterizes their common concern. In some cases the event may seem rather minor, but symbolic. In the development of the Civil Rights movement this event was the arrest of Rosa Parks, a black seamstress in Montgomery, Alabama, in 1955. Ms. Parks refused to give a white person her seat on a bus. In other cases, the event may be more dramatic such as the shooting of Vietnam War protestors on the Kent State University campus. The adoption of a new charter, a dramatic increase in inflation, the expulsion of group members, or even the rumor of impending action may also precipitate the formation of a new group. While the event itself may take different forms, precipitating events have some common characteristics. Each symbolizes important differences between the group members in power and the disenchanted members. Each event is distinctive and presents a common meeting ground for the alienated members. Each event suggests a clear issue around which protest can be organized. The precipitating events offer members hope that if they work together they can achieve change. Along these lines, the event reduces feelings of helplessness by identifying actions that can be taken.

Group Identification

The group in this stage becomes concerned with establishing an independent identity. Group members are discouraged from interacting with out-group members. There is a reluctance to accept new members into the group. Conflict with out-groups is often sought as a means of establishing clear ingroup/outgroup boundaries. Conformity is demanded and dissent is punished. Group members become very concerned with demonstrating that they belong in the group. In a recent study (Worchel, Coutant-Sassic, and Grossman, 1992), it was found that group members in this stage perceive similarity between ingroup members while viewing outgroups as being heterogenous. Groupthink is likely to occur in this stage of development. The group often adopts a rigid dogma, and attitudes become polarized. Group members may seek to establish the legitimacy of the group by exploring its roots and history. The ingroup is viewed as being better, often more moral, than the outgroups. The outgroups are viewed as being untrustworthy. The group may adopt a uniform and develop a language of its own. Members are excited about the group and a high state of arousal characterizes this phrase. Leadership is centralized and structure (norms and roles) made explicit. Group members are willing to sacrifice for the good of the group. Worchel, Hart, and Butemeyer (1987) found that individuals work harder in the group than alone (a finding opposite social loafing) at this point in group development.

Group Productivity

When the group feels that it has established an independent identity, the concern of the members turns to group productivity. The group members identify the goals for the group, and they begin to distinguish between members based on task ability. Leaders are chosen using the ability criteria. Interaction with the outgroups may be sought as a means of reaching productivity goals. New members will be accepted into the group if they possess needed skills. The overall level of arousal in the group is reduced as members focus on the task goals and avoid unnecessary conflict. Unlike the identification stage, group members in this stage began to make realistic assessments of the group and its resources.

Individuation

During this stage, attention shifts away from the group to the individual members. Group members examine their own needs and determine how well the group is meeting those needs. Members begin to demand that equity norms, rather than equality norms, be established. Individuals seek personal recognition and social comparison within as well as outside the group. Individuals begin to examine their alternative courses of action such as joining other groups or withdrawing from the group. New members that offer diversity and other points of view are accepted, indeed, often sought. Worchel et al. (1987) found that social loafing was likely to occur during this stage of development. Worchel et al. (1992) also found that members perceive high heterogeneity in the ingroup late in the group's development. This latter finding replicates earlier work showing that the ingroup is perceived as heterogenous while the outgroup is viewed as homogenous (Jones, Wood, and Quattrone, 1981).

Decay

The group begins to disintegrate as members question the value of the group. Competition between individuals is common and subgroups struggle for power. Attention focuses on the past failures or the lack of present direction. Leaders are blamed for group problems or other scape-goats are identified. Group members begin to hoard resources and social loafing becomes widespread. The group becomes the focus of attention, once again, but with the aim of discrediting it. Arousal is high and anger is common. This stage creates the conditions necessary for the stage of discontent. In that stage, motivation drops as members turn away from the group and become alienated.

Implications for Minority and Majority Influence

The basic assumption of this model is that groups develop through stages of development and at each stage the needs and concerns of the group and group members are different. As a result, the dynamics of the group are different at the various stages and in order to make accurate predictions about these dynamics, it is important to take into account the context of the group.

Because our present concern is minority influence, let's examine some of the predictions that may be derived from the model. The model suggests that the beginning of a group is largely characterized by alienated people who have little in common and no sense of belonging together. During the identification stage, the individuals become concerned with achieving cohe-siveness, clear boundaries, and a sense of togetherness. They resist fragmen-tation and demand loyalty. As the group matures, the concerns turn from identification to goal attainment and administering to the needs of individual members.

As Nemeth (1986) has pointed out, the presence of an unyielding minority creates internal conflict and divergent thinking. Although Nemeth's focus is on intrapersonal processes, the effect may also occur on an interpersonal level. According to our model, groups should be especially resistant to minorities during the identification stage and other times when cohesiveness is vital to the existence and identity of the group. During the productivity stage, when the group is concerned with goal attainment, group members should be more receptive to the deviant minority and the divergent thinking initiated by the minority, especially when the minority views involve task issues. During the individuation stage, the minority may also be very influential. During this time, the group members will be most receptive to minority views that involve personal values, different perspectives of the group and group structure, and information about alternative groups. Finally, groups in decay may reject minority views that do not involve identifying problems with the group. Minority positions that offer positive perceptions of the group or group unity will be met with hostility and minority views about task issues will be ignored. Hence, it can be predicted that influence of the minority on group members will be most pronounced either in aggregates where there is not yet concern for group identity and cohesiveness or in more mature groups where identity and group boundaries have been previously established. Further, the model suggests that the issues addressed by the minority position will influence its effectiveness. Group members will be affected by different minority messages at different times during group development.

Some Empirical Evidence

A number of predictions can be made from the stage model. Some of these predictions are being examined and preliminary evidence suggests the value of examining minority influence in the context of group development.

The Timing of Minority Presentation

The first study was designed to compare minority influence in aggregates and real groups. The study also compared the effects of minority influence during the early period of the group and late in its development. It was predicted that minorities would be more influential in aggregates than in groups and late in group development rather than during the early stages. Unlike much of the previous minority influence research, a major dependent measure was the immediate influence of the minority within the group context.

In the study, five subjects arrived at each experimental session. In the group conditions, the subjects were told that they would form a human relations court and decide the fate of a number of cases. Subjects were told that they were to work as a group and, if their performance was highly rated, they would have the opportunity to compete as a group for a cash prize at a later date. The members were given time to get acquainted and prepare for court. They were asked to choose a name for their court group and a "chief justice." In the early group condition subjects were presented with the Johnny Rocco case and told to decide the fate of Johnny, a young delinquent. They were to read the case and write an individual verdict (1 = very punitive treatment, 7 = very lenient treatment). The verdicts would then be shown to the other group members and each individual would write his or her final verdict. These final verdicts would constitute the "group product." Subjects were told that this would be the first case and there would be others later in the session.

The late group condition was similar to the early group condition except that the group worked together on a series of anagrams and word

105

tasks before being given the Johnny Rocco instructions. These groups, too, settled on a name and leader following the initial group discussion and expected additional cases to follow Johnny Rocco. In the aggregate condition, the five subjects were not given the opportunity to get acquainted nor did they expect to interact after the Johnny Rocco case. They were never referred to as a group and they were told their individual responses would be examined after the experiment.

After subjects gave the experimenter their initial "verdict," the experimenter appeared to write the verdicts down on a piece of paper and then passed them to the other subjects. In fact, the experimenter wrote bogus verdicts so that subjects believed that three other subjects were within one point of their verdict and one subject was at the extreme opposite end. Subjects were then given the opportunity to reconsider "the facts in the case in light of the initial verdicts" they received from the other group members. They were then asked to indicate their final verdict "which would only be seen by the experimenter." Hence, the final verdict was private. After subjects indicated their "final" verdict, they completed a questionnaire asking how much they enjoyed the task and group, how much a part of the group they felt, how well they felt their group (themselves) had done on the task, how they felt at the present time, and (in the group conditions) how well their group would perform on future tasks.

Manipulation checks showed that subjects felt more a part of the group in the two groups conditions than in the aggregate condition. Subjects felt more a part of the group and more similar to other group members in the early group condition than in the late condition. Subjects enjoyed the task and group more in the group condition than in the aggregate condition. They reported feeling happier and expected that the group would perform better in the early group condition than in either of the late group condition or aggregate condition.

The major dependent variable was the change of verdict. The change scores were computed by subtracting the final verdict from the initial verdict. Because subjects were run in groups, the mean group change was examined. Subjects in the aggregate condition moved significantly more toward the minority position (1.40) than subjects in the late group condition (.71). Subjects in the early group condition moved on the average away from the minority position ($-.43$) and this movement was significantly different than that shown in either of the other two conditions. Subjects in the early group condition reported themselves being more tense, angry, excited, and frustrated than subjects in either of the other two conditions.

Overall, these results showed the minority being able to influence other group members in the aggregate and late group conditions; the aggregate condition is most similar to the conditions faced by subjects in many minority influence studies. In the previous studies there is rarely an attempt to make subjects feel that they belong to a group in which the minority is acting. The minority was unsuccessful in moving the majority toward the expressed condition in the early group condition. Further, subjects in the early group condition expressed the most anger and frustration, and these feelings were attributed to the deviant during debriefing. The fact that early group members were committed to their group was shown in the positive ratings and expectations expressed about the group. The bottom line here is that the degree of minority influence can be determined by the nature of the group and that this is an important variable to consider when discussing minority influence.

A second study investigating the effects of the timing of the minority presentation involved fifty-seven longitudinal groups meeting a total of six one-hour sessions. It was predicted that a minority would be resisted or rejected in the early sessions, when identification and cohesion are believed to be important. The minority would gain influence as the group developed. The most influence would be found later, when a group is in the individuation stage.

Five subjects were randomly assigned to a group. Within the groups a confederate adopted a minority position during group discussions either in the first, third, or fifth session. This enabled us to investigate the effects of the minority opinion at early, middle, and late phases in the group's development. In each group condition the participants answered questions three different times during the session. First individually, then as a group, and again individually.

The group discussion items were two "risky-shift" choice-dilemma questions (Kogan and Wallach, 1964) in which participants were given a scenario and asked to choose the degree of risk that should be taken to solve the dilemma. In addition to the choice-dilemma questions, the participants were asked to give an answer to an objective question (i.e., How many ounces are in a quart?). These two types of questions were used to investigate the minority's influence on objective and subjective decision making in the group.

The confederate argued the most risky position on the choice-dilemma questions (1 = extremely risky, 10 = no risk) and an obviously incorrect answer on the objective question. The arguments used during the persuasion attempt included the same basic structure.

Group decisions were analyzed to indicate whether shifts in the overall group mean moved toward the minority's position. Difference scores were used, so that a positive mean indicates movement toward a minority position, a 0 indicates no movement, and a negative mean indicates movement away from a minority. In viewing the objective question, when answering in a group the minority opinion was rejected, with subjects actually moving away from their initial position in the opposite direction during the first session ($M = -2.70$). In the middle condition there is less rejection of the minority ($M = -0.87$), and in more mature groups the minority begins to have some influence ($M = 0.67$).

When difference scores on the objective question are examined between individual answers before influence and individual answers after influence, the means follow the same pattern of rejection of the minority during the first session ($M = -2.00$), a reduction in this rejection the third session ($M = -1.09$), and a slight influence in the fifth session ($M = .029$).

This pattern does not hold for subjective questions, however. In fact, there is consistent minority influence at all three stages of the group (session one $M = 1.44$; session three $M = 1.81$; session five $M = 1.63$). Similar means were found when individual answers before and after influence are compared on the subjective questions. Early meetings are not significantly less influenced ($M = 1.22$) than groups in middle meetings ($M = 1.59$) and late meetings are not significantly different than middle meetings ($M = 1.13$). These data suggest an interaction between the type of question a minority is influencing and the stage of a group's development that a minority attempts to influence.

Group Expectations and Issue Importance

The position that is being developed is that the minority may be influential in groups when the group is less concerned about its identity and more concerned about performance and meeting group members' needs. With this frame of reference, we can speculate about how expectations of future interaction should affect reactions to the minority. A group that meets together for only a short time with no expectations of being together in the future should have little concern about establishing its identity or developing structure. Such groups can focus on the task at hand. However, group members who expect to be interacting over a period of time are more likely to focus on identity, norms, roles, and interaction patterns. The immediate task the group is asked to perform represents only one activity of the many that will face the group. If we argue that the presence of a minority position causes group members to focus on the assigned task, it follows that the minority should be most influential in groups expecting to be together for only a short time, even if these groups are in the early stages of development.

This argument further suggests that other features in the environment that focus the group's attention on the task rather then on group identity and maintenance should enhance the influence of the minority position. One such variable should be the importance of the specific work task or the rewards associated with correct performance. Hence, we could predict that the minority will be more influential on important tasks than on less important ones and that this difference will be most pronounced when group members expect a limited group life.

In order to examine these hypotheses, an experiment was designed similar to the first study discussed. Groups of five subjects were given a ten-minute get-acquainted period. They were told that they would serve as a human relations court to make decisions about punishment in a case(s). The short duration group was told they would have one case to decide and the long duration group was told that they would have a number of cases to review. They were given the Johnny Rocco case and told to develop their own verdict. In this case the verdict was given in the number of years of juvenile detention the participant would recommend for Johnny. The range could be from 0 to 15 years. Groups in the high importance situation were told that their final verdicts would be examined to determine if they would win a $25 prize. Their answers would be compared against that given by a panel of experts. Subjects in the low importance condition were not told of the possible reward or of comparing their answer with the experts. After giving the experimenter their initial verdicts, the experimenter gave subjects bogus feedback showing four subjects agreeing with a position (within one point of agreement) and one subject holding an extreme position in the opposite direction. In general, subjects initially recommended lenient treatment (x = 1.84 years). Subjects were then asked to write a final verdict. The verdict, the amount of time it took the subjects to arrive at the final verdict, and ratings of the group served as the dependent variables. Again, subjects believed that only the experimenters would see their final questionnaire.

Table 5.1 Minority Influence as a Function of Expected Group Duration and Task Importance

		Importance of Task	
		High	**Low**
Expected Duration	Short term	1.93[1,2]	1.28
	Long term	.82	−.43

1. N = 8 groups per condition

2. Responses represent the difference in subjects' responses before learning of the position of other group members and after learning of this position. A (+) number indicates movement toward the minority position and a (−) number indicates change away from the minority position. The responses are given in terms of the number of years of juvenile detention recommended for Johnny Rocco.

As can be seen in table 5.1, both the expected duration of the group and the importance of the task affected the impact of the minority. The minority was least influential when subjects expected the group to continue beyond the present task and when the task was not important. In fact, there was a tendency to move away from the minority in the long duration/low important task condition.

Responses to other questions begin to shed some light on why this pattern of influence occurred. Subjects were more attracted to the minority in the short duration conditions than in the long duration conditions. However, they were more attracted to other majority members in the long duration conditions than in the short duration conditions. When asked how important it was for group members to support each other, subjects indicated higher importance in the long duration conditions than in the short duration conditions and higher importance in the low important task conditions than in the high important task conditions. Subjects in the high important task conditions were more likely than subjects in the low important task conditions to agree with statements that "everyone in the group should state his/her true feelings" and that "time should not be an important factor in reaching a decision." Finally, subjects in the short duration/high important task conditions were most likely to agree with the statement that "making a correct decision was the only factor that should guide group discussion."

Overall, these results suggest that people in groups meeting together for a short time to work on tasks that are personally important are most concerned with performing well and are most likely to be influenced by a minority opinion. This is an interesting combination of findings in light of Crano's suggestion (Gorenflo and Crano, 1989) that minorities are most influential on objective tasks. Indeed, concern about being right may enhance the willingness to consider minority opinions. On the other hand, concern about group cohesiveness may lead to rejection of the minority because the minority is viewed as being detrimental to group process. We can push this reasoning a bit further and consider the findings that minority influence is often delayed (Moscovici, Mugny, and Perez, 1985). When subjects are removed from the group or experimental setting, there is little need to consider group process issues. Their sole concern as they reconsider the task problem may be in finding a correct answer. In this case, individuals may be more willing to reconsider the minority position.

Previous Reaction to Minority and Outcome

Let us briefly consider a preliminary finding from another study before concluding. Most ongoing groups have a history of responding to deviant positions and have witnessed the consequences of their responses to the minority. These factors should influence their later reactions to the minority. The most straightforward prediction is that groups who have been influenced by a minority and been rewarded for accepting the minority position are more likely to be influenced by the minority in the future than groups who have experienced negative consequences from moving toward the minority position. Similarly, groups who have resisted minority influence in the past and have been rewarded for their perseverance should be less willing to go along with the minority than groups who have received negative consequences from their stubborn resistance.

An experiment was devised in which groups working on the Johnny Rocco case were led to believe that their final verdict was either influenced by the minority position or was not. Some groups were told that their final verdicts were "correct" while others were told that their verdicts were "incorrect." They were then given a second similar case in which they learned that there was a minority position.

The results strongly supported the hypotheses. Groups who were rewarded for moving in the minority direction did so on the second task. Groups who were not rewarded (punished) for moving toward the minority of the first task resisted minority influence on the second task. On the other hand, groups who were punished for not considering the minority position on the first task did move in the direction of the minority on the second task. Likewise, those rewarded for resisting the minority continued to resist the minority on the second task.

Conclusion

We have meandered through rather broad and diverse territory. Our major aim was to extol the virtues of the focus on theory and individual process taken in much of the minority influence research, and to caution against the tendency to study minority influence without considering the group and situational context. The group, like the individual, may have needs and goals that determine not only the success of the minority, but also the processes (intrapersonal and interpersonal) set into motion by the presence of the minority. Although the present research did not address the intrapersonal issue, it is possible that under some conditions the presence of the minority may be so threatening that it results in highly convergent (rather than divergent) thought processes. The minority not only represents a source of information, it also presents a norm for decision-making that may or may not be acceptable to individuals in the role as group members. As many investigators have pointed out, there is a fine line between acceptance and rejection of the deviant (Levine, 1988; Berkowitz and Howard, 1959).

In taking the contextual approach to minority influence, we have presented a tentative model of group development. The concern here is not to defend the specific model, but rather to make two points. First, when we discuss minority influence or any other social influence process in the context of "group behavior," it is vital not to lose sight of what a group is. There are distinct and real differences between groups and aggregates, and these differences may have profound effects on interpersonal dynamic. Our second point is that a group is not a static entity; it changes and develops over time. Just as we should avoid exclusively studying group processes outside of the group context, so too would it be a mistake to limit the study of groups to these aspects outside of their developmental context. Processes that occur in a group at one stage of its life may be very different from processes that occur at another stage within the same group. Moreland and Levine (1982) have made this point quite clear in their focus on the individual group member.

The aspect of the experimental work that we find so exciting is the variety of predictions that can be crafted by bringing together the theories of minority influence and the group development approach. Rather than present competing views of the process, they offer complementary approaches, each strengthening the other. Expanding the horizon of minority influence to include group and intergroup behavior should add new dimensions and richness to both focuses.

References

Asch, S. (1951). Effects of group pressure upon modification and distortion of judgment. In H. Guetzkow (Ed.), *Groups, Leadership and Men*. Pittsburgh, PA: Carnegie Press.

Baker, P. M. (1983). The development of mutuality in natural small groups. *Small Group Behavior*,14,301–311.

Bales, R., and Strodtbeck, F. (1951). Phases in group problem-solving. *Journal of Abnormal and Social Psychology*,46,485–495.

Bennis, W., and Shepard, S. (1956). A theory of group development. *Human Relations*,9,415–437.

Berkowitz, L., and Howard, R. C. (1959). Reactions to opinion deviates as affected by affiliation need (n) and group member interdependence. *Sociometry*,22,81–91.

Caple, R. (1978). The sequential stages of group development. *Small Group Behavior*,9,470–476.

Doise, W., and Moscovici, S. (1969–70). Approche et evitement du diviant dans des groupes de cohesion differente. *Bulletin de Psychologie*,23,522–525.

Forsyth, D. (1983). *An Introduction to Group Dynamics*. Monterey, CA: Brooks/Cole.

Goodman, M. (1981). Group phases and induced countertransference. *Psychotherapy: Theory, Research, and Practice*,18,478–486.

Gorenflo, D. W., and Crano, W. D. (1989). Judgmental subjectivity/objectivity and locus of choice in social comparison. *Journal of Personality and Social Psychology*, 57,605–614.

Gurr, T. R. (1970). *Why Men Rebel*. Princeton, NJ: Princeton University Press.

Hopper, R. (1950). The revolutionary process. *Social Forces*,28,270–279.

Jones, E. E., Wood, G. C. and Quattrone, G. A. (1981). Perceived variability of personal characteristics in ingroups and outgroups: The role of knowledge and evaluation. *Personality and Social Psychology Bulletin*,7,523–528.

Kelman, H. C. (1958). Compliance, identification, and internalization: Three processes of attitude change. *Journal of Conflict Resolution*,2,51–60.

King, C. (1969). *My Life with Martin Luther King, Jr.* New York: Holt, Rinehart and Winston.

Kogan, N. and Wallach, M. A. (1964). *Risk Taking: A Study in Cognition and Personality*. New York: Holt, Rinehart and Winston.

Levine, J. M. (1988). Reaction to opinion deviance in small groups. In P. Paulus (Ed.), *Psychology of Group Influence: New Perspectives*. Hillsdale, NJ: Earlbaum.

Malcolm X. (1973). *The Autobiography of Malcolm X*. New York: Ballantine.

Moreland, R. L. and Levine, J. M. (1982). Socialization in small groups: Temporal changes in individual group relations. In L. Berkowitz (Ed.), *Advances in Experimental Social Psychology*, vol. 15. New York: Academic Press.

Moreland, R. and Levine, J. M. (1984). Role transition in small groups. In V. Allen and E. van de Vhert (Eds.), *Role Transitions: Explorations and Explanations*. New York: Plenum.

Moreland, R., and Levine, J. M. (1988). Group dynamics over time: Development and socialization in small groups. In J. E. McGrath (Ed.), *The Social Psychology of Time*, pp 151–181. Newbury Park, CA: Sage.

Moscovici, S., Lage, E., and Naffrechoux, M. (1969). Influence of a consistent minority on the responses of a majority in a color perception task. *Sociometry*,12,365–380.

Moscovici, S., Mugny, G. and Perez, J. (1985). Les effects pervers du deni (par la majorite) des opinions d'une minorite. *Bulletin de Psychologie*,38,803–812.

Mugny, G., and Papastamou, S. (1980). When rigidity does not fail: Individualization and psychologization as resistances to the diffusion of minority innovations. *European Journal of Social Psychology*,10,43–62.

Nemeth, C. (1986). Differential contributions of majority vs. minority influence. *Psychological Review*,93,23–32.

Nemeth, C., and Staw, B. (1989). The tradeoffs of social control and innovation in groups and organizations. In L. Berkowitz (Ed.), *Advances in Experimental Social Psychology*, vol. 22. New York: Academic Press.

Nemeth, C., and Wachtler, J. (1974). Creating perceptions of consistency and confidence: A necessary condition for minority influence. *Sociometry*,37,529–540.

Paynton, C., and Blackey, R. (1971). *Why Revolution? Theories and Analysis*. Cambridge, MA: Schenkman.

Ross, L., Bierbrauer, G., and Hoffman, S. (1976). The role of attribution process in conformity and dissent: Revisiting the Asch situation. *American Psychologist*, 31,148–157.

Shaw, M. E. (1981). *Group Dynamics: The Psychology of Small Group Behavior.* New York: McGraw-Hill.

Toch, H. (1965). *The Social Psychology of Social Movements.* New York: Bobbs-Merrill.

Tuckman, B. W. (1965). Developmental sequences in small groups. *Psychological Bulletin*,63,384.

Tuckman, B. W., and Jensen, M. A. C. (1977). Stages of small-group development revisited. *Group and Organization Studies*,2,419–427.

Worchel, S., Cooper, J., and Goethals, G. R. (1991). *Understanding Social Psychology*, (5th ed.) Chicago: Dorsey Press.

Worchel, S., Coutant-Sassic, D., and Grossman, M. (1992). A developmental approach to group dynamics: A model and illustrative research. In S. Worchel, W. Wood, and J. Simpson (Eds.), *Group Process and Productivity.* Newbury Park, CA: Sage.

Worchel, S., Hart, D., and Butemeyer, J. The effects of rewards in future interaction in social loafing. Southwestern Psychology Association, Houston, TX, April 16-18, 1987.

CHAPTER SIX

MINORITY INFLUENCE EFFECTS: ASSIMILATION AND DIFFERENTIATION

Angelica Mucchi-Faina

A process of social influence does not invariably lead to increased conformism; that is, to greater uniformity of thinking and acting (Moscovici, 1976). On the contrary, it can give rise to diversified responses which develop in various modes.

While this assumption is generally shared, most of the research carried out in the field of influence has been devoted to investigate when and how a source contrives to bring about a change in its favor. Focus on this type of phenomenon has characterized studies on majority influence. Paradoxically, the same perspective has, for some time, also prevailed in research on minority influence whose raison d'etre lies in its attention to "diversity."

The limitations of such an approach have been variously pointed out (Montmollin, 1977; Nemeth, 1987), and today the theoretical cadre has been considerably extended, enabling us to examine minority influence in a wider spectrum than in the past.

In this chapter I shall review briefly the different effects which minorities can bring about, in an attempt to trace back for each the conditions which favor it, and to examine its underlying motivations. Finally, an interpretation of minority influence will be framed bearing in mind both the affective-motivational and the cognitive factors.

Terminologically speaking, I shall refer to the shift towards the minority source with the term *assimilation*. I shall instead use the term *differentiation* (Lemaine, 1974; Codol, 1984) for any change which develops in a direction other than that of the source.[1]

Assimilation

The Conversion Effect

Immediate assimilation with a minority source is a very rare phenomenon indeed. If a significant assimilation is to be produced, at the very least the source must be perceived as being consistent and confident, and this entails an adequate length of time.

Within these limits, *direct* and manifest assimilation, though not as strong as conformism to majority, has been observed ever since the first investigation in the field (Faucheux and Moscovici, 1967). During the first experiment, concerning the choice among four dimensions (size, color, form, and outline) of a visual stimulus, the presence of a confederate who declared consistently his personal preference for one of these, produced a significant increase in this choice. In the second experiment, in which the subjects were required to asssociate a stimulus word with a second word (a qualifying adjective or a superordinated noun), the confederate's consistent choice of the superordinated word caused an increase in this type of association. In both cases the responses of the subjects were voiced out aloud.

The authors related the success obtained by the minority to the social value of originality and protest. Although innovative processes are less frequent than conformity phenomena, a certain tension towards the modification of social rules and relations does exist in society. Hence, a consistent minority is appealing and can thus exert a social influence.

Most of the experiments which followed were not confined merely to verifying this effect, but also defined appropriate tools to perceive latent assimilation. With very few exceptions (e.g., a situation of sensory deprivation, Moscovici and Doms, 1982) the latter proved to be stronger than explicit influence.

First of all it was ascertained that assimilation was stronger at an indirect level (on a stimulus or problem different from, though connected with, that upon which the minority had expressed itself) than at a direct level (on the same stimulus). The first experiment to reveal this process was carried out towards the end of the sixties (Moscovici, Lage, and Naffrechoux, 1969). Here the minority influence was checked both on the same stimulus (color of the slides: green vs. blue), and also on a subsequent stimulus consisting in a series of colored cards in the blue-green color range (the Farnsworth test). In the experimental-group subjects, a shift in favor of green—the response given by the minority in the earlier session—in the discrimination threshold between blue and green was observed. This change (*indirect* influence) proved to be stronger than explicit adherence to the minority position (direct influence).

Later experiments confirmed the capacity of a minority to favor indirect assimilation, not only as concerns perceptive tasks (Moscovici and Lage, 1976), but also as to preferences and judgements. For example, in the research by Aebischer et al. (1984), the minority's choice in favor of new wave music led, at an indirect level, to an increase in preference for contemporary music, similar to the former in sound and harmony, and completely different from the hard rock music preferred by the subjects.[2] In the experiments carried out by Perez and Mugny (1986), target-judgment tends to go along the same lines as the minority, though not directly on the theme it proposes: rather, on an issue connected with it by an identical "organizing principle." The minority pro-abortion message, for instance, leads to a change in favor of birth control (thus going along the same lines) when tolerance (vs. morality) is introduced as the organizing principle.

Further investigation has revealed how a minority can cause an influence process which is not only more indirect, but generally more covert than that produced by a majority source. It has been found that a minority is more effective in a *private* situation rather than in a public one (Mugny, 1974–75; Mugny, 1976; Maass and Clark, 1983; Martin, 1987, 1988a, 1988b); at an *unconscious* level rather than a conscious one (Moscovici and Personnaz, 1980; Personnaz, 1981) after a *time delay* rather than immediately following the influence attempt (Moscovici, Mugny, and Papastamou, 1981). Taken together, these studies reveal that assimilation with minority is made easier when it is not evident (*conversion effect*, Moscovici, 1980; Moscovici and Mugny, 1987).

It should also be noted that some investigations have assumed or indicated the possibility of an inverse ratio, at least in trend, between manifest and covert assimilation, (Moscovici, Lage, and Naffrechoux, 1969; Moscovici and Doms, 1982; Mugny, 1984; Doise, Gachoud, and Mugny, 1986). Thus, it would appear that the subjects or groups which yield explicitly are more reluctant to assimilate at a latent level, and vice versa—as if there were a maximum assimilation threshold beyond which the subject will not go.

All considered, therefore, an assimilation process would appear to be facilitated when:

1. a certain period of time has elapsed
2. dependence is nonsalient and thus
3. the subject feels she or he is able to preserve sufficient personal autonomy.

This "caution" is supporting minority ideas, and the prevalent latency of assimilation, are explained by Moscovici (1980) as the "fear of losing face" and the desire to "avoid the risk of speaking or acting in a deviant fashion in the presence of others'' (p.211). In spite of the force of appeal of the minority, *assimilation with the minority is seen as threatening*: the influence target fears that *in toto* acceptance of the minority position would entail being charged with weakness and incompetence (Paicheler and Moscovici, 1984) or even worse, attribution to the self of stereotypical negative minority characteristics (Mugny, 1982) thus marring one's own image. Thus the subject who yields tends to adopt any type of *camouflage strategy* offered by the situation. The fact that generally assimilation is partial and often unconscious would suggest that the individual aim is not merely to keep under control the image that others have of them (*impression management*, Heilman and Toffler, 1976; Leary and Kowalski, 1990) in order to enhance themselves in the eyes of others, but also to maintain a positive concept of one's self (Mugny, 1982; Personnaz, 1984).

The Modelling Effect

A number of researchers have shed light on yet another indirect or partial assimilation mode. This consists, rather than approaching the minority message or position, in adopting its *behavior*, applying this, however, to other contexts or other contents.

To date, very little experimental work has been devoted to this phenomenon. In the course of a study carried out by Nemeth and Chiles (1988), it emerged that exposure to a dissident minority brought about, during a later session, greater resistance to majority pressure and an increase in personal independence. In this case, the minority provided a model of dissent. Following its example, the subjects managed to affirm their own ideas, and to act coherently with their personal vision of reality. Again, in an experiment conducted by Joule, Mugny, and Perez (1988), a minority breaking a rule also induced the subjects to break the rule, even though in a more moderate way.

A field research which aimed at investigating strategies used by the Italian feminist movement to obtain the decriminalization of abortion (Mucchi-Faina, 1984, 1987; Crespi and Mucchi-Faina, 1988) has shed light on how this process can be set going even outside the laboratory, when the minorities are social movements. The feminist movement proved a model of freedom and independence for women political activists. Indeed, far before influencing them directly—gaining explicit support for its ideas—it induced them to claim greater autonomy within their party (Mucchi-Faina, 1987). An active and dissenting minority would therefore appear capable not only of activating the target, but also of strengthening its capacity to resist majority pressure (*modelling effect*, Nemeth and Chiles, 1988).

The effect would seem to develop especially when the subject experiences a strong internal conflict between admiration for the source (viewed as "courageous" and "worthy of respect," Nemeth and Chiles, 1988) and the impossibility of accepting its position (considered wrong or too extremist, or also on account of self-image problems, Mucchi-Faina, 1987). In such a case, copying it in "another situation" could provide an efficacious strategy to maintain positive self- and hetero-evaluation.

Differentiation

The Boomerang Effect

While the various assimilation modes were being defined, a number of experiments were also beginning to reveal differentiation processes with regard to a minority source. In an experiment carried out by Nemeth and Wachtler (1973), the extreme pro-attitudinal position of a minority provoked a change in the opposite direction. In one of Mugny's experiments (1974, cit. by Moscovici, 1976), a differentiation of the subjects in the opposite sense occurred when a weak majority expressed a message, whether counterattitudinal (xenophobic) or pro-attitudinal (xenophilic: in the latter case the effect is weaker). In Paicheler's investigations (1976, 1977) the presence of a counternormative (antifeminist) minority gave rise to a bipolarization phenomenon in which the initially antifeminist subjects became even more so, while the position of the profeminist also was strengthened. In a later experiment (1979), Paicheler found a counterpolarization of the subjects (both in the consensus and in the postconsensus phases) in mixed groups in which a female confederate supported an antifeminist position. A similar effect occurred more recently in an experiment carried out by Clark and Maass (1988a, exp.3): subjects expressing an unfavorable attitude towards gay rights became more favorable towards gay rights in reaction to a homosexual minority which opposed gay rights.

In these investigations differentiation emerged as a counterpolarization of the subjects vis-à-vis the minority position, as a shift in the opposite direction to the one indicated by the source (*boomerang effect*).

Considering these studies as a whole, three elements would appear to encourage boomerang effect at an explicit level:

1. The item asks for attitudes and opinions rather than for more "objective" judgement.
2. The position expressed by the minority is similar or close to that of the target before exposure to the source.
3. The subject views the minority group in a particularly unfavorable manner (salience of diversity and deviance).

119

The "threatening" aspect of the minority now prevails over attraction: fear of being identified with the source increases and the target solves the problem by "changing its idea." As with the modelling effect considered earlier, the minority arouses an inner conflict but of an opposite nature: in the modelling case, an attractive source expresses an unacceptable message; in the boomerang case, aversion for the source induces subjects to negate a message with which they were formerly in agreement.

This differentiation mechanism would appear to develop just like *reactance* (Brehm, 1966): that is, negative attitudinal change occurring in the face of forceful persuasive communications. Indeed, in reactance, too, an essential prerequisite is the initial agreement of the subjects with the position held by the source (Worchel and Brehm, 1970; Wicklund, 1974).

The classic explanation of reactance is of a motivational nature: the subjects would appear to react in such a way as to restore their freedom which they believe to be endangered (*need for freedom*, Brehm, 1966). More recently, it has been surmised that people are interested above all in *giving an image* of autonomy and independence. According to this impression management interpretation, reactance is triggered by self-presentational concerns (Heilman and Toffler, 1976)—an explanation that has not always been confirmed (Wright and Brehm, 1982; Wright, 1986).

As for minority influence, the available data on boomerang effect are insufficient to permit definitive conclusions about the motivations underlying this phenomenon.[3] Anyhow, it is possible that, in this case too, the subject faces a dual problem: saving one's external image and protecting one's freedom.

The Divergency Effect

An experiment conducted by Moscovici and Lage in 1978 sheds light on a new phenomenon connected with minority influence. Making use once again of the blue/green paradigm, and inducing within this context an *originality* (vs. objectivity) *norm*, some of the subjects give a response which differs decidedly both from that of the majority and that of the minority (neither blue nor green: grey, white, yellow). These results, for the first time, reveal how in particular conditions the influence process can lead not only to a counterpolarization, but to a plurality (a diversification) of responses.

A series of investigations carried out by Nemeth and colleagues has made a valuable contribution to our knowledge of this process, shedding light on how differentiation can take on more articulate modes than simple opposition. It was found that a minority can stimulate detection of new and correct solutions (Nemeth and Wachtler, 1983), of original associations

(Nemeth and Kwan, 1985), and of alternative or better strategies (Nemeth and Kwan, 1987). It was also seen how this type of phenomenon does not occur when the source is the majority: in the presence of a majority, the subjects tend to adopt its same point of view (see Nemeth's chapter in this volume).

In these experiments, and notwithstanding the fact that the originality norm was not specifically recalled, the majority induced response diversification. Furthermore, and above all, differentiation did not manifest itself in reactive terms, in the form of rejection of the minority proposal. On the contrary, the minority proposal was taken into consideration as one of the possible alternatives. For example, an experiment carried out by Nemeth and Kwan (1987) employed a word composition task using letter-strings (e.g., tDOGe) in which subjects were asked to identify meaningful words. A minority (versus a majority) suggested an inverse sequence (e.g., GOD) as alternative to the more immediately perceptible sequence (DOG). In the majority condition, inverse composition strategy prevailed; in the minority condition, subjects made use of different composition strategies (direct, inverse, mixed sequences), thus adopting also, but not exclusively, the one suggested by the source. Similarly, in the experiment carried out by Moscovici and Lage (1978), the subjects who had been made to believe that they had obtained brilliant results on a creativity test gave both minority (green) and other responses.

In another series of experiments (Mucchi-Faina et al., 1991) in which the subjects were asked to formulate proposals concerning the best kind of representation to promote the image of the City of Perugia, it was found that the quality of a minority proposal can in fact favor divergence and originality. The presence of an original (vs. a conventional) minority proposal acted as an incentive for the subjects to formulate original alternative proposals. This, however, occurred only when the minority position was accompanied by a majority proposal of a conventional nature. Instead, when it was the majority which expressed an original position, or when both sources did, subjects elaborated fewer proposals and of a conventional nature.[4] This capacity to stimulate new and original production therefore appears to be a minority prerogative, and in particular, that of an innovative and unconventional minority.

Under certain conditions, therefore, differentiation is the fruit of independent elaboration and not merely the result of a reactive process of detachment from the source. In these investigations the minority did not represent a threat, but instead acted as a stimulus (Moscovici, 1976), prompting the subjects to assert their personal uniqueness (*divergence effect*, Nemeth, 1986).

Recently, it has been ascertained that the divergence effect can be

121

triggered not only on perceptive stimuli or creative problem solving, but also with regard to judgements and attitudes (Trost et al., 1989; Volpato et al., 1990). Inasmuch as the issue in these experiments concerned legislative reform, and consequently a proposal of change, in this case as well, the context involved an "innovation" norm. However, these studies also suggest that for divergence to occur it is essential that the issue involves the subjects directly and that the counterattitudinal minority message is expressed by a relatively close source (e.g., ingroup).

In summation, the divergence effect is encouraged when:

1. The context (norm of originality or innovation), the task, or the stimulus prompt the expression of independent ideas.
2. Subjects are directly involved in the task either because it is a competitive one—and so they are concentrated on their own performance—or because the issue is personally relevant for themselves.
3. Subjects were allowed ample time at their disposal.

Nemeth (1986) connects the divergence effect with the level of tension produced by the situation. Whereas excessive tension, such as that due to exposure to an opposing majority, hinders target performance, a minority engenders an "optimal" degree of tension (neither too high nor too low) which improves the outcome and favors a divergent way of thinking. The possibility of a relation between tension levels and differentiation processes has also been suggested by Codol (1984).

The Shifting Effect

The last type of differentiation gathered involved "closed" tasks—whereby the subject may not express personal opinions or estimations, but is obliged to select a preformulated reply—in a situation in which the target is exposed simultaneously to majority and minority sources, and can opt for one of at least three different answers. Differentiation in this case is expressed as shifting to an alternative not selected by either source.

An experiment performed by Kimball and Hollander (1974) demonstrated this phenomenon very clearly. The subjects were asked to express a series of judgements concerning highly ambiguous perceptive stimuli: they had to spot which of three lights went out first in a situation in which the time interval between the switching off of the first light and that of the others was totally imperceptible. The subjects could agree with the majority choice, or with that of a deviant subject (a confederate), or else opt for the third alternative. In the circumstance when the minority subject was portrayed as experienced (versus inexperienced) in the task, the researchers found a significant increase of the third choice, without there being any increase in direct minority influence. The authors interpreted this phenomenon as increased independence of the subjects in relation to the minority example (in fact, a case of modelling effect). However, they surmised that it could instead prove a negative reaction (*anticonformity*, Willis, 1965) rather than true independence (indifference to other people's replies).

An element in support of this second interpretation emerged in a more recent experiment (Mucchi-Faina et al., 1989). Subjects were required to express their opinion as to the geographical area in which Italian aid for developing countries should be concentrated. They were offered three options: Latin America, Asia, and Africa (at the time the most popular choice: in an extensive pre-test it received 65% of the answers). Subjects were asked to indicate their choice by making a cross on a sheet in one of three columns labelled Africa, Latin America, and Asia. In the experimental conditions which we are dealing with here (unpopular majority choice), the majority was represented by five crosses in the Latin America column. The minority choice was either absent or present with two crosses under the most popular choice (Africa). In the control group, no crosses appeared on the sheet.

The results (see table 6.1) show a significant difference between the two experimental conditions. When the minority was absent, subjects overwhelmingly chose Africa. Since the third choice (Asia) was totally neglected, it is possible that the problem was tackled in a bipolar manner (to accept the majority choice or to resist it; Nemeth, 1986) resulting in an independent choice. The presence of a minority instead led to an "escape" from the prevalent position with a shifting towards the third choice, besides a relative increase in the majority choice.

Since in this study the subjects' choices were unobstrusively timed, we

Table 6.1 Distribution Percentages of the Choice in Majority Unpopular Choice Conditions and in the Control

	Minority Absent	Minority Present	Control
Minority choice (Africa)	75%	53%	75%
	(24)	(17)	(24)
Majority choice (Latin America)	25%	31%	19%
	(8)	(10)	(6)
Third choice (Asia)	0	16%	6%
		(5)	(2)
	100%	100%	100%
	(32)	(32)	(32)

Note: Frequencies are bracketed.

have an additional element as to the "shifting" phenomenon compared with the Kimball and Hollander experiment (1974). On the average, the subjects who opted for the third choice (Asia) took far less time (12 seconds) than those who made the other choice (Africa: 20 seconds; Latin America: 31 seconds). Such a choice would therefore seem the fruit not of more independent behavior, or of greater reflection, but instead of an immediate standing aloof. While the conformist choice (Latin America) entailed a great decision-making effort for the subjects who chose it, the shift to the third option was a fairly simple way to resolving the problem.

Increase in reply diversification does thus not necessarily correspond to subjects' more intense cognitive activity. It should be noted that in both experiments the minority source is particularly trustworthy, inasmuch as it is declared to be "experienced" or makes a choice in line with social consensus. Paradoxically, it is precisely this reliability which produces the shifting effect.

The relationship between shifting and competence is no novelty. Outside the domain of minority influence, the work of Lemaine and colleagues (a synthesis in Lemaine et al., 1978) has frequently shed light on this phenomenon. For example, in one experiment (Personnaz et al., 1976–77) two subjects (one was a confederate) were required to give separate descriptions of a painting using a series of ready-made sentences divided into four thematic categories: "color," "form," "description," and "others." When the confederate was presented as an expert in painting techniques, and therefore specialized in "color" and "form," the experimental subject modified his original choice, which had been in favor of these categories, and from then on used category phrases differing from those of the expert. Thus, shifting occurred from one stimulus dimension to another, directly connected with the presence of a person having experience in the problem. The authors interpret this phenomenon as a strategy used by the subject when she or he finds her or himself in a state of inferiority, in order to avoid unfavorable comparison.

These studies enable us to formulate a preliminary interpretation of shifting which emerged from our investigation. When the subject is confronted with two sources and the minority position is somehow strengthened, she or he is faced with a dilemma. On the one hand, as we have seen, explicit assimilation to the minority position is difficult: to show dependence on a minority means to admit its superiority and this has negative repercussions on one's self-image. On the other hand, in this particular case, compliance to the majority is even more difficult. Since the target believes the minority to be right, a conformist choice becomes very evident and, hence, also causes self-image problems. Therefore, the third option is a way out for the subject which enables him or her to avoid both confrontation with the minority and the humiliation of compliance. Not surprisingly, this choice is relatively quick and easy.

A Two-Dimension Approach to Minority Influence

Can the same interpretative framework be used to account for the different effects which minority influence can produce? The factors which come into play in influence processes are many and varied. However, it is possible, following this analysis, to trace a theoretical pattern which takes into account affective/motivational factors in addition to cognitive elements.

Research in the field of information processing (Shiffrin and Schneider, 1977; Shiffrin and Dumais, 1981) has revealed how spontaneous answers and associations, assimilated at an early age and activated frequently in memory, are aroused unconsciously when a particular cue is given. These *automatic* processes differ from *controlled* processes, which instead are based on intentionality; they require the subject's attention and are endowed with greater flexibility. Controlled processes have the capability of inhibiting those automatically activated responses which the subject, for some reason, rejects (i.e., a judgement based on one's personal beliefs can substitute an automatically activated cultural stereotype, see Devine 1989). However, controlled processes, to come into operation, entail more time and sufficient cognitive capacities, and therefore cannot always be resorted to.

Whichever specific reference to the modes by which a persuasive communication can be processed, Petty and Cacioppo (1986) have drawn a distinction that, under certain aspects, is similar to the one just mentioned. According to their model, the message delivered by a source can be processed by means of either a *central* route or a *peripheral* route. The central route entails reflection and thorough evaluation of the content of the message transmitted. The peripheral route requires reduced cognitive effort since it does not go into the substance of the message but is instead based on other factors such as the attractiveness of the source, the style of the message, identification processes, heuristics (Chaiken, 1980), and so on.

The peripheral route, while representing a simpler form of information processing than the central route, does not merely imply automatic processes but also controlled ones. Both types of processing, however, can also be required by the central route (Sherman, 1987).

Automatic and controlled processes must therefore be considered as the two poles of a continuum and not as alternative modes. In this perspective, the central route comes very close to the controlled pole, whereas the peripheral route is set more closely to the automatic pole.

Returning to our issue, it is possible that the different effects of minority influence relate to the prevalent modes used by the subjects, besides motivations and affective states which prevail in turn.

We have seen that a minority is regarded by the individual as a threat (the fear of being associated with it, and thus considered deviant, represents a danger in term of self-image, identity, external impressions, etc.). At the same time, it exerts a strong appeal (referred to the values of independence and courage). A minority thus arouses two contrasting feelings in the subjects, *aversion* and *attraction*, which cause him to waver between a negative and a positive attitude, between rejection and acceptance.

It may feasibly be assumed that rejection of a minority source is a highly accessible attitude (Fazio, 1986), the outcome of precocious learning, often recalled to mind and therefore more stable and deeply rooted than the positive attitude. The latter would therefore seem relatively more recent and more directly connected to personal beliefs.[5] Figure 6.1 illustrates the various possibilities deriving from the factors examined.

In this perspective, the scant success enjoyed by a minority at an immediate and direct level may be attributed to an automatic type of process which is activated involuntarily (or almost involuntarily) whenever the target is exposed to a source of that nature. In turn, the shifting effect—at least when subjects react very promptly to the stimulus (e.g., see Mucchi-Faina, Maass, and Volpato, 1989)—can be interpreted as a partially automatic response brought about, when this is possible, in a double-threat situation.

Only a cognitive effort, based chiefly on his or her personal way of thinking and beliefs, enables the subject to overcome the immediate rejection and begin to take the source into more careful consideration.

Figure 6.1   Effects Produced by Minority Relating to the Prevalent Feeling and to the Type of Information Processing

		Feeling	
		Attraction	**Aversion**
	Automatic		
			Rejection (P)
			Shifting (P)
Process		Modelling (P)	Boomerang (P)
		Conversion (C)	Divergence (C)
	Controlled		

(P) = prevalence of the peripheral route
(C) = prevalence of the central route

The modelling and boomerang effects are both situated at a medium degree of complexity. They stem from the peripheral route since, as we have seen, they are linked above all with source-identification problems. Diametrically opposed, however, is their underlying feeling: in the case of modelling, attraction prevails and the subject is committed to imitate the behavior of his or her model in the hope that its courage and ensuing image will be transferred to him or her. To the contrary, in the boomerang effect, aversion prevails and the subject is bound to draw away from the source to avoid being identified with it. In these cases, therefore, the subject only brushes superficially the issues proposed by the minority, while mainly concerned with his or her own image and/or personal identity.

More complex cognitive processes, which lead to deeper changes (Petty and Cacioppo, 1986) can substitute responses of a peripheral type if the subject intends to commit him or herself, has the necessary capacity, and the circumstances are favorable (i.e., an adequate length of time). These are the central processes which accompany conversion and divergence. Here too, the main sentiment is different: the converging subject is deeply attracted by the minority message and appropriates it, even though she or he prefers to do so fairly covertly; divergence instead stems from individualism, from an urge to compete with the minority and prevail over it (Kruglanski and Mackie, 1990). Interest in the minority, which is fundamental in conversion, is purely instrumental in divergence.

Conclusion

The interpretative framework proposed, as is the case in all syntheses, greatly oversimplifies a series of phenomena which are in fact more complex. The picture is probably not an exhaustive one, nor can all the results obtained in this field be fitted in precisely. Moreover the different effects are "ideal-types" (Weber, 1922), and as such are seldom to be found in reality. For example, the modelling effect can go side by side with conversion and also with divergence, and the same applies to the boomerang effect. Specific effects could occur in relation with ambivalence of feelings or attitudes, rather than with the preponderance of a sentiment or of an attitude upon the other (i.e., a very extreme boomerang effect; see the ambivalence-amplification theory, Katz, 1981).

What I have attempted to show is how a minority, depending on the situation, can activate different qualities and quantities of information processing. If it is true that minorities frequently engender curiosity and have a "maieutic" function, it is also true that at times the effects they provoke are not the intended ones. The history of social movements demonstrates that in certain cases the innovative ferments of the minorities have ended up confirming and bolstering the current order instead of introducing social changes.

For this reason, I believe it to be essential that studies of social influence take yet a further leap forward, attempting to probe beyond the "dualist" and "monist" theories on majority and minority influence (Kruglanski and Mackie, 1990). Instead of concentrating our efforts on analyzing the existing similarities and differences between the two forms of influence, it would now appear more useful to try to gather the results which could stem from different types of interaction between the two sources. The effect produced by a minority cannot be investigated independently of the existence of a majority, and of the position it adopts. The simultaneous influence paradigm which, from the work of Maass and Clark (1983) onwards, has spread more and more during recent years, appears to be one promising tool for studies in this direction.

Notes

1. It has been observed (Sorrels and Kelley, 1984; Levine and Russo, 1987) that social influence does not necessarily entail movement, but can also adopt the aspect of lack of change. While bearing this possibility in mind, I shall not go into it here since minority investigations aim above all at understanding processes of innovation and change.

2. It should however be noted that in this experiment the source is defined as a "minority" only in terms of its (low) social status, but not numerically (on this point see also the chapter by W. Crano in this volume).

3. Research in which a differentiation process has been come across have rarely controlled the underlying mechanisms. The few exceptions have however revealed diversified results. In certain experiments, manifest differentiation is accompanied by underlying assimilation (e.g., Maass and Clark, 1986). In others, (e.g., Clark and Maass, 1988b) a differentiation process was found at both levels: a minority outgroup which expressed a position against abortion produced, both in private and in public, more positive attitudes to abortion. In an experiment carried out by Mugny (1982, exp.14) the subjects close to—as opposed to the ones distant from—a rigid minority differ at an explicit level, whereas at a covert level the effect is irrelevant. Finally, in an experiment carried out by Clark (1988), a minority which supported a position in favor of risk on an item recalling the value of prudence, obtains a weak direct assimilation and a significant differentiation at an indirect level compared with the control group.

4. The chapter by A. Maass and C. Volpato refers to this research in greater detail.

5. Although to my knowledge there is no specific research on this issue, from a number of studies emerge a series of indications which apparently reveal that at an early age subjects seek above all the similarities between themselves and the others. Acceptation of diversity, admiration and search for independence take over only at a

later stage. In an investigation on self-definition in a sample of adolescents of different ages which I carried out some years ago (Mucchi-Faina, 1983), it emerged with great clarity that the younger ones (aged fourteen) stressed their being "normal" and "like everyone else" more frequently (28% of that age-group) than the older teenagers (15% of the eighteen-year olds). Instead, the latter affirmed their "diversity" and "uniqueness" in greater numbers (10%)—an aspect almost totally absent in the younger adolescents (1%). These results would appear to show that acceptance and search for difference emerges only when one's own similarity with peers has been asserted. Considerations of this type have also been made by Tajfel (1981), Melucci (1982), and Codol (1984). The same "preference for the out-group" found in investigations conducted with children of minority groups (quote by Tajfel, 1981) could be read in this perspective: during childhood diversity is regarded above all as a disadvantage.

References

Aebischer, V., Hewstone, M. and Henderson, M. (1984). Minority influence and musical preference: Innovation by conversion not coercion. *European Journal of Social Psychology*,14,23–33.

Brehm, J. W. (1966). *A Theory of Psychological Reactance*. New York: Academic Press.

Chaiken, S. (1980). Heuristic versus systematic information processing and the use of source versus message cues in persuasion. *Journal of Personality and Social Psychology*,39,752–766.

Clark, R. D. (1988). On predicting minority influence. *European Journal of Social Psychology*,18,515–526.

Clark, R. D., and Maass, A. (1988a). Social categorization in minority influence: The case of homosexuality. *European Journal of Social Psychology*,18,347–364.

Clark, R. D., and Maass, A. (1988b). The role of social categorization and perceived source credibility in minority influence. *European Journal of Social Psychology*,18,381–394.

Codol, J. P. (1984). Social differentiation and non-differentiation. In H. Tajfel (Ed.), *The Social Dimension*, vol. 2, pp.314–337. Cambridge: Cambridge University Press.

Crespi, F., and Mucchi-Faina, A. (Eds.) (1988). *Le Strategie delle Minoranze Attive*. Naples: Liguori.

Devine, P. G. (1989). Stereotypes and prejudice: Their automatic and controlled components. *Journal of Personality and Social Psychology*,56,5–18.

Doise, W., Gachoud, J. P., and Mugny, G. (1986). Influence directe et indirecte entre groupes dans des choix esthetiques. *Cahiers de Psychologie Cognitive*,6,283–301.

Faucheux, C., and Moscovici, S. (1967). Le style de comportement d'une minorite et son influence sur les reponses d'une majorite. *Bulletin du C.E.R.P.*,16,337–360.

Fazio, R. H. (1986). How do attitudes guide behavior? In R.M. Sorrentino and E.T. Higgins (Eds.), *The Handbook of Motivation and Cognition: Foundations of Social Behavior*, pp.204–243. New York: Guilford Press.

Heilman, M. E., and Toffler, B. L. (1976). Reacting to reactance: An interpersonal interpretation of the need for freedom. *Journal of Experimental Social Psychology*,12,519–529.

Joule, R. V., Mugny, G. and Perez, J. (1988). When a compliance without pressure strategy fails due to a minority dissenter: A case of "behavioural conversion." *European Journal of Social Psychology*,18,531–535.

Katz, I. (1981). *Stigma: A Social Psychological Analysis*. Hillsdale, NJ: Erlbaum.

Kimball, R. K., and Hollander, E. P. (1974). Independence in the presence of an experienced but deviate group member. *Journal of Social Psychology*,93,281–292.

Kruglanski, A. W., and Mackie, D. M. (1990). Majority and minority influence: A judgmental process analysis. *European Review of Social Psychology*,1,229–261.

Leary, M. R., and Kowalski, R. M. (1990). Impression management: A literature review and two-component model. *Psychological Bulletin*,107,34–47.

Lemaine, G. (1974). Social differentiation and social originality. *European Journal of Social Psychology*,4,17–52.

Lemaine, G., Kastersztein, J., and Personnaz, B. (1978). Social differentiation. In Tajfel, H. (Ed.), *Differentiation between Social Groups: Studies in the Social Psychology of Intergroup Relations*, pp.269–299. London: Academic Press.

Levine, J. M., and Russo, E. M. (1987). Majority and minority influence. In C. Hendrick (Ed.), Group processes. *Review of Personality and Social Psychology*, 8,13–54.

Maass, A., and Clark, R. D. (1983). Internalization versus compliance: Differential processes underlying minority influence and conformity. *European Journal of Social Psychology*,13,197–215.

Maass, A., and Clark, R. D. (1986). Conversion theory and simultaneous majority/minority influence: Can reactance offer an alternative explanation? *European Journal of Social Psychology*,16,305–309.

Martin, R. (1987). Influence minoritaire et relations entre groupes. In S. Moscovici and G. Mugny (Eds.), *Psychologie de la conversion*. Cousset: Delval.

Martin, R. (1988a). Ingroup and outgroup minorities: Differential impact upon public and private responses. *European Journal of Social Psychology*,18,39–52.

Martin, R. (1988b). Minority influence and social categorization: A replication. *European Journal of Social Psychology*,18,369–373.

Melucci, A. (1982). *L'invenzione del presente. Movimenti, identita', bisogni individuali*. Bologna: Il Mulino.

de Montmollin, G. (1977). *L'influence sociale*. Paris: P.U.F.

Moscovici, S. (1976). *Social Influence and Social Change*. London: Academic Press; trad.fr. (1979), *Psychologie des Minorites Actives*. Paris: P.U.F.

Moscovici, S. (1980). Toward a theory of conversion behavior. In L. Berkowitz (Ed.), *Advances in Experimental Social Psychology*, Vol. 13, pp.209–239. New York: Academic Press.

Moscovici, S., and Doms, M. (1982). Compliance and conversion in a situation of sensory deprivation. *Basic and Applied Social Psychology*,3,81–94.

Moscovici, S., and Lage, E. (1976). Studies in social influence III: Majority versus minority influence in a group. *European Journal of Social Psychology*,6,149–174.

Moscovici, S., and Lage, E. (1978). Studies in social influence IV: minority influence in a context of original judgments. *European Journal of Social Psychology*,8,349–365.

Moscovici, S., Lage, E., and Naffrechoux, M. (1969). Influence of a consistent minority on the responses of a majority in a color perception task. *Sociometry*,32,365–380.

Moscovici, S., and Mugny, G. (Eds.). (1987). *Psychologie de la Conversion*. Cousset: Delval.

Moscovici, S., Mugny, G., and Papastamou, S. (1981). "Sleeper effect" et/ou effet minoritaire? Etude theorique et experimentale de l'influence sociale a' retardement. *Cahiers de Psychologie Cognitive*,1,199–221.

Moscovici, S., and Personnaz, B. (1980). Studies in social influence V: Minority influence and conversion behavior in a perceptual task. *Journal of Experimental Social Psychology*,16,270–282.

Mucchi-Faina, A. (1983). La definizione di se' nelle adolescenti. *Quaderni dell'Istituto di Studi Sociali*,20,171–180. Universitá di Perugia, Italy.

Mucchi-Faina, A. (1984). Stili di comportamento minoritario: Alcuni elementi di una rappresentazione sociale. *Giornale Italiano di Psicologia*,11,335–355.

Mucchi-Faina, A. (1987). Mouvement social et conversion. In S. Moscovici and G. Mugny (Eds.), *Psychologie de la Conversion*, pp.181–196. Cousset: Delval.

Mucchi-Faina, A., Maass, A., and Volpato, C. (1989). Social influence in popular vs unpopular source's choice. Unpublished manuscript. Universita' di Perugia.

Mucchi-Faina, A., Maass, A., and Volpato, C. (1991). Social influence: The case of originality. *European Journal of Social Psychology*,21,183–197.

Mugny, G. (1974-75). Majorite' et minorite': Le niveau de leur influence. *Bulletin de psychologie*,28,831–835.

Mugny, G. (1976). Quelle influence majoritaire? Quelle influence minoritaire? *Revue Suisse de Psychologie*,35,255–268.

Mugny, G. (1982). *The Power of Minorities*. London: Academic Press.

Mugny, G. (1984). Compliance, conversion and the Asch paradigm. *European Journal of Social Psychology*,14,353–368.

Nemeth, C. (1986). Differential contributions of majority and minority influence. *Psychological Review*,93,23–32.

Nemeth, C. (1987). Influence processes, problem solving and creativity. In M. P. Zanna, J. M. Olson and C. P. Herman (Eds.), *Social Influence: The Ontario Symposium*, vol. 5, pp.237–246.

Nemeth, C., and Chiles, C. (1988). Modelling courage: the role of dissent in fostering independence. *European Journal of Social Psychology*,18,275–280.

Nemeth, C., and Kwan, J. (1985). Originality of word associations as a function of majority vs. minority influence. *Social Psychology Quarterly*,48,227–282.

Nemeth, C., and Kwan, J. (1987). Minority influence, divergent thinking, and detection of correct solutions. *Journal of Applied Social Psychology*,17,786–797.

Nemeth, C., Mayseless, O., Sherman, J., and Brown, Y. (1990). Exposure to dissent and recall of information. *Journal of Personality and Social Psychology*,58,429–437.

Nemeth, C., and Wachtler, J. (1973). Consistency and modification of judgment. *Journal of Experimental Social Psychology*,9,65–79.

Nemeth, C., and Wachtler, J. (1983). Creative problem solving as a result of majority versus minority influence. *European Journal of Social Psychology*,13, 45–55.

Paicheler, G. (1976). Norms and attitude change I: Polarization and styles of behavior. *European Journal of Social Psychology*,6,405–427.

Paicheler, G. (1977). Norms and attitude change II: The phenomenon of bipolarization. *European Journal of Social Psychology*,7,4–14

Paicheler, G. (1979). Polarization of attitudes in homogeneous and heterogeneous groups. *European Journal of Social Psychology*,9,85–96.

Paicheler, G., and Moscovici, S. (1984). Suivisme et conversion. In S. Moscovici (ed.), *Psychologie Sociale*, Paris: P.U.F.

Perez, J., and Mugny, G. (1986). Induction experimentale d'une influence minoritaire indirecte. *Cahiers de Psychologie Sociale*,32,15–24.

Personnaz, B. (1981). Study on social influence using the spectrometer method: Dynamics of the phenomena of conversion and covertness in perceptual responses. *European Journal of Social Psychology*,11,431–438.

Personnaz, B. (1984). Perspectives sur les liens entre innovation et differenciation sociale, et reactance psychologique et "libertance." *Bulletin de Psychologie*, 37,501–506.

Personnaz, B., Kastersztein, J., and Lemaine, G. (1976–77). L'originalité sociale: Etude de la differenciation social dans un systeme semi-fermé. *Bulletin de psychologie*,30,451–454.

Petty, R. E., and Cacioppo, J. T. (1986). *Communication and Persuasion*. New York: Springer-Verlag.

Sherman, S. J. (1987). Cognitive processes in the formation, change, and expression of attitudes. In M.P. Zanna, J.M.Olson, and C.P. Herman (Eds.), *Social Influence: The Ontario Symposium*, vol.5. Hillsdale, NJ: Erlbaum.

Shiffrin, R. M., and Dumais, S. T. (1981). The development of automatism. In J. R. Anderson (Ed.), *Cognitive Skill and Their Acquisition*, pp.111–140. Hillsdale, NJ: Erlbaum.

Shiffrin, R. M., and Schneider, W. (1977). Controlled and automatic human information processing: II. Perceptual learning, automatic attending, and a general theory. *Psychological Review*,84,127–190.

Sorrels, J. P. and Kelley, J. (1984). Conformity by omission. *Personality and Social Psychology Bulletin*,10,302–305.

Tajfel, H. (1981). *Human Groups and Social Categories*. Cambridge: University Press.

Trost, M. R., Maass, A., and Kenrick, D. T. (1989). Minority influence: Ego involvement alters cognitive processes and reverses private acceptance. Unpublished manuscript. Arizona State University, Tempe.

Volpato, C., Maass, A., Mucchi-Faina, A., and Vitti, E. (1990). Minority influence and social categorization. *European Journal of Social Psychology*,20,119–132.

Weber, M. (1922). *Wirtschaft und Gesellschaft*. Tubingen: Mohr.

Wicklund, R. A. (1974). *Freedom and Reactance*. Hillsdale, NJ: Erlbaum.

Willis, R. H. (1965). Conformity, independence and anticonformity. *Human Relations*,18,373–388.

Worchel, S., and Brehm, J. W. (1970). Effects of threats to attitudinal freedom as a function of agreement with the communicator. *Journal of Personality and Social Psychology*,14,18–22.

Wright, R. A. (1986). Attitude change as a function of threat to attitudinal freedom and extent of agreement with a communicator. *Journal of European Social Psychology*,16,43–50.

Wright, R. A., and Brehm, S. S. (1982). Reactance as impression management: A critical review. *Journal of Personality and Social Psychology*,42,608–618.

CHAPTER SEVEN

THEORETICAL PERSPECTIVES ON MINORITY INFLUENCE: CONVERSION VERSUS DIVERGENCE?

Anne Maass and Chiara Volpato

Although minority influence had become a lively field of research long before 1980 (e.g., Moscovici, 1976), we believe that the
clearest formulation of minority influence theory was offered by Moscovici
in his seminal article under the cautious title of "Toward a Theory of
Conversion Behavior." Among the key predictions of conversion theory are
the following two: one refers to the process by which minority and majority
influence operate; the other refers to the outcome resulting from such
processes. As far as the underlying attentional and cognitive processes are
concerned, attention in minority influence is focused on the minority's
message which is tested against reality. The key process in minority
influence is the "examination of the relation between (the minority's)
response and the object or reality" (Moscovici, 1980, p.215). During the
interaction, the "main preoccupation is to see what the minority sees, to
understand what it understands" (Moscovici, 1980, p. 215). This *validation
process* requires the active generation of arguments and counterarguments by
the target of influence. Quite in contrast, majority influence induces a
relatively shallow *comparison process* in which the different opinions are
compared without further attention to the stimulus under discussion. Turning
to the differential outcomes resulting from these processes, majority influence is likely to become manifest in *public compliance* which is limited to
the influence setting and which persists only as long as the influence source
remains present. In contrast, the deeper processing of the minority message

produces a private and enduring *conversion* that will persist in the absence of the minority although it may not surface in public; in fact, the target itself may be largely unaware of the conversion that has taken place.

In 1986, Nemeth elaborated and further developed some ideas that were already hidden in Moscovici's earlier writings but that had largely been ignored in subsequent research. In particular, Moscovici had at different occasions alluded to the fact that minorities may, at times, stimulate original responses that go well beyond a pure conversion towards the minority position (see for example Moscovici, 1976, p. 157; Moscovici and Lage, 1978). It is exactly this idea that became the core of Nemeth's reformulation in 1986, according to which people exposed to a minority engage in *divergent* thinking, focusing on a wide stimulus array well beyond the minority's message. In contrast, majorities induce *convergent* thought processes in which people focus their attention on the majority's message without considering further aspects of the issue under discussion. Consequently, people tend to follow the majority regardless of whether the majority is correct or incorrect. In contrast, they are unlikely to adopt the minority position, but tend to detect new, alternative solutions that had not been proposed by the minority and that, in the absence of minority influence, would have gone undetected. Since these novel alternatives tend to be correct, minorities—contrary to majorities—not only stimulate creativity but also improve performance (for an opposite example where convergent rather than divergent thoughts were found to improve performance, see Nemeth, Mosier, and Chiles, 1992).

Just as the original minority influence theory, Nemeth's reformulation states that minorities induce active thought processes. Contrary to the previous approach, however, Nemeth's version stresses the divergent nature of these processes. Rather than facilitating the acceptance of the minority position (conversion), such divergent thinking is expected to stimulate the development of new positions.

Both conversion theory and Nemeth's theory—which we will here refer to as "divergence theory"—have received considerable empirical support suggesting that both approaches make valid predictions under specific circumstances. To this point, however, it remains unclear what exactly these circumstances are. Considering the remarkable experimental evidence for both lines of research, it becomes, indeed, essential to understand which situational and personality constellations are likely to produce conversion and which are likely to produce divergence effects. This question, we believe, is challenging both empirically and theoretically. From a theoretical perspective, hypotheses need to be advanced about when minorities will produce movements toward their position (conversion) and when they will stimulate divergent thought leading to new, original solutions. At the same time, a test of such predictions will require the development of new methodological tools.

In particular, a comparison of the two approaches requires that they be tested within the same conceptual framework and within the same experimental paradigm—whereas to date the two research traditions have employed distinct paradigms that render a comparison very difficult. Using Doise's (1986; Mugny and Doise, 1979) distinction between four levels of inquiry, one may argue that conversion theory has been investigated on various levels. Initially, conversion was predominantly studied on an "intra-individual" and "inter-individual" level (e.g., blue-green paradigm). Subsequently, however, research on conversion has quickly shifted towards the third level of investigation at which the social position and status of the protagonists involved in the social interaction is taken into account (see, for example, research on the minority's social category membership, such as Mugny, 1982; Pérez and Mugny, 1987; Volpato, Maass, Mucchi-Faina, and Vitti, 1990). One may even find occasional examples representing the fourth, so-called "ideological" level of investigation (see, for example, Moscovici's reinterpretation of Asch's effect, Moscovici, 1976; or the "naturalization" processes activated by the social system in defense against minority influence, Mugny and Pérez, 1986).

This is quite in contrast to research on divergence that tends to be located at the first two levels of inquiry. Nemeth's theory has almost exclusively been tested in the areas of cognition and problem-solving and where attempts have been made to generalize the theory to applied settings these tend to be fields such as organizational behavior and management (e.g., Nemeth and Staw, 1989).

As a result, studies on divergence lack the social component that is typical of conversion research. Conversion theory has often been tested in socially relevant contexts and social movements such as the feminist, green, or gay movement, or even the national movement of Le Pen's *front national* have frequently been cited as examples of conversion phenomena and have become the object of empirical investigation in a considerable portion of minority influence research (see, among others, Clark and Maass, 1988a, 1988b; Crespi and Mucchi-Faina, 1988; Kelly, 1990; Maass and Clark, 1983, 1986; Mucchi-Faina, 1987; Mugny and Pérez, 1986; Orfali, 1990; Paicheler, 1976, 1977, 1979, 1989; Paicheler and Flath, 1988).

Closely related to this general emphasis on social change vs. individual influence processes is the differential preference for experimental tasks in the two research traditions. With the exception of studies using the "chromatic after-effect paradigm" (see chapter by Personnaz and Personnaz in this volume), researchers in the conversion tradition have shown a strong preference for attitudinal and opinion measures. The majority of studies in the 1980s have employed social issues such as environmental pollution (Mugny, 1982; Mugny and Pérez, 1986), abortion (Maass, Clark, and Haberkorn, 1982; Mugny and Pérez, 1986) and gay rights (Maass and Clark, 1983). In contrast, Nemeth's theory has almost exclusively been tested in the areas of cognition and problem solving employing experimental tasks such as the discovery of embedded figures (Nemeth and Wachtler, 1983), word composition (Nemeth and Kwan, 1987), discovery of rules underlying number strings (Legrenzi, Butera, Mugny, and Pérez, 1991) or the Stroop test (Nemeth, Mosier, and Chiles, 1992; a fuller description of the relevant literature can be found in Nemeth's chapter in this volume).

Yet, we believe that Nemeth's theory may be applicable well beyond problem-solving tasks and that this theory may make important contributions to our understanding of social influence processes in the attitude change area, as well. The application of Nemeth's theory to the attitude area, however, requires not only a theoretical reorientation, but also a new methodology. In fact, traditional research paradigms in the attitude change area seem inadequate for an experimental test of Nemeth's approach. Whereas the differential predictions of Nemeth's and Moscovici's approach regarding the *cognitive processes* may well be studied with the same methodological tools (e.g., thought listing procedures, see Petty and Cacioppo, 1986; Trost, Maass, and Kenrick, in press; see also Trost and Kenrick's chapter in this volume), the different *outcomes,* namely conversion vs. the development of novel solutions, require entirely different measures. Traditionally, subjects in minority influence research are provided with two response options, namely either to maintain their pre-experimental viewpoint or to convert toward the minority position. Such prevailing measures (including so-called ''indirect'' measures) are well-suited for the test of conversion effects, but are unable to tap divergence effects since they generally do not allow for the development of new alternatives. Thus, an application of Nemeth's theory to the attitude change area requires new dependent measures that provide an explicit option for developing or adopting new and independent positions that are neither proposed by the minority source nor do they reflect the subjects' initial viewpoint.

In the remaining part of this chapter, we will advance some tentative hypotheses as to when divergence and conversion effects will occur, outline a number of ways how to test the two approaches within the same paradigm, and present preliminary findings in support of our hypotheses. Since conversion represents a well-established phenomenon whereas divergence effects have been explored to a lesser degree in the attitude change area, our discussion will concentrate on the latter. In particular, we will argue that divergence effects are most likely to emerge (a) in settings that foster creativity (e.g., normative pressure to be original), (b) when personal relevance is high, and (c) when people have a high probability to engage in and enjoy effortful cognitive endeavors (need for cognition).

Originality Norm

The first situational variable that should facilitate divergent thought processes is the normative context. To our knowledge, the first demonstration of divergent responses to a minority goes back to 1978, when Moscovici and Lage exposed subjects to the classical blue-green paradigm but, in addition, introduced an explicit norm of originality. Not only did the normative context of originality facilitate the adoption of the minority position ("green"), but it also induced divergent responses such as "grey," "white," or "yellow" that differed from both the majority and the minority position.

Such originality norm does not need to be induced explicitly, however, but may simply be inherent in certain tasks. Certain settings and tasks (such as brain-storming sessions and creativity measures) foster divergent and creative thinking implicitly, whereas others require binary decisions that leave little space for new alternatives (e.g., judgments of guilt vs. innocence). It is interesting to note that Nemeth has generally used tasks that encourage divergent responses such the search for embedded figures (Nemeth and Wachtler, 1983) or word-association tasks (Nemeth and Kwan, 1985). A person asked to discover an embedded figure in a series of drawings (Nemeth and Wachtler, 1983) or to provide word associations to a given color (Nemeth and Kwan, 1985) is certainly more motivated to search the whole stimulus array and to be creative than a person asked to choose between different legal proposals or to decide whether pollution is to be attributed to industry or to private consumers.

Finally, the norm of originality may not even be part of the situational context (be it explicitly or implicitly), but may be generated by the minority itself. A minority advocating an original position may introduce a new rule, replacing correctness with originality. An experiment by Mucchi-Faina, Maass, and Volpato (1991) illustrates how an original minority, unlike a conventional minority, may stimulate divergence. Subjects in this experiment were asked to provide different suggestions on "how to promote the image of Perugia internationally." Subjects were simultaneously exposed to a majority and a minority source of influence (supposedly participants of a previous survey on this topic). The majority had allegedly proposed a conventional representation of Perugia, namely a photograph of a well-known historical monument (Palazzo dei Priori). The minority was either described as having made an alternative, but equally conventional proposal (another famous monument, the Arco Etrusco),

Table 7.1   Number of Idiosyncratic Items and Mean Originality as a Function of
             Experimental Condition

	Number of idiosyncratic proposals	Mean Originality
Control Group	7	2.08
Conventional Minority	22	2.46
Original Minority	34	2.69

Note: The higher the mean, the greater the originality.
Source: Mucchi-Faina, Maass, and Volpato (1991). Adapted by permission of Wiley and Sons.

or as having made a highly unusual and original proposal (the escalator underneath the Rocca Paolina, representing a modern element in a medieval city). An additional control group was exposed only to the majority source. Besides privately expressing their agreement with the majority and minority proposal, subjects were also asked to indicate additional proposals that came to their minds as to how to promote the international image of Perugia. It is this latter measure that is of interest here.

The result pattern is quite clear. The conventional minority stimulates a greater number of proposals, but it is the original minority that stimulates greater originality (see table 7.1). In fact, subjects exposed to an original minority opposing a conventional majority are considerably more likely to generate original, that is, statistically infrequent, alternatives (as indicated by the mean originality of the responses as well as by the number of indiosyncratic responses, that is, responses indicated by only one subject).

It is important to note that it is neither originality per se nor minority influence per se that stimulates divergent thought processes, but rather the unique combination of the two. In fact, a second experiment (Mucchi-Faina, Maass, and Volpato, 1991, exp. 2; described in more detail in Mucchi-Faina's chapter in this volume) clearly indicated that an equally original majority is unable to stimulate creativity in others just as majorities in Nemeth's studies are unable to induce divergent thinking. Taken together, the above results suggest that, in minority influence, divergence effects are particularly likely to emerge in settings in which originality is stressed.

Personal Relevance

Considering that divergent thought processes are particularly demanding because they involve a wide range of alternatives and because they have to be actively generated by the recipient, we suspect that these thought processes require a particularly high level of motivation. Indirect evidence for this hypothesis comes from two studies which will briefly be described here (Trost, Maass, and Kenrick, 1992; Volpato, Maass, Mucchi-Faina, and Vitti, 1990).

The first study, which is described in more detail in Trost and Kenrick's chapter in this volume, investigated the role of personal relevance in minority influence. Although this study did not explicitly intend to compare Moscovici's and Nemeth's approach, it did include a cognitive activity measure (thought listing) that makes it possible to distinguish between thoughts that are directly related to the minority message and those that are generated by the recipient and that have no reference to the message. Subjects in this study were either confronted with a minority or a majority arguing for an unpopular proposal introducing a comprehensive examination in college. For half of the undergraduate subjects, the issue was highly relevant because the comprehensive examination was supposed to be implemented immediately; in case of approval, subjects themselves would be forced to take the exam. For the remaining subjects, the issue had less personal relevance since comprehensive examination was supposed to be introduced after they had already left school. Before indicating their favorability toward the proposal, subjects were asked to record the thoughts that had come into their minds while reading the proposal. These thoughts were then divided into those that simply restated or elaborated the message content message-related thoughts) and those that were relevant to the issue under discussion but were not traceable to the minority's or majority's arguments (recipient-generated thoughts). The results (see table 7.2) show that recipient-generated thoughts were relatively rare under majority influence independent of the level of personal relevance. In contrast, the minority proposal stimulated considerably greater recipient-generated thoughts when relevance was high than when it was low. With increasing personal relevance of the issue under discussion, people exposed to a minority tended to generate more of their own thoughts and fewer message-related thoughts. This suggests that personally relevant tasks tend to elicit the divergent thought processes suggested by Nemeth, whereas less involving issues typically used in minority influence research are likely to stimulate message-relevant thinking.

Table 7.2   Mean Difference Between Recipient-Generated and Message-Related Thoughts

	Minority	**Majority**
Low Relevance	1.52	2.53
High Relevance	3.55	1.58

Note: Higher scores indicate a relatively greater number of recipient-generated thoughts.
Source: Trost, Maass, and Kenrick, 1992.

Quite different, but largely converging evidence for our hypothesis comes from a study on minority influence and social categorization (Volpato, Maass, Mucchi-Faina, and Vitti, 1990). In this study, we compared the influence of in-group minorities (belonging to the subject's own social category) and what we have termed "dissident out-group minorities" (defined as a minority subgroup within a larger out-group category). As suggested also by other authors (Mugny and Pérez, 1986; Pérez and Mugny, 1987), the conflict between minority and majority within one's own group should be particularly relevant to the subject, whereas a similar disagreement within the out-group is personally less involving. In line with our previous argument, we therefore predicted that divergence effects will occur when people are exposed to influence from an in-group minority, whereas conversion effects are more likely to emerge when they are confronted with a dissident out-group minority (see also Martin, 1988a, 1988b, 1988c, for experimental evidence showing that such out-group minorities elicit greater private acceptance).[1]

We therefore exposed high-school students from Milan, Italy, to a minority advocating a revision of the final high-school examination intended to further increase the standards of the examination. The minority was either described as coming from the subject's own city (Milan) or from Rome. Note that these two cities have traditionally been in antagonism, with Milan representing industrial power, and Rome political power. Subjects were informed that the Ministry of Education had asked two student committees, one from Milan and one from Rome, to evaluate the proposed revision of the examination. They either received the alleged minority report from the Milan committee (in-group) or from the Rome committee (out-group). In either case, subjects believed that the committee had presented two separate reports, a majority and a minority report, and that they would receive only the minority report which was in favor of the new examination. After having read the minority report, subjects were asked to privately indicate their own opinion by selecting one of three response options, namely: agreement with the minority (conversion measure); agreement with the current regulation; or the proposal of a new alternative (divergence measure). Thus, contrary to traditional research in the area, subjects had the option to develop their own, novel proposals.

The results strongly support our predictions (see table 7.3). People tend to adopt the position advocated by a dissident out-group minority, but rather than going along with an in-group minority, they generate new alternative solutions. Apparently, dissident out-group minorities induce a conversion effect, whereas in-group minorities stimulate the divergent thought processes outlined by Nemeth. Assuming that the disagreement from an in-group minority is personally more relevant than a disagreement within the

Table 7.3   Percentages of Agreement with Minority Proposal, Traditional Regulation, and New Alternative Proposals as a Function of Experimental Condition

	In-group	Out-group	Control
Minority Proposal	53	76*	52
Traditional Proposal	10	7	31
Alternative Proposal	37*	17	17

Note: Cell frequencies with asterisk deviate significantly from their respective expected frequency (p. < .05).
Source: Volpato, Maass, Mucchi-Faina, and Vitti (1990). Adapted by permission of Wiley and Sons.

out-group, these results complement the previous ones. Interestingly, this pattern changes dramatically when people are confronted with a majority source (see Volpato et al., 1990, exp. 2). In this case, people adopt the position of the in-group majority while rejecting that of the out-group majority. In line with Nemeth's theory, neither in-group nor out-group majorities stimulate the development of new alternatives.

Taken together, the studies by Trost et al. (1992) and by Volpato et al. (1990) suggest that, as personal involvement increases, people become more likely to generate their own independent arguments and to develop new, alternative solutions whereas convergence is likely to occur under conditions of low involvement.[2]

Need for Cognition

Our third hypothesis regarding the differential domains of applications of Moscovici's and Nemeth's approach concerns individual differences, in particular, the need for cognition. Cacioppo, Petty, Kao, and Rodriguez (1987) have proposed that people differ with regard to their personal inclination to engage in and to enjoy effortful cognitive elaboration. Some have a high need for cognition, whereas for others thinking represents a joyless, though necessary activity. We suspect that people with a high need for cognition will be more likely to show the more demanding divergent thought processes suggested by Nemeth. On intuitive grounds, one may hypothesize that cognitively lazy individuals will limit their cognitive activity to the necessary by only scrutinizing the message of the influence source while carefully avoiding the more demanding consideration of the whole stimulus array from multiple perspectives.

Although we have only limited evidence for this hypothesis, it may be worthwhile to briefly describe the only experiment that has dealt with this issue (Vitti, 1989). After developing an Italian version of the Need for Cognition scale (Cacioppo, Petty, and Kao, 1984), this measure was added to one of our experiments in which subjects were exposed either to a majority or a minority source of influence advocating a rather unpopular revision of the final high school examination. Subjects had the choice between either adopting one of the existing legal proposals (the current regulation or the minority/majority proposal) or to develop their own alternative proposal. A correlation between the subjects' choice and their need for cognition indicated that subjects with a greater need for cognition were somewhat more likely to develop new, alternative proposals (r = .23). Although this correlation is not high, it clearly suggests that divergent thinking may, at least in part, depend on the individual's personal inclination to enjoy effortful thinking. More generally, these first results suggest that it may be worthwhile to consider personality variables in addition to situational ones. To our knowledge, individual difference variables have largely been ignored in minority influence research while such variables have been found to play an important role in majority influence and conformity (see, for example, Montgomery, Hinkle, and Enzie's, 1976, finding that individuals with an authoritarian personality are more susceptible to conformity pressure).

Taken together, our results suggest that Nemeth's theory may have a number of interesting applications beyond the problem-solving area and that time has come to give greater consideration to her theory in the attitude change area. We believe that, with appropriate methodological tools, we will be able to discover further hidden effects of active minorities that are not easily detectable with traditional prevailing measures.

More importantly, our findings suggest that Moscovici's and Nemeth's theory may have specific domains of applicability. Apparently, there are important situational and personality variables that determine the prevalence of one approach over the other. Although our research program is still at the beginning, we believe that our first results are encouraging enough to conclude that a systematic comparison between conversion and divergence is a worthwhile endeavor.

Notes

1. It is important to note that our argument is limited to "dissident out-group minorities" who generally enjoy a certain sympathy exactly because they are in opposition to the disliked out-group at large. We would not predict any conversion toward so-called "representative out-group minorities" that are representative of the out-group as a whole (e.g., gays—for a further discussion of the distinction between dissident vs. representative out-group minorities, see Volpato et al., 1990).

2. Although we have not yet addressed this issue experimentally, we suspect that the relation between personal relevance and divergent thought processes is a curvilinear one in which divergence increases up to a certain, optimal degree of involvement but declines beyond this point. Extremely high ego involvement may

well narrow the focus of attention to a small portion of the relevant stimuli (see also Easterbrook's (1959) cue utilization hypothesis).

References

Cacioppo, J., Petty, R., and Kao, C.S. (1984). The efficient assessment of need for cognition. *Journal of Personality Assessment*,48 (3),306–307.

Cacioppo, J., Petty, R., Kao, C. S., and Rodriguez, R. (1987). Central and peripheral routes to persuasion: An individual difference perspective. *Journal of Personality and Social Psychology*,51 (5),1031–1034.

Clark, R. D., III, and Maass, A, (1988a). Social categorization in minority influence: The case of homosexuality. *European Journal of Social Psychology*, 18,347–364.

Clark, R. D., III, and Maass, A. (1988b). The role of social categorization and perceived source credibility in minority influence. *European Journal of Social Psychology*,18,381–394.

Crespi, F., and Mucchi-Faina, A. (1988). *La strategia delle minoranze attive. Una ricerca empirica sul movimento delle donne*. Naples: Liguori.

Doise, W. (1986). *Levels of Explanation in Social Psychology*. Cambridge: The University Press.

Easterbrook, J. A. (1959). The effect of emotion on cue utilization and other organization of behavior. *Psychological Review*,66,183–201.

Kelly C. (1990). Social identity and levels of influence: When a political minority fails. *British Journal of Social Psychology*,29,289–301.

Legrenzi, P., Butera, F., Mugny, G., and Pérez, J. (1991). Majority and minority influence in inductive reasoning: A preliminary study. *European Journal of Social Psychology*,21 (4),359–363.

Maass, A., and Clark, R. D., III. (1983). Internalization vs. compliance: Differential processes underlying minority influence and conformity. *European Journal of Social Psychology*,13,197–215.

Maass, A., and Clark, R. C., III. (1986). Conversion theory and simultaneous majority/minority influence: Can reactance offer an alternative explanation? *European Journal of Social Psychology*,16,305–309.

Maass, A., Clark, R. D., III, and Haberkorn, G. (1982). The effects of differential ascribed category membership and norms on minority influence. *European Journal of Social Psychology*,12,89–104.

Martin, R. (1988a). Ingroup and outgroup minorities: Differential impact upon public and private response. *European Journal of Social Psychology*,18,39–52.

Martin, R. (1988b). Minority influence and social categorization: A replication. *European Journal of Social Psychology*,18,369–373.

Martin, R. (1988c). Minority influence and "trivial" social categorization. *European Journal of Social Psychology*,18,465–470.

Montgomery, R. L., Hinkle, S. W., and Enzie, R. F. (1976). Arbitrary norms and social change in high and low authoritarian societies. *Journal of Personality and Social Psychology*,33 (6),698–708.

Moscovici, S. (1976). *Social Influence and Social Change*. London: Academic Press.

Moscovici, S. (1980). Toward a theory of conversion behavior. In L. Berkowitz (Ed.), *Advances in Experimental Social Psychology*, vol. 13, pp. 209–239. New York: Academic Press.

Moscovici, S., and Lage, E. (1978). Studies in social influence IV: Minority influence in a context of original judgments. *European Journal of Social Psychology*,8,349–365.

Mucchi-Faina, A. (1987). Mouvement social et conversion. In Moscovici, S. and Mugny, G. (Eds.), *Psychologie de la Conversion*. Cousset: Del Val.

Mucchi-Faina, A., Maass, A., and Volpato C. (1991). Social influence: The Role of Originality. *European Journal of Social Psychology*,21,3,183–197.

Mugny, G. (1982). *The Power of Minorities*. London: Academic Press.

Mugny, G., and Doise, W. (1979). Niveaux d'analyse dans l'étude expérimentale des processus d'influence sociale. *Information sur les Sciences Sociales*,18(6),819–876.

Mugny, G., and Pérez, J. A. (1986). *Le Déni et la Raison. Psychologie de l'impact Social des Minoritiés*. Cousset: Del Val.

Nemeth, C. J. (1986). Differential contributions of majority and minority influence. *Psychological Review*,93,23–32.

Nemeth, C. J., and Kwan, J. (1985). Originality of word associations as a function of majority vs. minority influence. *Social Psychology Quarterly*,48,277–282.

Nemeth, C. J., and Kwan, J. (1987). Minority influence, divergent thinking, and detection of correct solutions. *Journal of Abnormal and Social Psychology*,17, 788–799.

Nemeth, C. J., Mosier K., and Chiles, C. (1992). When convergent thought improves performance: Majority versus minority influence. *Personality and Social Psychology Bulletin*,18,139–144.

Nemeth, C. J., and Staw, B. M. (1989). The tradeoffs of social control and innovation within groups and organizations. In L. Berkowitz (Ed.), *Advances in Experimental Social Psychology*, vol. 22. New York: Academic Press.

Nemeth, C. J., and Wachtler, J. (1983). Creative problem solving as a result of majority vs. minority influence. *European Journal of Social Psychology*,13,45–55.

Orfali, B. (1990). *L'Adhésion au Front National: De la Minorité Active au Mouvement Social*. Paris: Kimé.

Paicheler, G. (1976). Norms and attitude change I: Polarization and styles of behavior. *European Journal of Social Psychology*,6,405–426.

Paicheler, G. (1977). Norms and attitude change II: The phenomenon of bipolarization. *European Journal of Social Psychology*,7,5–14.

Paicheler, G. (1979). Polarization of attitudes in homogenous and heterogeneous groups. *European Journal of Social Psychology*,9,85–96.

Paicheler, G. (1989). *The Psychology of Social Influence*. Cambridge: Cambridge University Press.

Paicheler, G., and Flath, E. (1988). Changement d'attitude, influence minoritaire et courants sociaux. *Revue Internationale de Psychologie Sociale*,1,27–40.

Pérez, J. A., and Mugny, G. (1987). Paradoxical effects of categorization in minority influence: When being an outgroup is an advantage. *European Journal of Social Psychology*,17,157–159.

Petty, R. E., and Cacioppo, J. T. (1986). Communication and persuasion: Central and peripheral routes to attitude change. New York: Springer-Verlag.

Trost, M. R., Maass, A., and Kenrick, D. T. (1992). Minority influence paradigm: Personal relevance biases cognitive processes and reverses private acceptance. *Journal of Experimental Social Psychology,* 28,234–254.

Vitti, E. (1989) Influenza minoritaria é categorizzazione sociale. Master's thesis. University of Padova.

Volpato, C., Maass, A., Mucchi-Faina, A., and Vitti, E. (1990). Minority influence and social categorization. *European Journal of Social Psychology*,20,119–132.

CHAPTER EIGHT

EGO INVOLVEMENT IN THE MINORITY INFLUENCE PARADIGM: THE DOUBLE-EDGED SWORD OF MINORITY ADVOCACY

Melanie R. Trost and Douglas T. Kenrick

Nora Bredes was a fairly typical resident of Long Island, New York. She liked to sit at home "quietly reading or writing." Then, in 1979, the Long Island Lighting Company (LILCO) began building the Shoreham nuclear power plant down the road. Ms. Bredes organized her neighbors into a ratepayers' rights group and began to challenge the licensing of the plant. By June 1989, these few, tireless voices had convinced the majority of LILCO's shareholders to permanently close the plant. The Shoreham nuclear power station never generated one megawatt of electricity. The neighborhood organization effectively shut down the reactor (Tasini, 1990).

This is a shining example of successful minority group influence. It illustrates one of the most potentially valuable generalizations from this area of research: the hope that a small, minority voice can produce significant social change. In an early statement on the topic, Moscovici proposed that:

> The importance of minorities lies precisely in their being factors, and often originators, of social change in societies where social change is taking place. . . . It is the active individuals and groups who, being profuse in ideas and initiatives, express or create new trends. (Moscovici, 1976, p. 221)

149

The body of experimental evidence that has developed over the past twenty years has fairly convincingly confirmed that minorities, as well as majorities, can influence the decisions and beliefs of others (for reviews, see Levine and Russo, 1987; Maass and Clark, 1984; Maass, West, and Cialdini, 1987; Moscovici, 1980; Nemeth, 1986). Moreover, a minority appears to be primarily capable of eliciting private attitude change, whereas a majority is more adept at gaining public compliance than private acceptance (Maass and Clark, 1983; Moscovici and Lage, 1976; Moscovici and Personnaz, 1980). But, can laboratory findings on minority influence really generalize to an *important* social movement? Will people change their private attitudes in reference to a minority if it advocates a personally costly or unpleasant position? The purpose of this chapter is to examine a factor that seems to limit when a minority can successfully influence a majority's opinions: the target's personal involvement in the issue.[1]

Investigators in this area have relied primarily on laboratory experiments, using persuasion tasks that range from perceptual tasks (e.g., describing a slide color or finding an embedded figure) to attitudinal issues of low to moderate personal importance (e.g., advocating gay rights to heterosexual students). In general, the research has tended to overlook the likelihood that, in the real world, issues vary in importance to an individual. Although reviewers have acknowledged the idea that the personal relevance of an issue might mediate the effectiveness of the minority advocacy (Chaiken and Stangor, 1987; Maass, West, and Cialdini, 1987; Mugny, 1982), researchers have not systematically manipulated the personal relevance of the minority's message. There is, however, an even longer tradition of research in the persuasion area that suggests the relatively robust minority influence effect might wash out when the target is ego-invested.

Personal Relevance Limits Persuasion

Early persuasion researchers from the Yale school found increasing resistance to a counterattitudinal advocacy with increasing personal involvement (Sherif and Hovland, 1961). More contemporary researchers, who have adopted a *cognitive response approach* (Greenwald, 1968) to the study of persuasive message processing, have made several points that are particularly important for incorporating personal relevance considerations into theories of minority influence. First, messages can be processed in either an automatic, heuristic fashion, or in a more considered, systematic fashion, depending upon one's ability and motivation to think about them (Chaiken, 1980; Petty and Cacioppo, 1981). Second, high issue involvement is one factor that triggers more extensive argument scrutiny, as indicated by the typically high correspondence between thoughts and attitudes, and the ability to discriminate between compelling and weak arguments (Petty and Cacioppo, 1986b). Third, high personal relevance can induce *biased* thinking that either supports one's initial attitudes or protects one's self against a counterattitudinal message. For instance, a personally relevant, counterattitudinal appeal can generate more negative thoughts, resulting in decreased persuasion (Burnkrant and Howard, 1984; Howard-Pitney, Borgida, and Omoto, 1986). Finally, when the persuasive message does trigger careful processing, information about the message source can augment the effects of argument strength on attitudes. For instance, an advocacy from someone who obviously benefits by persuading the target is likely to be attributed to selfish motivations, leading to counterarguments and resistance to social influence (Petty and Cacioppo, 1986a; 1986b; 1990).

Personal involvement in an issue, then, not only increases the motivation to engage in careful and extensive cognitive processing but also can affect the direction of the thoughts that are expressed. In particular, people express more unfavorable and fewer favorable thoughts about a message of great personal relevance whenever (a) the personal consequences of the message are truly negative, and (b) the message is processed at one's own pace, as with a written message versus an audiotape (Burnkrant and Howard, 1984). The more aversive the potential consequences of the advocacy, the greater the incentive to counterargue and the lower the likelihood of persuasion. For example, Minnesota students opposed to an increase in the state's drinking age, and whose social behaviors would be limited by the change, were more likely to exhibit biased message processing after viewing a debate on the issue. These highly involved students were more likely to remember opposing arguments and list negative thoughts than those whose behavior would not be limited by the higher drinking age (Howard-Pitney et al., 1986). Therefore, important, negative consequences can lead to biased or selective argument processing, as opposed to objective consideration of a persuasive message, especially when the source is suspect.

Implications of Relevance for the Processing of Minority Advocacies

Minority influence researchers have also taken a cognitive processing approach to explaining the minority influence effect, proposing that minorities and majorities exercise influence by stimulating different types of thinking. According to Moscovici (1980), a minority gains a persuasive advantage over a majority because it elicits a *validation process*: attention is focused on the minority's position, stimulating an active evaluation of the message arguments and, ultimately, internal acceptance if the position is reasonable. A majority, on the other hand, elicits a *comparison process*:

attention is focused on comparing the discrepancies between one's own opinion and the majority opinion. This engages shallow processing of the message and uncritical acceptance of the majority opinion, as the target has attended more to the self-presentational conflict than the message arguments. An alternative representation of how people process minority positions in decision-making tasks differentiates the types of thinking by focusing more on the process of argument elaboration than on the outcome. Nemeth (1986) has shown that minority advocacies stimulate more *divergent* thinking, leading to the discovery of novel solutions that are qualitatively better than those stimulated by a majority source. The solutions may or may not coincide with the minority's position, and the target's acceptance of the minority's opinion is less important than the processes that led to the decision. Majorities, on the other hand, elicit *convergent* thinking that narrows the target's focus to the majority message, resulting in unreflective and common responses to the task. Both Moscovici and Nemeth advocate dual-process models of minority influence, referring to the idea that a minority stimulates different types of thoughts than a majority. Nemeth, however, focuses on how targets think about the issue, while Moscovici emphasizes their ultimate judgments.

We decided to investigate the consequences of incorporating personal relevance into the minority influence paradigm, and present two studies designed to meet those goals. In the first study, we tested several predictions from a combined model of the persuasion processing findings and the minority influence models (Trost, Maass, and Kenrick, 1992). First, we expected personal relevance to moderate the minority influence effect. Given that previous minority influence studies have used issues that are not highly important to subjects, a low involvement, minority advocacy should replicate the classic effect: acceptance of the minority position. When a minority advocated a highly relevant issue, however, we expected subjects' thoughts to be negatively biased, similar to the responses elicited by deviates in earlier research (Festinger, 1950; Schachter, 1951), leading to resistance to the minority advocacy (Burnkrant and Howard, 1984; Petty and Cacioppo, 1986a). Alternatively, according to Moscovici's (1980) conversion model of social influence, a majority advocacy was expected to stimulate minimal thought processing and show little influence under either high or low relevance.

Second, subjects' thoughts about the issue were expected to support their attitudes (Greenwald, 1968). Although a minority's stance elicits primarily favorable thoughts under conditions of low to moderate personal relevance (Maass and Clark, 1983), we proposed that introducing high personal relevance would cause the minority influence pattern to be reversed. Specifically, minority advocacy of a position that has high personal relevance should elicit predominantly negative thoughts (following Burnkrant and Howard, 1984). In contrast, people exposed to a majority advocacy should be largely unaffected by the level of personal relevance if, as suggested by conversion theory (Moscovici, 1980), a majority's message is processed in a shallow, superficial manner.

In summary, we expected the manipulation of issue relevance not only to limit minority influence, but also to provide important evidence concerning the issue of distinctive processing for minority versus majority messages. We investigated these predictions over a series of two studies. As expected, in the first study we found that the classic difference between minority and majority sources reversed under conditions of high personal relevance because the minority triggered effortful, and biased, cognitive processing.

An Examination of Personal Involvement

The first study used a common manipulation of personal relevance from the persuasion literature. The issue, introduced in Cialdini, Levy, Herman, Kozlowski, and Petty (1976), recommended that all undergraduate seniors should pass a comprehensive examination to be eligible for graduation. Issue relevance was manipulated by recommending that the mandatory exams be instituted either within one year (affecting the graduation requirements of all subjects, and thereby inducing *high personal relevance*), or after nine years *(low personal relevance)*. Participants were told that a student discussion group had generated both minority and majority reports on the issue of instituting mandatory examinations. Half of the time, subjects were told that a *majority* of the group (nine of eleven members) had written a favorable report about the exams; the remaining half of the subjects were told a *minority* of the group members (two of eleven members) had written a favorable report. They were also told that, to save time, half of them would read the majority report (either favorable or unfavorable) and half would read the minority report (either unfavorable or favorable). In reality, all 104 subjects read the same report favoring comprehensive exams. It was simply attributed to either a minority or a majority.

The report was a mixed message, including four strong arguments (e.g., comprehensive exams would increase teaching effectiveness, enhance the school's reputation, and increase average starting salaries by $4,000 after graduation) and one weak argument (the exams increase student anxiety by 39%) advocating mandatory comprehensive exams for seniors (from Petty and Cacioppo, 1986a). The mixed message was used so that subjects could generate both positive and negative comments about the proposal (Petty, Harkins, and Williams, 1980), allowing their opinions to move in either direction. Also, a mixed message was expected to be more realistic, as argument quality is rarely either purely strong or weak. Subjects in a no-persuasion control group read a short description of the proposal that did not include the persuasive arguments, source, or relevance information. Thus, all subjects read the same short description of the exams, but only the experimental groups read the supporting arguments.

Once they had read the proposal, students first rated their favorability toward the proposal and then listed their thoughts about the idea using a technique that measures the content and valence of the recipients' thoughts (Cialdini et al., 1976; Howard-Pitney, Borgida, and Omoto, 1986; Maass and Clark, 1983; Petty and Cacioppo, 1986a). All ratings were made in a private response setting.[2]

As shown in figure 8.1, we replicated the classic finding for the minority source. Students in the low relevance conditions were more favorable toward the mandatory comprehensive exams when the recommendation was made by a minority than a majority. Under high personal relevance conditions, however, the effect was reversed. The minority's advocacy resulted in less favorable ratings of the mandatory comprehensive exams by those students who thought that the exams started during the next year than by those students believing that the minority proposal was to start in nine years. Control subjects, on average, rated the idea significantly lower than the minority/low relevance condition, and marginally lower than the two majority conditions ($M = 4.96$). When the minority's arguments were highly involving, however, they produced no more influence than if the subjects had heard no favorable arguments at all.

Although the total number of thoughts was unaffected by the source or the level of relevance, the valence of those thoughts varied for the minority source condition but not for the majority source condition. Regardless of the level of personal relevance, the majority advocacy resulted in a similar

Figure 8.1: Favorability ratings for Study 1, as a function of personal relevance and minority/majority advocacy.

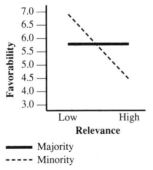

number of positive and negative thoughts about the majority report. The minority advocacy, however, prompted markedly different proportions of positive and negative thoughts under the high and low relevance manipulations. When the exams were not to start for nine years, subjects exposed to the minority report recorded relatively more positive than negative thoughts concerning the proposal (replicating the results of Maass and Clark, 1983), indicating that their more favorable attitudes were based on more favorable thoughts about the exams. When the examination requirement would apply to themselves, however, the recipients' response pattern flipped and they recorded significantly more negative than positive thoughts, corresponding to their unfavorable attitudes.

The results of this first study clearly show that the minority influence phenomenon is affected by ego-involvement, but they also raise several new questions. The minority advocacy results are relatively straightforward. The minority obviously stimulated negatively biased information processing under conditions of high personal relevance, and appeared to elicit objective, controlled processing of the minority message under low relevance. This is in contrast to contemporary persuasion models that would not predict a minority advantage under conditions of low relevance, when automatic information processing should favor the more numerous, and therefore heuristically accurate, majority opinion (Nemeth, 1986; Petty and Cacioppo, 1986b). Explaining subjects' responses to the majority advocacy is more difficult. The contemporary persuasion models would predict that subjects should be more favorable to the majority opinion under low relevance, and they should be more responsive to argument quality under high relevance, regardless of the source. As there was no significant difference between the high and low relevance responses to the majority report, it is difficult to determine the type of processing elicited by the majority, if any. Were subjects truly not processing the majority message even when it was a very costly proposition for them, as would be predicted by the conversion model of social influence (Moscovici, 1980)? Or, did they think about the highly involving majority information to the same extent as the minority information, but the majority label simply elicited more conformity to the idea? Or were the subjects simply showing a moderate level of agreement to a mixed message, indicating that they were processing the message objectively under both high and low relevance conditions? We conducted a second study to examine these issues more closely.

An Examination of Personal Involvement and Argument Quality

As mentioned earlier, we used a mixed message in the first study to allow greater variability in the responses. Unfortunately, this created some ambiguity in interpreting responses, especially in the majority conditions. The follow-up study manipulated a third variable, *strength of the message arguments,* to better distinguish careful message processing from heuristic processing in the majority conditions, and objective processing from biased processing in the minority conditions (Petty and Cacioppo, 1986b).

In the second study (Trost and Ybarra, 1994), subjects were asked to read one of two messages. One message included only four strong arguments favoring the exams (similar to those used in the first study). The second message included only four weak arguments (e.g., the university would be following the tradition of Plato, someone's brother took them and now feels that he has a better job, and the exams increase anxiety). According to contemporary persuasion models, a low involvement issue should produce little thought about the message. Therefore, subjects would not be expected to discriminate between the strong and weak messages, and their favorability ratings should be based more directly upon the credibility of the source (Petty and Cacioppo, 1986b).

We just showed, however, that the minority apparently elicited controlled information processing under low relevance conditions. Therefore, subjects exposed to a minority source should be more persuaded by four strong arguments than those who read four weak, specious arguments favoring the exams. The results of the previous study also indicated that highly involved subjects exposed to a minority report were biased against that minority, even when the minority presented a reasonable position. So, the minority might be expected to trigger negative attitudes when the topic is highly involving, regardless of whether their arguments are strong or weak. A slight advantage might accrue to the stronger arguments, but overall, both the strong and weak minority advocacies ought to be rejected when they are of high personal relevance.

The questions posed by the first study indicate that several patterns of responses are possible in the majority conditions. In the first study, subjects gave the exams a moderately favorable rating under both low and high relevance. But, given that the mixed message was designed to be moderately favorable, it is unclear if the ratings in the majority condition were due to the fact that people were not really thinking about the arguments or that they were thinking about them objectively and rating them accordingly. In the persuasion literature, being highly involved in an issue can cause people to think more about the message and to elaborate on it more carefully, resulting in more favorable opinions of strong arguments than of weak arguments. So, the strong versus weak arguments variable was added to better explain thought processing in the majority conditions. If the subjects were processing the majority's message, they should discriminate between the strong and weak messages, but only when the issue is highly involving. If, on the other hand, they were not thinking about the message, the subjects should not differentiate between the strong and weak arguments under conditions of either high or low relevance.

Some of the second study's results confirmed the predictions made from the minority influence model and some confirmed the predictions made from the persuasion models of information processing (see figure 8.2). As conversion theory would predict, under low relevance, the minority advocacy obviously elicited controlled, but objective information processing. The subjects rated the strong arguments more favorably than the weak arguments. The corresponding comparison in the majority condition indicated that subjects were more likely engaged in heuristic processing, as the strong and weak proposals were rated as being equally favorable. As implied by the results of the first study, when the aversive minority advocacy would affect the respondents, it was uniformly resisted. Even though there was a slight advantage to the stronger arguments under high relevance, the difference between the two types of argument quality was not reliable, and the minority apparently engaged biased processing aimed at discrediting the minority's opinion. On the other hand, subjects' responses to the majority advocacy appear to fit better with the contemporary persuasion models than the minority conversion model. The subjects did not discriminate between strong and weak arguments under low relevance; they were equally acceptable. When the students would have to take the comprehensive exams to graduate, however, they did process the majority's arguments, but did so relatively objectively, rating the strong arguments more favorably than the weak arguments.

In general, the minority appears to trigger controlled, objective information processing when its position is not threatening, and controlled, negatively biased information processing when its position is personally

Figure 8.2: Favorability ratings for Study 2, as a function of personal relevance, minority/majority advocacy, and argument strength.

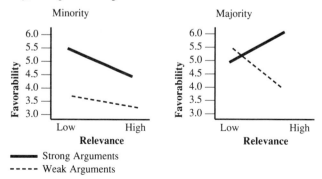

threatening to the respondents. The majority, on the other hand, appears to elicit relatively heuristic, favorable information processing when the issue is not threatening, and objective, controlled processing of a more personally threatening proposal.

Conclusions: Personal Relevance Limits a Minority's Influence

Taken together, these results suggest an important limitation on the existing minority influence paradigm: the impact of a minority on a recipient's private attitudes reverses when the issue is of high personal relevance. High relevance apparently transforms the phenomenon of minority conversion into something more aptly described as resistance to the minority opinion, and it does so by altering recipients' thoughts. Moscovici's (1980) formulation has portrayed influence targets as privately favoring the ''underdog'' minority. Our findings support this viewpoint in the low relevance context. However, the findings under high relevance indicate that the minority's underdog advantage is a tenuous one. When the advocacy presents a direct threat to the individual, differential reactions to minorities and majorities are more reminiscent of findings on hostility toward deviates (Schachter, 1951). Compared with a majority, a threat from a minority is more likely to elicit a counterattack. Personal relevance appears to be as central to the minority conversion phenomenon as it is to other areas of social influence, and should be incorporated into future reconceptualizations of the models of minority influence.

As always, these conclusions must be tempered with a note of caution. In both of these studies, as in most minority influence research, we exercised strict laboratory control to establish the general processes that underlie minority influence. The tradeoff for the heightened control was that we had to move away from the phenomenon's roots in basic, interactive group settings. The information processing and motivational moderators outlined in this paper could differ when people are confronted with real minorities advocating counterattitudinal positions. Future research investigating the differential cognitive processes engaged by a minority and majority should extend the external validity of this line of research by investigating the influence of a physically present group to see if similar processes govern the influence of both imagined and real groups.

So, let us return to the question posed at the outset of this chapter. Can advocates of minority positions hope to spark real social movements? Moscovici's (1980) theory and research were inspired by his desire to understand how innovation occurs in *society*. Integrating ego involvement into minority influence theory is only one step toward forming a more general understanding of how real activists, such as Nora Bredes, do or do not influence others. Margaret Mead once said, "Never doubt that a small group of thoughtful, committed citizens can change the world. Indeed, it's the only thing that ever has." Based upon our findings, when the issue is of relatively little personal importance, Mead's intuitively appealing words are supported by hard evidence. Yet, our data suggest that dissident groups will have difficulty spreading their ideas unless they can convince the masses that it is in their own self-interest to challenge the status quo. Nora Bredes and her ratepayers' coalition were able to convince LILCO shareholders that continued construction of the nuclear reactor would only further deplete their pocketbooks. When it comes to important global issues like peace and environmental protection, we may be advised to heed the double-edged sword of minority advocacy. Our very survival may depend upon better understanding the advantages and limitations governing those small groups of committed citizens in their efforts to produce social change.

Notes

1. Although recent reviews of the persuasion literature have proposed several different types of personal involvement (see Johnson and Eagly, 1989), we will use the terms "personal relevance," "issue involvement," and "ego involvement" interchangeably (see also Petty & Cacioppo, 1990).

2. The results were gathered under private measurement conditions. A public condition was not included because previous research has found that minority influence operates only on privately held attitudes (Chaiken and Stangor, 1987; Maass and Clark, 1984; Maass, West, and Cialdini, 1987).

References

Burnkrant, R. E., and Howard, D. J. (1984). Effects of the use of introductory rhetorical questions versus statements on information processing. *Journal of Personality and Social Psychology*,47,1218–1230.

Chaiken, S. (1980). Heuristic versus systematic information processing and the use of source versus message cues in persuasion. *Journal of Personality and Social Psychology*,39,752–766.

Chaiken, S., and Stangor, C. (1987). Attitudes and attitude change. *Annual Review of Psychology*,38,575–630.

Cialdini, R. B., Levy, A., Herman, C. P., Kozlowski, L. T. and Petty, R. E. (1976). Elastic shifts of opinion: Determinants of direction and durability. *Journal of Personality and Social Psychology*,34(4),663–672.

Cialdini, R. B., and Petty, R. E. (1981). Anticipatory opinion effects. In R. E. Petty, T. Ostrom, and T. Brock (Eds.), *Cognitive Responses in Persuasion*, pp. 217–235. Hillsdale, NJ: Erlbaum.

Cialdini, R. B., and Richardson, K. D. (1980). Two indirect tactics of image management: Basking and blasting. *Journal of Personality and Social Psychology*,39,406–415.

Eagly, A. H., and Chaiken, S. (1984). Cognitive theories of persuasion. *Advances in Experimental Social Psychology*,17,268–359.

Festinger, L. (1950). Informal social communication. *Psychological Review*,57,271–282.

Greenwald, A. G. (1968). Cognitive learning, cognitive response to persuasion, and attitude change. In A. G. Greenwald, T. C. Brock and T. M. Ostrom (Eds.), *Psychological Foundations of Attitudes*, pp. 147–170. New York: Academic Press.

Howard-Pitney, B., Borgida, E., and Omoto, A. M. (1986). Personal involvement: An examination of processing differences. *Social Cognition*,4,39–57.

Johnson, B. T., and Eagly, A. H. (1989). Effects of involvement on persuasion: A metaanalysis. *Psychological Bulletin*,106,290–314.

Levine, J. M., and Russo, E. M. (1987). Majority and minority influence. In C. Hendrick (Ed.), *Review of Personality and Social Psychology*, vol. 8, pp. 10–54. Newbury Park, CA: Sage.

Maass, A., and Clark, R. D., III. (1983). Internalization vs. compliance: Differential processes underlying minority influence and conformity. *European Journal of Social Psychology*,13,197–215.

Maass, A., and Clark, R. D., III. (1984). The hidden impact of minorities: Fifteen years of minority influence research. *Psychological Bulletin*,95,428–450.

Maass, A., West, S. G. and Cialdini, R. B. (1987). Minority influence and conversion. In C. Hendrick (Ed.), *Review of Personality and Social Psychology*, vol. 8, pp. 55–79. Newbury Park, CA: Sage.

Moscovici, S. (1976). *Social Influence and Social Change*. London: Academic Press.

Moscovici, S. (1980). Toward a theory of conversion behavior. In L. Berkowitz (Ed.). *Advances in Experimental Social Psychology*,13,209–239.

Moscovici, S., and Lage, E. (1976). Studies in social influence IV: Minority influence in a context of original judgments. *European Journal of Social Psychology*,8,349–365.

Moscovici, S., and Personnaz, B. (1980). Studies in social influence V: Minority influence and conversion behavior in a perceptual task. *Journal of Experimental Social Psychology*,16,270–282.

Mugny, G. (1982). *The Power of Minorities*. London: Academic Press.

Nemeth, C. (1986). The differential contributions of majority and minority influence. *Psychological Review*,93,23–32.

Petty, R. E., and Cacioppo, J. T. (1979). Issue involvement can increase or decrease persuasion by enhancing message-relevant cognitive responses. *Journal of Personality and Social Psychology*,37,1915–1926.

Petty, R. E., and Cacioppo, J. T. (1981). *Attitudes and Persuasion: Classic and Contemporary Approaches*. Dubuque, IA: W. C. Brown.

Petty, R. E., and Cacioppo, J. T. (1986a). *Communication and Persuasion: Central and Peripheral Routes to Attitude Change*. New York: Springer-Verlag.

Petty, R. E., and Cacioppo, J. T. (1986b). The elaboration likelihood model of persuasion. In L. Berkowitz (Ed.), *Advances in Experimental Social Psychology*, vol. 19, pp. 123–205. New York: Academic Press.

Petty, R. E., and Cacioppo, J. T. (1990). Involvement and persuasion: Tradition versus integration. *Psychological Bulletin*,107,367–374.

Petty, R. E., Harkins, S. G., and Williams, K. D., (1980). The effects of group diffusion of cognitive effort on attitudes: An information processing view. *Journal of Personality and Social Psychology*,38,81–92.

Schachter, S. (1951). Deviation, rejection, and communication. *Journal of Abnormal and Social Psychology*,46,190–207.

Sherif, M., and Hovland, C. I. (1961). *Social Judgment: Assimilation and Contrast Effects in Communication and Attitude Change*. New Haven, CT: Yale University Press.

Sorrentino, R. M., and Higgins, E. T. (1986). Motivation and cognition: Warming up to synergism. In R. M. Sorrentino and E. T. Higgins (Eds.), *The Handbook of Motivation and Cognition: Foundations of Social Behavior*, pp. 3–19. New York: Guilford Press.

Tasini, J. (1990). Shutting down Shoreham's nuke. *Mother Jones*,15,30–31.

Trost, M. T., Maass, A., and Kenrick, D. T. (1992). Minority influence: Personal relevance biases cognitive processes and reverses private acceptance. *Journal of Experimental Social Psychology, 28,234–254*.

Trost, M. T., and Ybarra, O. (1994). Further evidence for distinctive processing of minority and majority arguments. Arizona State University, Tempe.

PART THREE

Methodological
Issues

CHAPTER NINE

PERCEPTION AND CONVERSION

Marie Personnaz and Bernard Personnaz

At what level does a source of influence exert an impact and how can it be meaningfully assessed? For years, research on social influence has been satisfied with recording the manifest responses provided by subjects, either in oral or written form within the influence setting. Strange phenomena accompanying "compliance" were often revealed with these types of rating. It could be observed that the subjects publicly changed opinions, and yet the very nature of the change raised still another question. Would subjects return to their previous point of view once the source of influence had left? Interviews following experiments conducted by Asch (1951) revealed that a number of subjects yielded to the point of view of the majority, either from fear of being different or fear of being ridiculed or belittled. Yet, they did not honestly believe the majority. Pretending to conform may be a means of avoiding pressure or belittlement; but the individual does not fully give up his or her original point of view. Indeed, to a certain degree it somehow remains hidden along with the complete reference system on which it is based (Personnaz, 1979)—at least until a less threatening situation comes along. Such strategies demonstrate that the individual's explicit opinion is somewhat unreliable and that other means of analysis must be implemented if hidden processes are to be better understood.

In seeking to identify possible minority influence, early research on this subject (Moscovici, Lage, and Naffrechoux, 1969; Lage, 1976; Moscovici and Lage, 1976) showed that a minority source consistently asserting that a color slide everyone took to be blue was green had little influence in terms of the subjects' manifest responses (between 8 and 11 percent of green responses according to the experiments). Conversely, if subjects were asked to rate the color of a series of disks ranging from blue to green, a shift in thresholds of perceptual discrimination from blue to green was observed, especially for those subjects who had not been overtly influenced. They considered the blue disks to be significantly greener than did subjects who had not been confronted with a minority source.

However, the ratings which these assessments provided were also manifest judgments. Did they merely correspond to a generalization of green responses or did they imply a deeper modification of the perceptual code? In short, does the individual who says she or he sees "green" actually see green? How and when does conversion to another judgment take place? By conversion, we mean "the subtle process of cognitive or perceptual modification the person continues to apply to his or her usual response even after implicitly adhering to the views and responses of others, although he may not be aware of it, nor feel a particular urge to do so." (Paicheler and Moscovici, 1984, p. 153). Furthermore, how can such a conversion be assessed?

The Blue-Green Paradigm and the Study of Perceptual Conversion

The reader may wonder about the choice of perceptual stimuli in research on minority influence. In fact, their effectiveness can be attested to by a long tradition that goes back to the nineteenth century. Perceptual stimuli offer specific advantages. Compared to "ideological" ratings such as opinions which depend on the "Zeitgeist" or the outlook at an historical moment, perceptual stimuli allow for a persistence of rating which goes beyond the immediate present and power struggles.

Whether in the form of the autokinetic spot of light, as used by Sherif (1936) for his experiments on normalization, or the unequal vertical lines for the conformity study by Asch (1951), or that of blue-colored slides, as in the experimental paradigm in research on minority influence which shall be examined here, none of these methods has become "outdated," in comparison to prevailing opinions in vogue over the last decades. It is a commonly accepted fact that within the "ideological" realm, what was once a popular opinion is often no longer valid later on.

Many will say that the utilization of perceptual stimuli in this period of social change is a weakness. Yet, is it really a weakness? Should we not, on the contrary, deal with much more internalized norms rather than those related to ideology? Norms of color perception are usually handed down through culture at an early age and shared by individuals within that culture to the point that colors are often considered to be objective appellations and we often overlook that they are in fact social norms. Challenging norms of perception creates great confusion, as we were able to witness during our experiments. If norms of perception relating to colors, so deeply and so unanimously endorsed, can be changed, more recently acquired ideological norms should likewise be prone to change.

Furthermore, perceptual stimuli provide an extremely accurate means of assessment. If the equipment used is methodologically sound, rigorous and precise, assessments may be achieved and the degree of change in the subjects' ratings resulting from influence can be evaluated with great precision. As we will see later, perceptual stimuli also allow to measure changes the subjects themselves are unaware of.

Finally, another advantage of this paradigm is that it allows for the assessment of change at multiple levels. When crossed with the experimental and post-experimental phases, it makes it possible to observe the convergence and divergence in the levels of change at any given time. In other words, one is in a position to undertake a study of the dynamics of change (Personnaz and Guillon, 1985) and thereby to take into account the nature of intervening processes in the observed phenomena. The blue-green paradigm has been useful to identify and understand a number of psychosocial processes which would have been difficult to observe otherwise (Personnaz and Personnaz, 1987). An attempt was made to answer the question raised at the beginning of this chapter; i.e., "Does a person actually see what she or he claims to see?" When a subject changes his or her rating of an object, does she or he bring into play cognitive processes that are susceptible to modify his or her perception of the object or does she or he merely change his or her rating? What are the stages involved in the conversion to another system of values or point of view? When is there convergence between what the person says he or she sees and what the person genuinely sees?

The Consecutive Effect or How Do We Know What a Person Claims He or She Sees Is Genuinely What He or She Sees?

In order to answer this question, Moscovici and Personnaz (1980) developed a method which allowed them to measure indices of perceptual change independently of manifest responses. It was in this way that the measurement of the consecutive effect was brought into the blue-green paradigm. This method is based on a well-known visual phenomenon found in studies on perception, that is, when a colored light is projected onto a white surface and is subsequently switched off, there appears a fleeting image of its contrasting complementary color, referred to as the afterimage or aftereffect.

The procedure for each test in these experiments consists of projecting a blue-colored slide onto a white screen in a dark room. The subjects are asked first to rate the color, either verbally or in writing. Once the slide is switched off, they then have to identify in writing the color of its afterimage by way of a color scale ranging from yellow to violet through intermediate colors. If the subject sees the slide as blue, the corresponding afterimage would be in a color range of yellow to orange, which is the complementary color of blue. However, if the blue colored slide is perceived as green, the afterimage would obviously be within the red to red-violet range. Most people are unaware of the complementary link between the projected colored slide and its afterimage. Moreover, this procedure allows the measurement of the subject's possible perceptive changes of which the subject is unaware or does not want to reveal.

The research is usually presented as a study in color perception and its procedure is closely similar to the one in other studies by Personnaz (1976, 1979) on public and private influence. During the first phase, the subjects—usually a naive subject and a confederate—perform a test-series of written ratings on the color of a slide and its afterimage. This reveals the initial perception of the subjects prior to the influence attempt. The experimental conditions are subsequently introduced. The source of influence (i.e., the confederate) and its target represent either a majority or a minority. To this effect, fictitious results from earlier studies conducted on a larger population are presented. They vary depending on the condition in which they are to be placed. Instructions, for example, indicate that:

1. 18.2 percent of the people saw the slide as green, and 81.8 percent saw it as blue (condition in which the confederate is the minority and the naive subject is the majority), and
2. 18.2 percent of the people saw the slide as blue, and 81.8 percent saw it as green (condition in which the confederate is the majority and the subject is the minority).

Immediately after, the influence phase begins. At this point, the subjects are instructed to announce the color of the slide that is presented several times. In each of the tests, the confederate consistently asserts that the slide is green. In the third phase, the subject once more mentions, but in writing this time, the color of the slide and that of its afterimage. At the end of this phase, the confederate gives a plausible reason for leaving the room and does so. From that point on (phase four), the subject is left alone and asked to supply written answers. Phases one, three, and four therefore make it possible to obtain the private and latent ratings of the subjects, that is, before the influence attempt in phase one, immediately after, with the source of influence present in phase three, and after the source of influence has left in phase four. The only public phase in which the ratings deal exclusively with the color-slide is phase two.

Following phase four, the subject usually fills out a post-experimental questionnaire which not only covers the ratings of the stimuli, but also the way in which the subject perceived the situation including the source of influence and him- or herself in the situation.

Minority and Majority Influence: Two Influences of a Different Nature

The minority and the majority neither exert influence in the same manner nor at the same levels. The majority appears either as a reference because of its size or as representing a dominating norm. It seems to focus the subjects' cognitive activities on social positions (Guillon and Personnaz, 1983) by a comparison process (Moscovici, 1980). This focalization tends to blur the perception of the stimulus (Personnaz, 1976, 1986). Conformity does not necessarily imply a change in the perception of the object. The post–experimental interviews of Asch (1951) reveal that most of the subjects who conformed to the majority did so for "social" reasons. Either the subjects were afraid of being excluded or marginalized or they felt the opinion of the majority was closest to the truth. Whatever the case may be, it seems they still did not manage to see the stimulus as the majority did.

Personnaz (1979) obtained results showing that when social pressures are high during interaction it becomes quite easy to make subjects dependent on the norms of others. Yet, this dominating norm is dismissed when the source is absent. In certain cases, dependence may hinder influence. These studies indicate that if the subjects change their public response during interaction, they still see the stimulus as they did previously. By so doing, they retain a so-called "clandestine" reference system (Personnaz, 1976, 1981, 1988). The minority does not apparently have an impact comparable to the majority's. In fact, it would even appear to lack persuasive power altogether. In particular it cannot exert influence by way of power, prestige, or competence. Compared to the majority, whose attributes are generally positive, the minority arouses little attraction or desire to be identified with it. Its attributes appear negative and even create resistance. One neither wishes to be similar to the minority or to be associated with it for fear of being labelled as a deviant. However, if the minority defends a point of view opposite to that of the majority with determination, it may disturb, puzzle, and progressively bring the individual to have a closer look at the stimulus, thereby center him- or herself cognitively on it and eventually explore it from a different angle than that from which it is usually perceived. The stimulus may ultimately be seen in a totally different way because of the information provided by the minority. This focusing process, together with the progressive appraisal of an object from the standpoint of the source of influence, known as validation (Moscovici, 1980), often leads to conversion.

Moreover, access to the object becomes easier with the departure of the minority source because interpersonal conflict between the source and its target would become blurred at this stage (Moscovici and Nève, 1971; Personnaz, 1979).

In the experiments conducted by Moscovici and Personnaz (1980), the influence of the minority was assessed at the manifest and latent levels by the ratings of the color slide and the ratings of the chromatic afterimages. It was found that the influence of the minority was effective at the latent level during phase three when the source was present. This influence was maintained during phase four after the departure of the source. Subjects responded that still saw the slide as "blue" at the overt level, though they shifted their rating of the consecutive effect to "red" (the complementary of green). This response was quite in contrast to the one during phase one, when they saw it as orange or red-orange (complementary of blue). In other words, they claimed to see blue, but in fact, they were beginning to perceive the color of the slide close to green.

These results suggest that the minority produces a latent influence which the subjects may be unaware of. It suggests moreover that a change in the subjects' perception of the stimulus may occur without actually producing a change in their judgment, that is, conversion, as defined earlier. The findings of another study conducted by Doms and Van Avermaet (1980), using the same experimental procedure, support these results, and at the same time, reveal that a majority is also likely to induce conversion.

Further light has been shed on the problem in a partial replication of this conversion experiment (Sorrentino, King and Leo, 1980). Subjects were classified after the experiment in terms of their degree of suspicion—high, moderate, or low; it was found that the moderately suspicious subjects were the ones who most often changed their ratings toward the complementary of green. These results suggest that minority influence leads to increased attention being directed toward the object. Yet to do so, the source of influence must challenge the target sufficiently to avoid creating indifference (as is certainly the case when suspicion is low) and raising attribution biases (which may be the case when suspicion is high).

A Study of the Dynamics of Conversion by the Minority: The Different Stages of the Process

The investigations reported earlier led to the discovery of conversion phenomena through changes in scaled ratings. Would it be possible to implement perceptual recordings which do not depend on language? The spectrometer method, introduced by Personnaz (1981), made it possible to observe convergence and divergence of the effects of influence at three levels of response, thereby providing a better grasp of the underlying processes involved. The spectrometer used in this study is an instrument that enables the subjects to gradually unroll the whole spectrum through a little window and to stop the knob at the exact color corresponding to the slide color and that of the afterimage they perceived. A numbering counter, used as an onmeter, indicates to the experimenter the precise wavelength of the color selected by the subject. In Personnaz's study (1981) subjects were instructed to pair the color on the spectrometer with that of the color slides, then with the afterimage they had just seen, for each trial of each phase— except for the interaction phase two. More reliable than methods involving verbal ratings or rating scales, often subject to distortion, this method revealed what the subject actually saw without resorting to "highly socialized" verbalization. In accordance with Asch's (1940) words this procedure allows to observe the object of the judgment and not the judgment of the object.

This research has uncovered several important clues to the dynamics of conversion phenomena resulting from minority influence. The findings show that conversion unfolds over three successive stages. It starts at the latent level when the subjects are influenced by the minority via the consecutive effect, immediately after the interactive phase. In other words, when they are in the presence of the source of influence they begin to shift their rating of the afterimage color toward the complementary color of green. So it appears that subjects begin to change at a level where conflict with the minority is not manifest.

At another level the subjects maintain the response but, in the absence of the source, they adjust the color spectrum toward green, the color asserted by the minority. At this point, conversion takes place at the manifest perceptual level. Conversion effects appear at the judgment level, at the end of the experimental session. The rating of the subjects submitted to minority influence are thus closer to green than those of the subjects submitted to majority influence. This study suggests that the dynamics of conversion therefore begin at a nonconscious level, then proceed to a nonsocialized overt level, and finally emerge at the manifest judgment. It should be mentioned that few of the subjects who were asked admitted that they had been influenced by the minority confederate. Instead, they claimed that changes were self-initiated.

The dynamics of minority influence conversion seem to imply a process of conflict internalization for which the successive stages must allow the individual to externalize the norms of others as if they originated from him- or herself. The stages which have been identified in a laboratory setting seem somewhat similar to those studied in social movements (Mucchi-Faina, 1987).

Facilitation and Limitation of Minority Influence: Conflict—A "Sine Qua Non" Condition for Conversion to the Minority Point of View

The studies just reported, as well as others using the same paradigm, have attempted to assess the factors which enhance minority influence. One of its central elements is conflict. It seems that the more intense the cognitive conflict created by the minority source is, the more influence it has. This conflict may be reduced or increased in different ways. Let us now have a closer look at the processes involved in arousing and reducing conflict in the case of minority influence.

Sensorial Deprivation: A Strategy for Reducing Conflict

Since the Korean War, numerous experiments on sensorial deprivation have shown that subjects left in total isolation display perception troubles of varying degree along with an alteration of their intellectual aptitude which makes them prone to persuasion (see McGuire, 1986; Haythorn, 1973 for a review). Moscovici and Doms (1982) examined to what extent subjects placed in sensorially deprived settings were prone to minority or majority influence.

This study was exactly the same as that of Moscovici and Personnaz (1980) except that at the end of phase one, that is, after receiving the fictitious percentage of ratings, subjects were left in total darkness for forty-five minutes, supposedly to eliminate the effects of their initial perceptions. The influence phase and the post-influence phases followed this period of deprivation.

The results showed a significant increase in green ratings, which corresponds to manifest influence. This effect took place from the outset of the interaction phase when there was a majority source and immediately afterwards, whether the source was a majority or a minority. This shows that sensorial deprivation increases compliance whatever the source of influence is. Nevertheless, no latent influence was found on the afterimage. A posteriori analyses of these data suggest that it was the subjects who openly resisted the influence attempt who changed their consecutive-color ratings the most, but only when the source was absent. However, when these subjects were confronted with a majority, they tended to polarize their initial ratings by seeing an even bluer afterimage. This suggests that a latent process of counter-influence took place which corresponds to a reinforcement of their "clandestine" referent (Personnaz and Guillon, 1985). This research stresses the necessity for the target of influence to internalize the conflict in order to be converted to minority influence. Subjects who, at the manifest level resisted the most in the presence of a minority, were the ones who were the most readily converted at the latent level after the minority left. However, those who solved the conflict at the manifest level, by letting themselves be influenced in their overt responses, were not influenced by the minority at the latent level.

High or Low Self-Esteem as Reducer or Activator of Conflict

Another way of reducing or increasing the target's conflict consists of acting upon his or her self-image by giving the target either minority or majority status as well as a positive or negative image of him- or herself. Several studies that attempted to correlate self-esteem with susceptibility to influence attempts (e.g., Easterbrook, 1959; McGuire, 1968) have shown that individuals who were made to have a poor self-image were less receptive to influence than those with a favorable self-image. In fact, having a poor image of themselves (as opposed to what happens in the case of sensorial deprivation) makes the subjects focus on self-examination (Duval and Wicklund, 1972) and to experience internal comparison conflicts. This, in turn, makes them less prone to influence. Conversely, subjects who have high self-esteem and who do not experience internal conflict would be more receptive.

An investigation conducted by M. Personnaz (1988) examined the impact of positive or negative self-esteem on minority or majority influence at the perceptual level. The experimental procedure was identical to that of Moscovici and Personnaz (1980) with the difference that at the end of phase one the subjects received fictitious results of a test of creativity and an analysis of their hand writing. Both results which allegedly converged provided the subjects with either a positive or a negative image of themselves. They were made to believe that they had received an above-average or a poor score on both tests. After the positive or negative image had been induced, subjects were exposed to the influence source. The results showed the subjects with positive self-esteem to be the most susceptible to influence whatever the source was. Seeing themselves positively may have lead to a "fair-play" behavior. At the latent level, the minority had a greater impact on subjects with high self-esteem, though the effect weakened after the source left. However, it is only after its departure that the minority influenced subjects with low self-esteem. It may be a sign that these subjects internalized the conflict more deeply, which in turn led to a delay in information processing. When the source was the majority, it did not influence the subjects at the latent level. A tendency toward latent-level polarization was seen whenever the target exposed to majority influence was given a positive self-image.

A similar tendency was observed in the Moscovici and Doms's (1982) study. Whenever the subjects with high self-esteem were confronted with a majority, they committed themselves either to outward conformity or to reactive counter-influence. It seems therefore that in the presence of the minority a positive image reduces cognitive conflict and leads to short-lived *quick conversion*, whereas the negative image heightens intrapersonal conflict and gives rise to *slow conversion*. As seen in the previous studies, an increase or decrease in conflict resulting from a minority source may be modulated by factors linked to the target of influence. It may likewise be achieved by factors linked to the source of influence, namely, by emphasizing explicitly or implicitly its social or psychological characteristics. These characteristics may also reduce the intensity of the conflict and consequently lower the minority's influence. Different types of characteristics were manipulated, one of which being the *psychologization* of the minority.

Psychologization of the Minority as a Limiting Factor of Influence

A number of studies conducted (Mugny and Papastamou, 1980; Papastamou, 1988) in the field of attitudes have shown that if the opinions or judgments of a minority were explained by its psychological and personal characteristics (in other words, if the minority was *psychologized*) its influence could be reduced. It appeared that no cognitive conflict could longer be created. In the realm of perception, Moscovici and Personnaz (1986) tested the effects of psychologizing a minority and a majority. Their experiment used the spectrometer approach (Personnaz, 1981) to record judgments as well as spectral adjustments concerning the color slide and its afterimage. The subjects were confronted either with a minority or a majority source of influence. In one condition—personality condition—they were informed that the purpose of the study was to determine the interaction between personality and color perception. To persuade them, the experimenter showed them a book entitled *The Color Test: Your Personality Revealed by Colors*. In the other condition—the aesthetic condition—the study was presented as an investigation concerning the aesthetic value of colors. While the personality condition involved psychologization, the aesthetic condition involved a common cultural norm. Results showed, as predicted, that the minority had no influence at any level in the personality condition whereas the majority influenced the subjects' color perception. When the source was absent, this influence took place both at the manifest and latent levels. Results which were the opposite in the aesthetic condition, replicated those of Personnaz's (1981): when the minority was present, it exerted influence at the latent level, and in its absence, at the manifest level. A majority source exerted influence at the manifest level only when it was present.

Psychologization had opposite effects depending on the source of influence. It reduced minority influence but increased majority influence. In the case of the minority source, psychologization seems to eliminate conflict and its influence because its judgments are then attributed to personality traits. But what Moscovici and Personnaz's study (1986) points out is the impact of a psychologized majority source. In this case, the majority has lost credibility, one of its most important attributes. The majority does not appear any more as a reliable social reference. As Moscovici and Personnaz (1986) said, "it becomes necessary to investigate to what extent the majority's opinion or perception is reasonable" (p.356). When faced with a psychologized majority, subjects do not find themselves confronted with a unanimous majority but merely with an aggregate of individuals whose influence is very different.

Discrimination as an Activator of Conflict

Conflict seems to emerge primarily from minority influence. Minorities may be studied in terms of individuals belonging either to one's own group or to an outside group. If we turn to the field of intergroup relations (Tajfel, 1978) and identity theory (Turner, 1981; Mugny, 1981; Mugny and Papastamou, 1982), we would conclude that an individual would be more likely to act favorably toward a member of his own group than to someone who is not. One would therefore be more likely to identify with the socially more attractive influence source from one's own group and adopt its ways of doing and saying things, rather than with an unattractive outside source. However, as will be seen, minority influence paradoxically does not follow this pattern. Instead, even if it is unattractive the out-group minority has more influence than the in-group minority. In other words, the more discrimination the minority displays, the stronger its influence is.

To what extent will conflict be increased or reduced by a source of influence which belongs to an out-group or an in-group? If an individual is faced with an in-group source which defends a point of view different from that of the majority, he might fear to be likened to that idiot or dissenter if he adopts the latter's point of view. This individual will usually do everything to avoid such attributions. Reactions of social comparison (Festinger, 1954) or differentiation (Lemaine, 1974) make the target center on social interaction. If the source belongs to the in-group, questions may be raised about the normative substructure of the group itself. A French proverb: "I can defend myself from my enemies, but please protect me from my friends . . ." illustrates the difficulties of avoiding centering on group relations in such a situation. The more important group cohesiveness is, the more difficult it is for the individual to innovate and to be recognized by the individual's own group. In order for the individual to dissociate the content of his response from his own self, it often becomes necessary to create a new group where the individual may exert real influence.

Whenever an individual is faced with an out-group source whose response differs from the individual's own and that of the majority, the individual is much less likely to identify or associate him- or herself with it. If the source belongs to a group socially categorized as an out-group distant from oneself, the transition from social conflict to cognitive conflict then can occur. Only then may the source's point of view be looked upon, detached from social comparison, taken into consideration, and perhaps even adopted. This dissociation (Perez and Mugny, 1987) of the source from its response should allow for conversion to take place, particularly after the source of influence has been removed. The social proximity of the source and target would tend to make the source and its response indistinct and to hide the stimulus. Conversely, as the social distance between the source and the target grows, the dissociation between the object and the source becomes more salient and the object itself can be investigated.

An experiment conducted by Personnaz and Personnaz (1989) showed that an out-group source of influence that consistently defends a new point of view has more influence than an *in-group* source. Using the blue-green procedure described earlier, social categorization was induced by varying both the sex of the source and of the target of influence: same sex or opposite sex. Categorization along gender lines was made salient by presenting the experiment as a study of the influence of sex on color perception. The results showed that the in-group source was influential at the manifest level, but only when it was present. The same sex source did not lead to conversion, but to superficial and short-lived influence. When the source was of the opposite sex, the process of change proved to be totally different. Conversion phenomena occurred first at the latent level and then at the manifest level. The dynamics of change were, therefore, gradual (Personnaz, 1981). Similar results were obtained in Great Britain by Cole (1989), who conducted an experiment using the blue-green paradigm in order to determine the impact of minority and majority sources belonging to the in-group (same sex) or to the out-group (opposite sex). The out-group minority had more influence than did the in-group minority on the perception of the afterimage, which implies that the out-group has more influence at the latent level than an in-group one.

Both of these studies clearly showed that, in the case of categorization by sex, only the minority outgroup source only produced conversion and thus support our theoretical contentions about the hidden impact of a source of influence which does belong to the in-group.

Another experiment performed by Personnaz and Orii (1989) clarified this social labeling process. The study, which used the blue-green paradigm once more, took place in an intercultural perspective (Orii and Personnaz, 1990). It was performed in small groups consisting of five French subjects and a Japanese confederate who confronted them with the green response. It included two experimental and one control condition in order to make the minority characteristic implicit or explicit. In the first condition, the fictitious percentage of people who had seen the slide as blue or green was not given, thus making categorization implicit and to be assessed subjectively by the subjects. In the second condition, the source was explicitly categorized as belonging to a minority. Prior to the influence phase, subjects were told that according to the results of a "fictitious" study conducted in Japan, 18.2 percent of the subjects had seen the slide as green, as did the actual source of influence, and 81.8 percent as blue. By so doing, the source of influence was explicitly identified as an out-group minority. In the control condition the responses were recorded in writing only.

The results showed that the source of influence, which had not been categorized as a minority, exerted influence only at the manifest level, after the source left. However, the explicitly categorized minority source exerted an influence at the latent level as the subjects' responses were more strongly oriented toward the complementary of green but only after the source's departure (slow conversion). Influence persisted after the experiment, since these subjects remembered the color of the afterimage as being closer to the complementary of green than did the subjects in the other conditions. The explicit social categorization not only increased conflict at the response level but it also elicited attributions of psychological characteristics specific to minorities. The post-experimental questionnaire revealed that the minority source was perceived to be more self-confident than the noncategorized source. It suggests that the social categorization of the minority source sharpened the perception of its consistent behavior style and increased its impact. No such influence was found in the control condition. The social gap between the minority and its target of influence as well as the labeling of the minority source both contribute to heightening the cognitive conflict and facilitate conversion.

Attractiveness as Deterrent of Minority Influence

The attractiveness of a source of influence may also be conducive to influence. Research on majority influence has shown that the more attractive the source of influence is the greater the likelihood that it will exert influence. And yet, contrary to what one might think, attractiveness does not facilitate minority influence. The attractiveness of the source of influence will cause the target to focus on it at the expense of the object of interaction. It creates a "masking effect" that hinders cognitive appraisal.

177

One may give the same response as the attractive source without necessarily accepting it as one's own. Therefore, the influence effect may be found at the manifest level but without conversion. On the other hand, an unattractive source does not draw attention on itself but on its response by creating cognitive conflict, rather than social comparison. It should more likely create a validation process which would then lead to conversion.

This hypothesis was tested in an experiment (Personnaz and Personnaz; 1989) using the blue-green paradigm. The subjects—all female—were faced with a female confederate who was dressed, groomed, and made-up either attractively or unattractively. Different clothing and appearance styles had been tested beforehand. As usual, the source asserted that the slide was green whereas the naive subjects saw it as blue. The results supported the hypothesis. When she was attractive, the subjects were openly influenced whether she was present or not. Conversely, no latent influence was found. While the unattractive confederate did not openly influence the subjects, she brought the subjects to see the complementary of green independently of her presence. She was, therefore, responsible for conversion. The findings suggest that in order for the minority to have a latent influence it does not need to be attractive. Quite the contrary, by monopolizing attention, an attractive source may distract the subjects from the cognitive conflict related to the response and therefore prevent conversion.

Majority and Minority Conflict

Throughout the different studies reported so far, it has been shown repeatedly that the conflict initiated by a minority is of a different nature from the conflict produced by a majority. Both types may even be considered as the opposite of each other. What exacerbates the conflict on the one hand reduces it on the other. Turning to their effects, the minority brings about more conversion and the majority more compliance (Maass and Clark, 1984).

To sum it up, majority influence is felt at the manifest level rather than at the latent level. This overt influence is facilitated by all those factors that attract attention to its image and lead to social comparison rather than focusing on the new response. Proximity of group members and attractiveness give rise to this quasi-exclusive centration. The conflict created by the majority is essentially interpersonal, and whether it determines compliance or resistance, the stimulus is seldom actively explored at the cognitive level. When one adopts the majority's response, it likely involves compliance, forced submission, or mere imitation, since the majority's point of view is seen as a truth which can hardly be questioned and is even considered to be law. It is possible, as we have seen, to facilitate majority influence by putting the target in a state of double dependence, as in the case of sensorial deprivation. The target who is unable to process information adopts the majority's point of view without questioning it. In some exceptional instances the majority may lead to conversion. Looking back at the blue-green experiments reported earlier, the majority produced conversion in two instances. Doms and Van Avermaet (1980) found that the minority as well as the majority brought about conversion, though the majority produced this effect only after its departure. It is interesting to compare these findings with other ones from the same study. At the end of the experiment, subjects were asked to state what percentage of people they thought would agree with their own response or with the opposite one. This provided a manipulation check on the information given at the end of phase one concerning the fictitious percentage of people who had seen blue or green. Whenever the source was a minority, the subjects thought that 70.5 percent of the people would see blue as they did and 24.5 percent would see it as green. Conversely, when the source was a majority, the subjects thought that 45 percent of the people saw blue as they did and 54 percent saw green as the source did. The majority which influences at the latent level after it leaves is underestimated, suggesting that it has lost one of its most important attributes: its numerical strength.

The second study that showed the latent majority influence is the one conducted by Moscovici and Personnaz (1986). At the condition that it was psychologized, the majority exerted latent influence; otherwise, it did not. The psychologized majority lost the credibility of its point of view which is usually considered to be fundamental truth. The majority no longer appeared to be monolithic, infallible, and unanimous, but rather as consisting of individuals with differing personal characteristics. It suggests that social comparison processes became blurred and that the individual was able to actively grasp the point of view defended by the majority.

The majority would therefore produce conversion but at the condition that its normal attributes are questioned or that it has nonspecific characteristics. Minority conflict, on the contrary, is of an entirely different nature. To sum it up, its force resides in creating a cognitive conflict, at the response level, and internalized, which drives the subject to explore it. In order for the conflict to emerge, the cognitive investigation of the stimulus must somehow be facilitated while it can be prevented by factors which encourage social comparison, particularly identification with the source of influence. Belongingness to the in-group and social attractiveness may also contribute to social comparison. In order to exert influence, the minority must additionally be identifiable and even socially categorized, a factor which makes distinctiveness salient and conflict socially obvious. This essentially social conflict is both the starting point of the process of conversion and its driving force. Problems in identifying the minority reduce its influence, whereas its labeling points out to its difference and reinforces it. Factors related to the influence target when it is opposed to the minority do not have the same effects as when it is opposed to the majority. Sensorial deprivation prevents the conflict from occurring by leaving the target without cognitive resources, a situation which, in turn, limits minority influence. Conferring a positive or negative self image to the target of influence speeds up or delays conversion to the minority's point of view while at the same time it shortens or extends it.

Conclusion

While the findings of all these studies show that the majority can modify the judgment of a subject (but usually superficially without modifying its underlying frame of reference), the minority modifies the subject's judgment at the deepest levels through a chain of cognitive activities. It appears that conversion is essentially a psychological resultant of social conflict. The nature of the conflict is linked to the social asymmetry of the actors involved in the confrontation. The more exacerbated the social conflict is, the more effective the conversion will be. Likewise, any factor that stirs conflict will induce conversion to the minority's point of view. The individual has to internalize the social conflict through unconscious processes in order to be converted. Conversion modifies the response which originated the conflict but, furthermore, it arouses intense cognitive activity which changes the individual's thought patterns (Nemeth, 1986). Only at this expense does the minority have an impact. In contrast to the popular belief that "strength is found in numbers," the minority *that refuses to give up* may prevail.

References

Asch, S. E. (1940). Studies in the principles of judgments and attitudes II: Determination of judgments by group and by ego standards. *Journal of Social Psychology*, 12, 433–445.

Asch, S. E., (1951). Effects of group pressure upon the modification and distorsion of judgment. In H. Guetzkow (Ed.), *Groups, Leadership and Men.* Pittsburgh, PA: Carnegie Press.

Cole, D. H. (1989). Minority influence and intergroup relations in a perceptual task. 3rd Year Social Psychology Project, Canterbury, University of Kent, Institute of Social and Applied Psychology.

Duval, J., and Wicklund, R. A. (1972). *A Theory of Objective Self-Awareness.* New York: Academic Press.

Doms, M., and Van Avermaet, E. (1980). Majority influence, minority influence and conversion behavior: A replication. *Journal of Experimental Social Psychology*, 16,283–292.

Easterbrook, J. A., (1959). The effect of emotion on cue utilization and the organization of behavior. *Psychological Review*,66,183–201.

Festinger, L. A. (1954). A theory of social comparison processes. *Human Relations*, 7,117–140.

Guillon, M., and Personnaz, B. (1983). Analyse de la dynamique des représentations au cours d'une interaction d'influence avec une minorité et une majorité. *Cahiers de Psychologie Cognitive*,3,65–87.

Haythorn, W. W. (1973). The miniworld of isolation: Laboratory studies. In J. Rasmussen (Ed.), *Man in Isolation and Confinement*. Chicago: Aldine.

Lage, E. (1976). *Innovation et Influence Minoritaire*. Paris: E.P.H.E. Thèse de 3ème cycle.

Lemaine, G. (1974). Social differentiation and social originality. *European Journal of Social Psychology*,4,17–52.

Maass, A., and Clark, R. D. (1984). The hidden impact of minorities: Fourteen years of minorities influence research. *Psychological Bulletin*,95,428–450.

McGuire, W. J. (1968). The nature of attitudes and attitude change. In G. Lindzey and E. Aronson (Eds.), *Handbook of Social Psychology*. Reading, MA: Addison-Wesley.

Moscovici, S. (1980). Toward a theory of conversion behavior. In L. Berkowitz (Ed.), *Advances in Experimental Social Psychology*, vol. 13. New York: Academic Press.

Moscovici, S., and Doms, M. (1982). Compliance and conversion in a situation of sensory deprivation. *Basic and Applied Social Psychology*,3,81–94.

Moscovici, S., and Lage, E. (1976). Studies in social influence III; majority versus minority influence in a group. *European Journal of Social Psychology*, 6,149–174.

Moscovici, S., Lage, E., and Naffrechoux, M. (1969). Influence of a consistent minority on the responses of a majority in a color perception task. *Sociometry*,32,365–380.

Moscovici, S., and Neve, P. (1973). Studies in social influence II: Instrumental and symbolic influence. *European Journal of Social Psychology*,3,461–471.

Moscovici, S., and Personnaz, B. (1980). Studies in social influence V: minority influence and conversion behavior in a perceptual task. *Journal of Experimental Social Psychology*,16,270–282.

Moscovici, S., and Personnaz, B. (1986). Studies on latent influence using spectrometer method: Psychologization effect upon conversion by a minority and a majority. *European Journal of Social Psychology*,16,345–360.

Mucchi-Faina, A. (1987). Mouvement social et conversion. In S. Moscovici and G. Mugny (Eds.), *Psychologie de la Conversion*. Cousset: Del Val.

Mugny, G. (1981). Identification sociale et influence sociale. *Cahiers de Psychologie Cognitive*,1,124–126.

Mugny, G., and Papastamou, S. (1980). When rigidity does not fail: Individualization and psychologization as resistances to the diffusion of minority innovations. *European Journal of Social Psychology*,10,43–61.

Mugny, G., and Papastamou, S. (1982). Minority influence and psychosocial identity. *European Journal of Social Psychology*,12,379–394.

Nemeth, C. (1986). Differential contributions of majority and minority influence. *Psychological Review*,93,23–32.

Orii, M., and Personnaz, B. (1990). Inter-cultural innovation experiment. 1: The effect of a Japanse minority source upon the process of perceptual conversion among French subjects and the influence of social categorization. *Research in Social Psychology*,5(2).

Paicheler, G., and Moscovici, S. (1984). Suivisme et conversion. In. S. Moscovici, S. (Ed.), *Psychologie Sociale*. Paris: Presses Universitaires de France.

Papastamou, S. (1988). La psychologisation. L'us et l'abus de l'explication psychologique dans l'appréhension des phénomènes de la persuasion. Thèse de Doctorat d'Etat, Paris, E.H.E.S.S.

Perez, J. A., and Mugny, G. (1987). Comparison et construction sociale de la réalité. In S. Moscovici and G. Mugny (Eds.), *Psychologie de la Conversion*. Cousset: Del Val.

Personnaz, B. (1976). Conformité, consensus et référents clandestins: La dépendance en tant que processus annulateur de l'influence. *Bulletin de Psychologie*, 29,230–242.

Personnaz, B. (1979). Niveau de résistance à l'influence de réponses nomiques et anomiques, étude des phénomènes de référents clandestins et de conversion. *Recherches de Psychologie Sociale*, 1,5–27.

Personnaz, B. (1981). Study on social influence using the spectrometer method: Dynamics of the phenomena of conversion and covertness in perceptual responses. *European Journal of Social Psychology*,11,431–438.

Personnaz, B. (1986). Changements normatifs manifestes et latents dans les phénomènes d'influence minoritaire et de dissimilation. *Bulletin de Psychologie*,38,177–189.

Personnaz, B. (1988). Zmiany normatywne i percepcyne jako stutky wplywu spolecznegro i diferencjacji. *Przglzad Psychologiczny*,31,167–183.

Personnaz, B., and Guillon, M. (1985). Conflict and conversion. In S. Moscovici, G. Mugny and E. Van Avermaet (Eds.), *Perspectives on Minority Influence*. Cambridge: The University Press.

Personnaz, B., annd Orii, M. (1989). Conversion effect of a french majority by a japanese minority. *Colloque International sur l'influence sociale des minorités*. Perugia: Universita of Perugia and E.A.E.S.P.

Personnaz, B., and Personnaz, M. (1987). Un paradigme pour l'étude expérimentale de la conversion. In S. Moscovici and G. Mugny (Eds.), *Psychologie de la Conversion*. Cousset: Del Val.

Personnaz, B., and Personnaz, M. (1989). Contextes intergroupes et niveaux d'influence. *Colloque International sur l'Influence des Minorités*. Perugia: Universita di Perugia and E.A.E.S.P.

Personnaz, M. (1988). Représentation de soi, centration cognitive et influence sociale. Actes du Colloque Européen: *Construction et Fonctionnement de l'Identité*. Aix-en-Provence: CREPCO and the University of Provence.

Sherif, M. (1936). *The Psychology of Social Norms*. New York: Harper.

Sorrentino, R. M., King, G. and Leo, G. (1980). The influence of the minority on perception: A note on possible alternative explanation. *Journal of Experimental Social Psychology*,16,293–301.

Tajfel, H. (1978). *Differentiation between Social Groups: Studies in the Social Psychology of Intergroup Relations*. London: Academic Press.

Turner, J. C. (1981). Towards a cognitive redefinition of the social group. *Cahiers de Psychologie Cognitive*,1,93–118.

Chapter Ten

INTEGRATING MINORITY AND MAJORITY INFLUENCE: CONVERSION, CONSENSUS, AND UNIFORMITY

Juan A. Pérez, Gabriel Mugny, Fabrizio Butera, Claude Kaiser, and Patricia Roux

Is the robot the prototype of true influence? Can one conceive of influence as equivalent to a touch which is sufficient to reverse the direction of movement? It is true that the individual is often conceived as a "response machine" (Moscovici, 1972), lacking any autonomy, a simple reflection of external pressures which, according to circumstances, cause him or her to hold completely opposed views with equal conviction. A vision of this kind certainly inspired the first studies on influence, studies based on such notions as suggestion and hypnosis (see Aebischer and Oberlé, 1990; Paicheler, 1988; Moscovici, 1985). In contrast to this vision an alternative was developed (cf. Asch, 1948), that of a person at once "psychological" and "rational," encouraging us to look for the explanation of genuine influence in the reasons which have to do with a particular conception of "objective reality." One idea, shared by many researchers, derives from the principle that deep, latent changes flow from the perception that the views of others provide a proof of objectivity and truth (Festinger, 1950, 1954).

On the one hand, we approve of expert, credible, majority, and in-group sources, and reject minority, incompetent, out-group sources at the overt level for normative reasons or in the name of heuristics of simplification (cf. Chaiken, 1987; Cialdini, 1987). These normative influences (Deutsch and Gerard, 1955) depend on the degree of (symbolic) power available to the source, power to provide social approval, and on the extent to which the

185

target can be identified by the source (cf. Allen, 1965). The conformity of the subject, whether it takes the form of compliance or identification (Kelman, 1958) fulfills an instrumental function here (to permit an escape from punishment or to ingratiate) or a symbolic function (to affirm solidarity or a community of identity—cf. Turner, Hogg, Oakes, Reicher, and Wetherell, 1987—or more simply a special relationship). On the other hand, however, we would only genuinely appropriate the response, we would only internalize it (Kelman, 1958) for informational reasons (the source informs us about objective reality—Goethals, 1972). This informational influence is a function of the degree of competence or credibility of the source and of targets' uncertainty about their own judgments or beliefs or opinions, in particular by virtue of the ambiguity of the stimulus or the complexity of the task (Festinger, 1950). The source is the pledge of truth and reducer of uncertainty, certainly for reasons linked to its social characteristics (its superior numbers, credibility, expertise, trustworthiness), but it is the content of its message which has informational value.

However, we are in the presence of an "epistemological nightmare" here (cf. Paicheler, 1988). Without overstating the influence actually obtained, it must be asked how influence is possible at all when, as in the Asch (1956) majority influence paradigm, responses depart from any evidence of objective reality, when they are clearly erroneous (cf. Friend, Rafferty, and Bramel, 1990)? In the name of what normative force can an erroneous majority exercise influence overtly? In the name of what informational force can a message without objective foundations exercise an influence, be it only indirect? It is this question that we shall address in the present chapter. We shall defend the hypothesis that in reality rational man may be brought to change even his most confident and objective judgments, not because of some loss of consciousness or as a result of the play of irrational forces residing in the group, but probably because of the very social psychological foundations of his rationality or what one might call his "epistemo-ideology" (Mugny and Doise, 1979).

Asch Revisited: Just Compliance?

Let us take Asch's (1951, 1956) experiment on conformity and independence and push the reasoning to the limit. The essential characteristic of the situation is that the stimuli are entirely without ambiguity; subjects responding in isolation almost never make mistakes. Subjects anticipate a perfect consensus in responses, and this expectation is then confirmed at the beginning of the experiment because for the first two items the source responds in the same way as the subject, which is to say correctly, ("in order to lend a quality of trustworthiness to the majority," Asch, 1956, p. 7;

additionally, "the errors of the majority were smallest on the early trials, generally increasing as the experiment progressed," p. 6). When subjects then discover all the other participants, with whom they share the same background (they belong to the same college), giving responses which unanimously depart from this objective reality, they display two common psychological reactions or sentiments. On the one hand, there is confusion and perplexity, given that the others are seen as having the same motivations and the same abilities as themselves, and because they are assumed to see the same reality that the subjects see. This is all the more true as the task presented is in reality not difficult, and subjects correctly perceive this and given that there is only one correct response which can be determined without the slightest ambiguity.

In practice, all subjects respond to this perplexity by searching for an explanation for the absence of consensus. The post-experimental interviews are most revealing on this point. The subject can question himself and ask himself for example if he has properly understood the instructions; faced with the unanimous persistence of the others in their error, he might imagine that the others have mutually influenced one another (see, for example, Wilder, 1977) or that perhaps the difference in responses reflects the different perspective one has depending on where one sits, or again that it is a test of psychological illusions which are produced in some persons. But the lack of hesitation, certainty, and calmness with which the others respond, the absence of any evident cultural differences between the partners to this interaction, and the fact that from time to time the others do give the correct response (on average, one time in three), thereby occasionally verifying the consensus, all these elements converge so that one by one the plausibility of these various explanations is undermined. The consequence is that if one is not able to agree with the majority then one finds oneself needing to change the representation of the nature and role of consensus, in brief questioning the definition of what is an "objective reality."

There thus arises a socio-cognitive dilemma: the subject must choose between remaining faithful to his perception or submitting to the erroneous judgment of the majority. We know that subjects resolve this conflict in various ways (see also Cruchfield, 1955). Some subjects, with more or less confidence in their judgments, maintain their independence throughout the experiment. Most of the others show some compliance either on just a few trials or on a majority of the trials. Among these overtly influenced subjects there are some who say they have changed their answers only to avoid spoiling the experiment, and others who do it in order not to appear different from the group and to avoid ridicule or confrontation. Others continue to deny that they went along with the group judgment either because they do not wish to acknowledge their conformity or because they were influenced without being aware of it. Whichever the case, two conclusions can be drawn from this more qualitative analysis of Asch's experiments, conclusions which are often touched upon in his accounts. The first seems inevitable: if one gives subjects a plausible explanation for the differences between their judgments and those of the source, there will be no influence. The second is that one should not be too troubled by these influence effects because for the most part they are only compliance effects, they do not involve genuine influence (in variant four, for example, a plausible pretext is constructed for subjects giving their responses in writing and this substantially reduces the influence obtained; see also Allen, 1965). However, one of the fundamental principles of research practice is not to trust appearances too much and at least to test the implausibility of the null hypothesis.

This was the task undertaken in an experiment which used Asch-type material, but also allowed the assessment of indirect influence (Mugny, 1984). Subjects were given the incorrect response of a majority (88 percent of a population of college students) or a minority (12 percent of that population). Additionally, half of the subjects were told that the experiment was a study of perceptual illusions and were provided with some dramatic examples of such illusions. The others, in a manner more akin to the Asch experiments, received no such information. As regards the effects of a minority source, these were totally intelligible within the framework of psychological conversion (Moscovici and Mugny, 1987; Mugny and Pérez, 1991). First of all, compared to a control condition in which there was no influence pressure, the minority achieved no overt influence in any of the situations. However, it did achieve a hidden or latent influence (cf. Maass and Clark, 1984; Maass, West, and Cialdini, 1987) in accord with the pattern of conversion described by Moscovici (1980), but only if no explanation was introduced for the minority error in terms of visual illusions. When this was the case, even the indirect influence disappeared, an effect similar to that of psychologization (cf. Papastamou, 1983). In this situation, invalidation of the minority response wiped out any influence. All this seems very reasonable.

Things look radically different, however, when one considers the majority. Three things can be observed. First of all, compared to the control condition in which there was no influence attempt, the majority source produced an overt influence when no reference was made to visual illusions. But as would be expected on the basis of comparable work on majority and minority influence (cf. Levine and Russo, 1987; Moscovici, 1985), a majority had no latent influence. Moscovici and Personnaz (1980, 1986) have claimed that overt majority influence cannot be accompanied by any deeper influence. Next, the fact of introducing an explanation (in terms of illusions) for the majority errors did not noticeably diminish its overt influence, which contradicts the first conclusion drawn earlier. Finally, and this result would seem to be even more challenging, the introduction of such an explanation caused the appearance of a latent influence by the majority, which contradicts the second assumption. Thus, the invalidation of the informational value of the source's response does not counteract all its influence.

This is not an isolated observation in our literature; notably Sperling (in Asch, 1952), DiVesta (1959), Pollis, Montgomery, and Smith (1975), and even Nemeth and Wachtler (1983) who have reported a stronger majority influence when the majority is in error than when it is correct, all provide indications that despite being discredited in tasks which involve facts or precise answers a source can continue to exert a significant influence. Thus, it would seem that the effects observed in the Asch paradigm are more complex than one might have imagined at first sight.

These effects seem, however, to contradict those observed in studies on *denial*. Let us recall that in these latter studies subject must as a general rule determine which four arguments out of five summarizing the message of a minority or majority source are improbable, unworthy of belief and not to be taken into consideration. In brief, denial consists of placing the credibility of a source's message in doubt. Now, somewhat in the same manner as in the paradoxical effect of "thought suppression" (Wegner, Schneider, Carter, and White, 1987), we have observed two things. First, if denial counteracts the overt influence of a source, it also increases its delayed and/or indirect influence (Moscovici, Mugny, and Pérez, 1984–85). If these paradoxical effects of denial seem to be of sufficiently general significance, it emerges nonetheless that they only occur when the source is a minority and not when it is a majority (Pérez and Mugny, 1992; Pérez, Mugny, and Moscovici, 1986; Pérez, Moscovici, and Mugny, 1991).

On the basis of these results the conclusion would be different from that drawn from conformity research (Mugny, 1984; Nemeth and Wachtler, 1983). In the latter, when the system of responses of the majority is invalidated (perceptual illusion) and has no basis recognizable by the target (incorrect majority), then majority sources seem to be able to generate indirect influence effects similar to those usually produced only by minority sources. Studies on denial show that indirect influence can also be exerted by minority sources, under the paradoxical condition that they lose any credibility. In conclusion, in some cases denial seems to facilitate the indirect effect of minority sources but not of majority sources; in others, the reverse seems true.

Our hypothesis is that this difference might be due to the nature of the norm which is salient in the various issues chosen to build up the influence situation. In particular, studies on denial favoring minority sources (Pérez et al., 1986) have been carried out basically using opinion issues which admit of subjective responses, while the Asch-like study by Mugny (1984) and the Nemeth and Wachtler (1983) experiment have employed tasks demanding objectively correct solutions. In the former, influence is based on a preference norm; in the latter, it involves a norm of objectivity (Moscovici, 1976). Thus, when the influence situation is based on an objectivity norm, which is to say, when it induces the subjects to expect only one response to be correct, then denial would increase indirect influence of a majority. Conversely, when the situation of influence allows for a certain pluralism (i.e., when the subject is not led to anticipate a full consensus but to regard a variety of responses as having some orienting value), then denial would favor indirect influence by a minority.

The basis for this hypothesis lies on our view that there may be an intervening effect of some representation of knowledge (either that implied in the task by the nature of the stimuli used or that induced by some characteristic of the context), according to which the existence of a given consensus (majority source) must correspond to a uniform reality or entity. On the other hand, if minority viewpoints emerge that differ from those of the majority, they would imply that reality must be multiform in nature. Thus when a particular situation of influence (majority and objective stimulus, minority and subjective stimulus) arouses either one kind of correspondence (consensus and uniformity) or another (lack of consensus and diversity), then the subjects will adopt a cognitive functioning and orient their responses in a convergent or a divergent way, similar to the processes described by Nemeth (1986, her chapter). This is the core of the theoretical problem that led us to conceive the study reported next (Brandstaetter, et al., 1991).

The "Cheese" Experiment

After filling in a personal questionnaire, subjects were shown successively, for five seconds each, nine figures with a varying angle (72.5, 50, or 27.5 degrees) and lines (varying in length from 16.5 to 17.5 cm.). Subjects had to estimate the angle (in degrees), the length of the horizontal and of "the other line" (in centimeters). They were also asked to imagine that the figure represented a piece of cheese, and to estimate its weight (in grams). In a post-test run after the experimental phase, the same data were collected for a second time, allowing for the evaluation of changed scores. After completing the post-test run, subjects were asked some questions concerning their evaluation of the task as well as of the source of influence.

During the experimental phase subjects were shown successively six figures with an angle of 90 degrees (unity conditions) or 85 degrees (plurality conditions). The rationale for this manipulation was that with 90 degree figures, subjects would expect to a greater extent a correct answer, that is, a higher consensus and uniformity of responses, while with 85 degree figures the correct response would not be so clear and, therefore, an absence of total consensus and the emergence of some divergence in the responses would be more readily accepted. For each figure subjects were informed that either 88 percent of the people (majority conditions) or 12 percent (minority conditions) previously studied had estimated the size of the angle as around 50 degrees, subjects then having to give their own estimation of the angle.

Before starting the influence phase, we sought to invalidate the credibility of the source's responses. The experimenter showed the subjects a picture with two lines, one obviously longer than the other, and announced that either 88 percent or 12 percent of subjects who participated in the previous experiments had incorrectly judged these lines to be equal in length. Thus, in all conditions, the source is presented as less competent than the subjects. A possible explanation of these "errors" was then provided: they could have been due to the occurrence of a visual illusion. In order to make this explicit, subjects were demonstrated two sets of illusions where seemingly differing lines or circles were actually of equal size. The question is whether, in spite of these manipulations, the source still constitutes a reference point, as the early observations by Sperling (1946, cited in Asch, 1952) suggest. He found that despite the explicit indication that the autokinetic effect was a perceptual illusion, some interindividual convergence still occurred.

Direct influence was evaluated from the estimates of degrees of the angles in the figures during the experimental phase, underestimation constituting a direct positive influence of the source. Indirect influence was measured along two dimensions: the length of the two lines, and the weight of the "piece of cheese." According to Robinson (1972), the decrease of an acute angle implies an increase in the length of the lines, thus an increase in length between the pre- and post-test can be considered a positive indirect influence. The second index of indirect influence is the weight of "the piece of cheese" (the lower the weight estimated at the post-test run, the greater the indirect positive influence).

Our main hypotheses were that despite the denial of the source's informational power (incorrectness and perceptual illusion), majority sources should produce an indirect influence when the stimulus calls for a uniform response (90 degree angle), while the same should be true for minority sources with a less compelling angle (85 degrees). The predictions for direct influence were more trivial: on the base of the classical effects observed in studies on conformity (cf. Allen, 1965), a greater influence should be found

Table 10.1 Difference between Post- and Pretest in the Weight of the Piece of Cheese
(– Means more Influence) and Length of Lines (+ Means more Influence).

	Majority		Minority	
	90°	**85°**	**90°**	**85°**
Cheese	49.26	129.95	151.55	−46.60
Horizontal line	1.03	−0.46	−1.10	−0.45
Other line	0.86	−0.22	−1.27	0.62

Source: Brandstaetter et al. Copyright 1991 John Wiley. Adapted by permission of the publisher.

in conditions implying higher ambiguity (85 degrees), and, on the base of studies of innovation, one should expect majorities to achieve more direct influence than minorities.

Let us consider the results. We calculated in how many of the six items of the experimental phase subjects did underestimate the size of the angle (90 degrees or 85 degrees depending on the experimental stimulus). One condition yielded a larger number of subjects underestimating the angle; in the majority-85 degree condition which induced more direct influence than each of the other three (p < .05), eleven of the twenty-one subjects are influenced for at least one item, nine of these being influenced for five or six items. With respect to differences between pre-test and post-test we calculated a mean difference over the nine items for the weight of the piece of cheese and the length of the two lines of the figure. Results indicate that for the three indices there is an interaction between type of source and type of stimulus, for weight of piece of cheese (p < .02); length of the horizontal line (p < .01); length of "the other line" (p < .02).

As table 10.1 shows, the strongest influence on the weight estimates was found in the minority-85 degree condition, estimates in this condition being reduced compared to the majority-85 degree condition (p < .06) and the minority-90 degree condition (p < .03). As regards the changes observed in horizontal line length, the condition which really shows a greater indirect influence was that of majority source-90 degrees which differed from the minority-90 degree condition (p < .02), and tended also to differ from the majority-85 degree condition (p < .09). No other contrast approached significance, although we should note that the minority-85 degree condition had a slight positive effect. With respect to the effects in the length of "the other line," the effects are rather similar: the majority-90 degree differs from the minority-90 degree condition (p < .04), which in turn tended to differ from the minority-85 degree condition (p < .06).

These results support part of our hypotheses. First, we observed very little direct influence. At this level, majority produced a significant influence, but only when stimulus was 85 degrees. Here we find a most characteristic result (e.g., Crutchfield, 1955): when there is a decrease in the degree of confidence, then dependence with respect to the more consensual response (that of the majority in this case) increases. However, as the majority is explicitly erroneous one must suppose that there is some residual effect of power symbolized by the majority status, consistent with the fact that subjects are less influenced but can nonetheless be significantly influenced when there is no explicit normative or informational dependence (cf. Deutsch and Gerard, 1955; Sperling, in Asch, 1952; Hogg and Abrams, 1988). This residual power is expressed elsewhere in the fact that the minority for its part exercises no influence under the same conditions, the behavior of subjects expressing a dissimilarity with the source (cf. Mugny, Butera, Pérez, and Huguet, 1993). It is understandable that there is no influence in the 90 degree conditions at this direct level. Both majority and minority lacked a certain normative "power" (subjects responded anonymously; cf. Deutsch and Gerard, 1955). Informational pressure was also explicitly reduced by the incorrectness of the source and by the demonstration of the perceptual illusions. Finally, the distinctiveness of the 90 degree angle provided subjects with more confidence in their own responses than the 85 degree angle.

Nevertheless, several kinds of indirect influence are apparent. A majority source, with a 90 degree stimulus, produced an indirect influence effect on the perception of length of the lines, and a minority source, with a 85 degree stimulus, influenced weight estimates. These indirect influence effects are difficult to explain in terms of either the notion of normative influence or the notion of informational influence. The former seems inappropriate because the indirect nature of this influence means the target cannot be controlled directly by the source. Informational influence is also unlikely to account for these indirect effects. First, the information from the source was obviously wrong and subjects had a correct perception, and second, the source's manner of perceiving was explicitly invalidated as due to visual illusion. Furthermore, even though the source might have a certain informational value, it would still be necessary to explain why subjects do not integrate such information into their responses on the same dimension where the source gives the information.

Two Representations of Knowledge: Unity and Pluricity

To integrate this new effect theoretically, an effect we regard as a majority conversion (the latent majority influence is greater than the overt influence), we believe it is necessary to refer to the concept of representation of knowledge. A representation of knowledge functions according to a two-fold logic, the assumption being that majorities induce a representation of unity and that minorities induce a representation of multiplicity. The representation of unity will involve a belief that the existence of a given consensus will correspond to a unique, uniform reality, this belief being activated by the simple reference to a majority judgment. From the point of view of the representation of plurality, the belief will be that the absence of consensus corresponds to a diverse, plural reality. This belief will normally arise as a result of consistently expressed minority perspectives.

The representation of unity would operate in two ways: one reflects conformity or compliance and relates to what Nemeth (1986) refers to as the dynamics of convergent thinking: in the face of a majority, subjects tend to adopt its response, discarding other possible (even more correct) alternative responses (cf. Nemeth and Staw, 1989). But another outcome is possible: instead of adapting their own responses to the propositions made by the source in order to ensure that just one point of view dominates (restoring of consensus), subjects can also redefine or change their perception of the object properties so that they fit the source's point of view and reconstruct the unity of the specific knowledge (restoring of uniformity). Thus, when the representation of unity is activated, subjects will tend to cause its intervention at a direct level. If, however, it is not possible for them at this level for whatever reason (e.g., when there is a manifest informational deficiency in the source) then the intervention will occur at an indirect level. Thus, subjects would not accept the source's responses, but they would exhibit a perceptual conversion.

The activation of this representation of unity is a function of the majority nature of the source and of the type of stimulus. That is, it requires that the task in the influence situation leads subjects to believe that only one point of view must predominate, that only one response must be correct, because the judgments are interdependent (Pérez and Mugny, 1989, 1990), because a norm of objectivity is operating (cf. Moscovici, 1976; Kaiser, 1989; Papastamou, Mugny, and Kaiser, 1980), or simply because the type of judgment makes it possible to determine exactly what is the correct response (cf. Goethals, 1972; Crano, 1989, his chapter).

On the other hand, the representation of multiplicity, relating to a divergent functioning of thinking, would account for the indirect changes occurring in response to minority sources in various influence situations. Such would be the case when a norm or originality predominates (cf. Maass and Volpato, 1989; Moscovici and Lage, 1978), or when judgments are given in a multidimensional way or in a plural social space (Pérez and Mugny, 1989, 1990). This would cover the case of our minority source-85 degree condition. Two reasons can be advanced for the occurrence of such an effect in this condition. This first is that it is a condition where subjects are provided with no consensual response, where on the contrary, they are told that the response originates from a minority. Second, the stimulus itself is less normative (85 degrees). In these specific influence conditions (a minority and a non-normative stimulus) the correspondence between lack of a majority consensus and diversity of ways of defining the object becomes highly salient, leading targets to adopt divergent cognitive functioning and to orientate their influenced responses to indirect dimensions. This occurs only at an indirect level, due partly to an antiminority intergroup bias and to the identification conflict commonly induced by minorities (cf. Pérez and Mugny, 1990).

Explaining Majority Conversion

Despite the impressive number of studies conducted on majority influence (cf. Allen, 1965, 1975), one rarely finds conditions in which subjects adopt the response of another because that response is ascendant (restoration of consensus) or in order that the definition of the object should become more uniform (restoration of uniformity). In order to determine whether persons change in order to reestablish consensus rather than because they are dependent, it would be necessary to confront the targets of influence with a majority stripped of its normative and informational power; for example, a majority consisting of nothing but a reference percentage. Could one still expect any influence, especially on judgments about an unambiguous physical reality? The answer would seem to be in the negative, if one accepts the view that influence is a function of dependence. However, on the basis of the hypothesis that targets can also construct the consensus and not merely submit to it, a positive answer might be expected.

So, do targets change only because the source possesses normative and informational credentials, or do they perhaps sometimes modify their own positions in order to construct or strengthen a valid norm for the condition of uniqueness and consensuality (Hogg and Turner, 1987; Turner, 1991)? In effect, when subjects find themselves confronted with a situation in which a source questions the principle of unity by a response that is novel for the targets, they have three possible means of restoring the principle:

a. They can resort to a strategy of reciprocally influencing the source; in particular, by more firmly asserting their own position. The likelihood of pursuing this solution is reduced to the extent that the source enjoys a normative or informational ascendance over the targets. Even if the latter are able to express themselves symbolically by some polarization of responses in opposition to those of the source, this is not readily compatible with the type of paradigm considered here because subjects have no possibility of communicating with the source. Such a study, however, would be highly desirable (cf. Rule and Bisanz, 1987; Pérez, Mugny, and Roux, 1989; Mugny, Maggi, Leoni, Gianinazzi, Butera, and Pérez, 1991).

b. They can reestablish overt consensus by concurring with the source's explicit responses. This is the most commonly considered option. This strategy amounts to generating consensus without any process of uniformity with respect to the object; that is, without a constructive redefinition of its properties by the targets. Attention is centered on the relation with the source, whether this be one of submission (Milgram, 1974), attraction, identification (including in the sense specified in Turner et al., 1987), or internalization (Kelman, 1958). This strategy for reestablishing consensus cannot constitute a solution with respect to minority sources because these do not define the most consensual position; they constitute forms of out-group. Nor can it operate in relation to majority sources when these are devoid of normative and informational power. In effect, as we have seen with the "cheese experiment," once the majority is discredited (the subjects knowing that the majority can be wrong, that it can be the victim of an illusion, etc.), this outcome becomes less likely. The question which arises is as follows: how can subjects validate their judgments when confronted with majorities or minorities if each in their own fashion has been discredited? We have already described, with reference to studies on denial, the manner in which processes of validation could operate in relation to minority sources. Now we focus on discredited majority sources, and we must consider a third solution, one already envisaged by Allen and Wilder (1980): the target reconstructs reality.

c. It is necessary to recognize that the target can also become engaged in a cognitive activity of redefining the properties of the object (whether this involves a perceptual stimulus or a social judgment), so as to accommodate to the majority point of view. By this means, the majority error is converted into a new reality which satisfies, at a latent level, the imperatives of the representation of unity. The nature of this influence is such as to release a particular cognitive activity with respect to the properties of the object with the aim of reestablishing a latent uniformity between the targets' own responses and the overt responses of the majority to which subjects have not been able to adhere overtly. This restores belief in the unity of the object, temporarily shaken by the majority's disturbance of the consensus.

If it is allowed that this third strategy, which has been the focus of very little research beyond the level of anecdotal observation (cf. Asch, 1956), may be related to some of the conditions accompanying the preceding strategy (cf. Mackie, 1987; Mugny, 1984), our general hypothesis is that *consensus* (case b) and *uniformity* (case c) constitute two quite distinct processes, largely independent of one another. When, therefore, does each occur? First, it is necessary that in the two cases the representation of unity be made psychologically salient by associating the nature of the influence relationship, in particular the majority identity of the source, with the expectation within the debate of a consensual response linked to knowledge (for example, objective rather than subjective, cf. Gorenflo and Crano, 1989).

Second, it is necessary to recognize that a majority identity renders social comparison with the source salient (Moscovici, 1980). Influence can take the form of an explicit expression of consensus, in so far as the social comparison between source and target is favorable to the source. In this case, influence, as is typically the case in studies of majority influence, will be limited to an overt level, since this form of approach behavior reestablishes consensus and defuses the conflict. As for uniformity, our conclusions are derived from reasoning about the inverse case: influence takes the form of a reconstruction of the object when social comparison between target and source, unfavorable to the latter, rules out the expression of overt consensus while at the same time the representation of unity remains salient. Influence under these conditions is expressed not directly but indirectly.

In the experiment on the "cheese effect" we played with the nature of the stimulus. In front of the majority, an ambiguous stimulus (85 degrees) produced more search for consensus, while a totally unambiguous stimulus (90 degrees) imposed a process of uniformity. In the study we are going to present next, we only employed completely unambiguous perceptual stimuli so as to hold constant the strong degree of consensus in the anticipated response. We were concerned to exclude the possibility that direct majority responses could be due to the properties of the stimulus itself, something which the use of different angles (90 degrees and 85 degrees) did not allow us to control in the preceding experiment.

We attempted to induce a search for consensus via categorization of the majority, assuming that common category membership would be more likely to lead to the reestablishment of consensus (and this at an overt level) than to the construction of uniformity of the object (at a latent level). This outcome is possible through self-categorization (cf. Turner and Oakes, 1989), but it would be blocked in the case of an out-group majority with which one would not identify. Confronted with such a source, targets could then become engaged in a process of uniformity, and thus change at a latent level, without having conceded anything at the manifest level. Apart from this, we directly induced belief in either the unity or the plurality of responses, assuming that the above effects will only be observed when a principle of universality in perception is believed to cut across the categorical differences which otherwise exist.

On the basis of the preceding argument interaction effects between the two variables were predicted, the direction of effects varying according to the level of influence considered. We anticipated that within the framework of a representation of unity, the salience of one common category membership would lead more strongly to the reestablishment of consensus (thus at a manifest level), and that the salience of a differentiating category would, in contrast, lead to a construction of the uniformity of the object at a latent level.

The "Race" Experiment

One hundred eight subjects with a median age of twenty-two, of whom two-thirds were women and all were white, participated in the experiment which lasted about three quarters of an hour. They answered in groups of six to eight. The material and the procedure for this experiment are similar to those of the preceding experiment (Branstaetter et al., 1991) in all respects but one: the angles used in the experimental phase are all 90 degrees. The experiment was presented as bearing on either the universality or variation of perception across races, by suggesting to subjects that scientific work has demonstrated the existence of either a single form of perceptual apparatus or instead forms that vary across races. In the unity conditions the experimenter asserted "it appears evident today that there are no differences in perception between races, and that the visual apparatus is the same for all human beings. In brief, each individual perceives things in a manner that is independent of his or her race." In the plurality conditions, the experimenter claimed "it appears evident today that there are differences in perception between the races and that the visual apparatus is not the same for all human beings. In brief, each individual perceives things in a manner that varies according to his or her race."

Subjects were then exposed to pressure from a majority source (88 percent in all experimental conditions) either of the white race (in-group) or the black race (out-group). The results to be reported were derived from identical measures to the "cheese experiment" except for a test of embedded figures (inspired by the task used by Nemeth and Wachtler, 1983), in which subjects must twice determine which of four very complex figures contain a standard figure. Each time, two of the complex figures contain this standard figure. We regarded their performance as providing us with information about their degree of cognitive activation.

First of all it should be noted that the racial membership of the source was correctly perceived, a white race source being described as having a more white identity than a black race source. In addition, if subjects were as a whole disinclined to attribute the sources' responses to racial characteristics, they were nonetheless more inclined to do this with respect to a black than a white source, and more so in the conditions involving interracial differences in perception than in those in which universality of perceptual processes was claimed. In effect, the two experimental inductions were correctly decoded. Let us note next that a white source attracted more negative descriptions than a black source. Thus they were rated as less agreeable (p < .01), more rigid (p < .04), and as having less accurate vision (p < .02).

The effects of the two independent variables accumulate when subjects express the degree to which the responses of the source either help or disturb them. White sources disturb them more (7 means these responses disturb me; m = 3.80) than black sources (m = 3.35; p < .07), and do this more so when it is claimed that the perceptual process is the same for all humans (m = 3.85) than when it is claimed that there are interracial differences (m = 3.38; p < .07). The most disturbing source is therefore one with a white identity under the condition of similarity (m = 3.98), while a source with a black identity when perceptual differences are proposed is rated the most helpful (m = 3.02).

Let us now consider the estimates of the six 90 degree angles in the influence phase in which the source alleges that it is 50 degrees. The data are characterized by an interaction effect (p < .04). As table 10.2 shows, a single condition differed from the others, that in which the white majority responded in a context of similarity. In this condition, a smaller angle was estimated. Thus, there was more direct influence here than by the black source under otherwise similar circumstances (p < .02) or by the white source under the presupposition of racial differences in perception (p < .01).

As regards indirect effects, reflected in estimates of the weight of the cheese, these also give rise to an interaction (p < .04). As predicted, these are most marked for the black source when similarity across races is assumed (cf. table 10.2). Indirect influence here is significantly greater than for the black source when racial dissimilarity is assumed. This latter combination produced the least influence (p < .02), and less than the white source when dissimilarity was assumed (p < .08).

For the hidden figures task, we simply subtracted the number of figures wrongly identified (a maximum of four) from the number correctly identified (also a maximum of four). First there was an effect for racial membership of the source. A black source induced better cognitive functioning

Table 10.2   Mean Estimates of 90 Degree Angles, Mean Changes in Weight Estimates
(– Means more Influence), and Embedded Figures Test Performance
(Number of Correct Figures Minus Number of Incorrect Figures)

	White Majority		Black Majority	
	Similarity	Difference	Similarity	Difference
Angles	80.89	88.73	88.98	87.28
Cheese weight	+33.47	−27.83	−187.32	+296.13
Hidden figures	−0.48	+0.55	+1.04	+0.43

Table 10.3   Mean Change (in Grams) of the "Cheese" Weight (– Indicates a Positive Influence) as a Function of Subjects' Belief That There Is or Is Not a Single Correct Response

	Similarity	Difference
Subjects thinking there is a single correct response		
White majority	+201.44	–56.08
Black majority	–321.29	+373.01
Subjects thinking there is not only one correct response		
White majority	–123.31	+6.06
Black majority	–41.17	+176.54

with more correct responses ($F1/104 = 7.759$, $p < .01$). An interaction effect also appeared here ($F1/104 = 11.061$, $p < .01$). On this measure, the white source in the similarity condition induced significantly poorer performances than either a black source under the same condition ($t/104 = 4.326$, $p < .001$) or a white source in the condition of assumed interracial differences ($t/104 = 3.197$, $p < .01$).

On the basis of a complementary analysis, we divided our sample into two groups according to whether they thought there was (or was not) a single correct response to the task. Table 10.3 indicated for these two categories of subject, and as a function of experimental condition, mean changes in estimates of the weight of the "cheese." The results indicate a modest second-order interaction ($p < .10$), and decomposition of the interaction effect reveals that the first order interaction had its greatest effect on subjects who thought there was a single correct solution. For these subjects a black source under conditions of similarity induced a greater influence than a black source under conditions of difference ($p < .01$), but also more than a white source in the similarity condition ($p < .05$). As regards a white majority, this achieved more influence than a black majority source in the difference condition ($p < .08$), but did not differ significantly from a white majority source in the similarity condition. For those subjects who did not believe in the existence of a single correct response, there were no significant effects.

Thus, we now know a little bit more about the factors responsible for targets either reestablishing consensus without modifying their perception of the object or reestablishing uniformity at a latent level without conceding any manifest influence when confronted with majority dissension. First and most important, these contrasting dynamics can appear in a single context, in this case the one asserting the universality of perception (similarity across racial groups). This is the condition in which the representation of unity is explicitly induced. In this context, an intragroup majority induces a consensus effect which takes the form of greater manifest influence, while it is the out-group majority which is responsible for the latent uniformity effect.

Several indices suggest that subjects confronted with an intragroup majority will be preoccupied with reestablishing a consensual relation with their fellows, to the detriment of the accuracy of their perceptual estimates of the correct angle. For one thing, they felt more uncomfortable under such circumstances. The responses of a majority from their own group disturbed them more; they judged the majority more disagreeable and incorrect, and more stress provoking (Maass, 1987; Nemeth, 1986). This did not prevent these same subjects from conforming more strongly and overtly; they protested, but they consented. However, this was only the case if subjects were led to believe in the universality of perception. Clearly, majorities were only effective, even at the manifest level, in the condition where they appeared coercive. In contrast, the out-group majority concerned the targets less in terms of the latters' relation with the source, because they had no fear of being assimilated (Lemaine, 1975). They focused their attention more upon the object and perhaps on a search for indices capable of informing a more adequate vision. The best proof seemed to us to be that subjects faced with an out-group had a higher number of correct responses on the hidden figures task than those confronted with an in-group.

In Nemeth's (1986) terms, we are able to confirm that an intragroup context encourages a convergent mode of thinking oriented towards accounting for the majority response to the detriment of attention given to the characteristics of the task presented. In other words, it encourages a convergent form of functioning corresponding to the restoration of consensus. In an out-group context, subjects are more likely to become engaged in a divergent form of thinking in which overt opposition to the source's response does not prevent careful attention to the tasks, thus allowing a superior performance in the hidden figures task. This divergent process induced by the out-group culminates in the effect of constructivism (reduction in weight estimates) in which the new properties of the object ensure a uniformity of judgments, without targets having overtly adopted the majority point of view.

Consistent with our hypothesis concerning the representation of unity, one way of reestablishing this representation consists in redefining the object to make it conform to the interpretation given by the majority. It appears that two conditions must be fulfilled if this phenomenon of majority conversion is to be observed. One condition is that unity cannot be realized via the route of overt consensus because this ends with heterogeneity of points of view, this last strategy being the case with respect to an in-group but not an out-group. The other is that subjects believe the existence of a single and unique response is a requirement of being right, and thus that they are convinced of the unity of the object, of its necessary uniformity. This has already been demonstrated in the preceding experiment (Branstaetter et al.,

1991), because the search for consensus occurs in the context of an ambiguous stimulus, allowing variations in responses that are more or less correct, and because the latent creation of uniformity (via the majority) occurs in the context of a totally unambiguous stimulus. In the present experiment, we were also able to make a complementary analysis which showed that it is primarily subjects who are persuaded of the existence of a correct response, and not those who doubt this, who become most involved in this process of uniformity of the object.

Finally, in the out-group source condition, in which interracial differences were asserted, subjects not only refused to concur openly with the source. They also modified their responses at a latent level in the direction of an increased differentiation from the position deriving from the source. It is in this context of intergroup differentiation, where differences of response from the out-group are congruent with the categorization, that the subjects have actively reconstructed a differentiation at a latent level. They are unable to express their differentiation at a manifest level, being limited by evidence and the "good form" of the right angle. This effect is similar to the "latent polarization" or "counter conversion" reported by Moscovici and Doms (1982) and Personnaz and Personnaz (1987). Has one activated a modern form of racism (Dovidio and Gaertner, 1986), given that beyond their overtly egalitarian values, subjects have reintroduced differences even if these are symbolic? Another interpretation would be that the desire of subjects to respond to the source expresses a wish to influence it. Further experiments will perhaps allow us to distinguish between these possibilities. Be that as it may, reciprocal influence constitutes another possible means for individuals to reconstruct normative uniformity when this has been put into doubt in a context of unity.

Conclusions

The set of studies we have reported here allow us to draw some more general conclusions about processes of social influence. First of all, it must be conceded that majority and minority influence are complementary. Several researchers have argued that they are different processes, that they operate at different levels; one involves the most public level of judgment while the other operates in the sphere of private opinions. There is not the least paradox here in asserting that a minority can, to a greater extent than a majority, influence private or unconscious judgments at a much deeper psychological level within the individual. However, while not contradicting this initial intuition, our results require recognition that majorities can likewise have deeper effects, but under quite different conditions from those which apply for minorities and on the basis of radically different social-psychological dynamics. To appreciate this, one must consider another form of complementarity between these sources.

In effect, when one confronts subjects with information and supplies sufficient reasons for not taking it into account, a source described as majority can continue to exert influence in the domain of "facts" in which a single unanimous collective judgment is expected and when the judgment to be decided is considered as objective. Under the same conditions, minorities seem to be more effective in the domain of "opinions" or when judgments are legitimately subjective and diverse, which is to say within the context of a norm of preference. Thus, it is possible to draw conclusions about the most suitable type of source when the issue is to change beliefs that are scientifically contradicted by experts, or when the issue is one of changing opinions in a direction that would be more advantageous for the development of society.

Nonetheless, influence is not solely a function of credibility. The value of the source's judgment—which makes the others' judgment a frame of reference for the social psychological construction of a new reality—will in reality be determined by what might be considered a complex naive or common sense epistemology, according to which following the judgment of the majority sometimes constitutes the only way to be correct, the only means to be in the right, while on other occasions the only guarantee is to do other than the majority (which is not to do as the minority).

These two cases, however, have the same precondition: to influence latent judgments it is necessary to strip the source of its credibility and free it from the dynamics of identification and self-categorization. While this has the effect for minorities of removing the usual logic of resistance while they confront, for majorities this takes on the appearance of a high price they are willing to pay in order to convince. In the terms of the Elaboration Likelihood Model (Petty and Cacioppo, 1986) one might say that it leads to deep change by a central route, except that this is not accessed by the force of the argument but by the fact that the source is stripped of heuristics which it would otherwise be inclined to use in some way (Chaiken, 1987; Cialdini, 1987).

Finally, these influences do not seem to rest on the informational value of the source's response any more than they do on its power or its normative force. The rationality of influence appears here most strongly in the process of validation itself, rather than in the validity imputed to the responses. Individuals are not in the habit of ignoring majority judgments, nor are they accustomed to the possibility that a stimulus which they consider to be objective could allow more than one correct response requiring unanimity. The constructivist process which flows from this allows reestablishment of the validity of judgments shaken by the erroneous judgments of a legitimate source, via either consensus or uniformity according to the availability of heuristics. For the future, these effects, which were unanticipated in classic analyses of social influence, will enable us to study and explore the strength of beliefs, or at least to establish more explicitly the logic of social thought which causes adherence to false ideas (cf. Boudon, 1990; Moscovici, 1992).

References

Aebischer, V., and Oberlé, D. (1990). *Le Groupe en Psychologie Sociale*. Paris: Bordas.

Allen, V. L. (1965). Situational factors in conformity. In L. Berkowitz (Ed.), *Advances in Experimental Social Psychology*, vol. 2. New York: Academic Press.

Allen, V. L. (1975). Social support for nonconformity. In L. Berkowitz (Ed.), *Advances in Experimental Social Psychology*, vol. 8. New York: Academic Press.

Allen, V. L., and Wilder, D. A. (1980). Impact of group consensus and social support on stimulus meaning: mediation of conformity by cognitive restructuring. *Journal of Personality and Social Psychology*, 39, 1116–1124.

Asch, S. E. (1948). The doctrine of suggestion, prestige and imitation in social psychology. *Psychological Review*, 55, 250–276.

Asch, S. E. (1951). Effects of group pressure upon the modification and distortion of judgment. In H. Guetzkow (Ed.), *Groups, Leadership and Men*. Pittsburgh, PA: Carnegie Press.

Asch, S. E. (1952). *Social Psychology*. Englewood Cliffs, NJ: Prentice-Hall.

Asch, S. E. (1956). Studies on independence and conformity: A minority of one against an unanimous majority. *Psychological Monographs*, 70, no. 416.

Boudon, R. (1990). *L'art de se Persuader*. Paris: Fayard.

Brandstaetter, V., Ellemers, N., Gaviria, E., Giosue, F., Huguet, P., Kron, M., Morchain, P., Pujal, M., Rubini, M. Mugny, G., and Pérez, J. A., (1991). Indirect majority and minority influence: an exploratory study. *European Journal of Social Psychology*, 21, 199–211.

Cialdini, R. B. (1987). Compliance principles of compliance professionals: Psychologists of necessity. In M. P. Zanna, J. M. Olson, and C. P. Herman (Eds.), *Social Influence: The Ontario Symposium*, vol. 5. Hillsdale, NJ: Erlbaum.

Chaiken, S. (1987). The heuristic model of persuasion. In M. P. Zanna, J. M. Olson, and C. P. Herman (Eds.), *Social Influence: The Ontario Symposium*, vol. 5. Hillsdale, NJ: Erlbaum.

Crutchfield, R. S. (1955). Conformity and character. *American Psychologist*, 10, 191–198.

Deutsch, M., and Gerard, H. B. (1955). A study of normative and informational social influence upon individual judgment. *Journal of Abnormal and Social Psychology*, 51, 629–636.

Di Vesta, F. J. (1959). Effect of confidence and motivation on susceptibility to informational social influence. *Journal of Abnormal and Social Psychology*, 5, 204–209.

Dovidio, J. F., and Gaertner, S. L. (1986). *Prejudice, Discrimination and Racism.* Orlando: Academic Press.

Festinger, L. (1950). Informal social communication. *Psychological Review*, 57, 271–282.

Festinger, L. (1954). A theory of social comparison processes. *Humana Relations*, 7, 117–140.

Friend, R., Rafferty, Y., and Bramel, D. (1990). A puzzling misinterpretation of the Asch "conformity" study. *European Journal of Social Psychology*, 20, 29–44.

Goethals, G. R. (1972). Consensus and modality in the attribution process: The role of similarity and information. *Journal of Personality and Social Psychology*, 21,84–92.

Gorenflo, D. W., and Crano, W. D. (1989). Judgemental subjectivity/objectivity and locus of choice in social comparison. *Journal of Personality and Social Psychology*, 57, 605–614.

Hogg, M. A., and Abrams, D. (1988). *Social Identifications: A Social Psychology of Intergroup Relations and Group Processes.* London: Rutledge.

Hogg, M. A., and Turner, J. C. (1987). Social identity and conformity: A theory of referent informational influence. In W. Doise and S. Moscovici (Eds.), *Current Issues in European Social Psychology*, vol. 2. Cambridge: The University Press.

Hovland, C. I., Lumsdaine, A. A., and Sheffield, D. F. (1949). *Experiments of Mass Communication.* Princeton, NJ: Princeton University Press.

Kaiser, C. (1989). Consistance diachronique et contextes normatifs dans l'influence minoritaire. Doctoral diss., University of Geneva.

Kelman, H. C. (1958). Compliance, identification and internalization, three processes of attitude change. *Journal of Conflict Resolution*, 2, 51–60.

Lemaine, G. (1975). Dissimilation and differential assimilation in social influence (situations of "normalization"). *European Journal of Social Psychology*, 5, 93–120.

Levine, J. M., and Russo, E. M. (1987). Majority and minority influence. In C. Hendrick (Ed.), *Group Processes.* Newbury Park, CA: Sage.

Maass, A. (1987). Minorites et processus de conversion. In S. Moscovici and G. Mugny (Eds.), *Psychologie de la Conversion.* Cousset: DelVal.

Maass, A., and Clark, R. D., III. (1984). The hidden impact of minorities: Fourteen years of minority influence research. *Psychological Bulletin*, 95, 428–450.

Maass, A., and Volpato, C. (1989). Theoretical perspectives on minority influence: Conversion vs divergence? Paper presented at the Third Workshop on Minority Influence, Perugia, Italy.

Maass, A., West, S. G., and Cialdini, R. B. (1987). Minority influence and conversion. In C. Hendrick (Ed.), *Group Processes.* Newbury Park, CA: Sage.

Mackie, D. M. (1987). Systematic and nonsystematic processing of majority and minority persuasive communications. *Journal of Personality and Social Psychology*, 53, 41–52.

Milgram, S. (1974). *Obedience to Authority*. New York: Harper and Row.

Moscovici, S. (1972). L'homme en intéraction: Machine à répondre ou machine à inférer? In S. Moscovici (Ed.), *Introduction á la Psychologie Sociale*, vol. 1. Paris: Larousse.

Moscovici, S. (1976). *Social Influence and Social Change*. London: Academic Press.

Moscovici, S. (1980). Toward a theory of conversion behaviour. In L. Berkowitz (Ed.), *Advances in Experimental Social Psychology*, vol. 13. New York: Academic Press.

Moscovici, S. (1985). Social influence and conformity. In G. Lindzey and E. Aronson (Eds.), *The Handbook of Social Psychology*, vol. 2. New York: Random House.

Moscovici, S. (1992). The psychology of scientific myths. In M. Von Cranach, W. Doise, and G. Mugny (Eds.), *Social Representations and the Social Bases of Knowledge: Proceedings of the 1st Congress of the Swiss Society of Psychology*. Bern: Huber.

Moscovici, S., and Doms, M. (1982). Compliance and conversion in a situation of sensory deprivation. *Basic and Applied Social Psychology*, 3, 81–94.

Moscovici, S., and Lage, E. (1978). Studies in social influence IV: Minority influence in a context of original judgments. *European Journal of Social Psychology*, 8, 349–365.

Moscovici, S., and Mugny, G. (Eds.). (1987). *Psychologie de la Conversion*. Cousset: Del Val.

Moscovici, S., Mugny, G., and Pérez, J. A. (1984–85). Les effets pervers du déni (par la majorité) des opinions d'une minoritié. *Bulletin de Psychologie*, 38, 803–812.

Moscovici, S., and Personnaz, B. (1980). Studies in social influence V: Minority influence and conversion behaviour in a perceptual task. *Journal of Experimental Social Psychology*, 16, 270–282.

Moscovici, S., and Personnaz, B. (1986). Studies on latent influence using spectrometer method I: Psychologization effect upon conversion by a minority and a majority. *European Journal of Social Psychology*, 16, 345–360.

Mugny, G. (1984). Compliance, conversion and the Asch paradigm. *European Journal of Social Psychology*, 14, 353–368.

Mugny, G., Butera, F., Pérez, J. A., and Huguet, P. (1993). Les routes de la conversion: influences minoritaires et majoritaires. In J. L. Beauvois, R. V. Joule, and J. M. Monteil (Eds.), *Perspectives Cognitives et Conduites Sociales*, vol. 4. Neuchatel, Paris: Delachaux et Niestlé.

Mugny, G., and Doise, W. (1979). Niveaux d'analyse dans l'étude expérimentale des processus d'influence sociale. *Information sur les Sciences Sociales*, 18(6), 819–876.

Mugny, G., Maggi, J., Leoni, C., Gianninazzi, M., Butera, F., and Pérez, J. A. (1991). Consensus et stratégies d'influence. *Revue Internationale de Psychologie Sociale*, 4, 403–420.

Mugny, G., and Pérez, J. A., (1991). *The Social Psychology of Minority Influence.* Cambridge: Cambridge University Press.

Nemeth, C. (1986). Differential contributions of majority and minority influence. *Psychological Review*, 93, 23–32.

Nemeth, C., and Staw, B. M. (1989). The trade of social control and innovation in groups and organization. In L. Berkowitz (Ed.), *Advances in experimental social psychology*, vol. 22. New York: Academic Press.

Nemeth, C., and Wachtler, J. (1983). Creative problem solving as a result of majority vs minority influence. *European Journal of Social Psychology*, 13, 45–55.

Paicheler, G. (1988). *The Psychology of Social Influence.* Cambridge: Cambridge University Press.

Papastamou, S. (1983). Strategies of minority and majority influences. In W. Doise and S. Moscovici (Eds.), *Current Issues in European Social Psychology*, vol. 1. Cambridge: Cambridge University Press–L.E.P.S.

Papastamou, S., Mugny, G., and Kaiser, C. (1980). Echec à l'influence minoritaire: La psychologisation. *Recherches de Psychologie Sociale*, 2, 41–56.

Pérez, J. A., Moscovici, S., and Mugny, G. (1991). Effets de résistance à une source experte ou minoritaire, et changement d'attitude. *Revue Suisse de Psychologie*, 50 (4), 260–267.

Pérez, J. A., and Mugny, G. (1989). Discrimination et conversion dans l'influence minoritaire. In J. L. Beauvois, R. V. Joule and J. M. Monteil (Eds.), *Perspectives Cognitives et Conduites Sociales*, vol. 2. Cousset: Del Val.

Pérez, J. A., and Mugny, G. (1990). Changement d'attitude, crédibilité et influence minoritaire: Interdépendance et indépendance de la comparaison sociale. *Revue Suisse de Psychologie*, 49, 150–158.

Pérez, J. A., and Mugny, G. (1992). Social impact of experts and minorities, and smoking cessation. In M. von Cranach, W. Doise, and G. Mugny (Eds.), *Social Representations and the Social Bases of Knowledge: Proceedings of the 1st Congress of the Swiss Society of Psychology.* Bern: Huber.

Pérez, J. A., Mugny, G., and Moscovici, S. (1986). Les effets paradoxaux du déni dans l'influence sociale. *Cahiers de Psychologie Sociale*, 32, 1–14.

Pérez, J. A., Mugny, G., and Roux, P. (1989). Evitement de la confrontation idéologique: Quelques déterminants psychosociaux des stratégies persuasives. *Revue Internationale de Psychologie Sociale*, 2, 153–163.

Pérez, J. A., Mugny, G., Roux, P., and Butera, F. (1991). Influences via la comparaison sociale, influences via la validation. In J. L. Beauvois, R. V. Joule and J. M. Monteil (Eds.), *Perspectives Cognitives et Conduites Sociales*, vol. 3. Cousset: Del Val.

Personnaz, B., and Personnaz, M. (1987). Un paradigme pour l'étude de la conversion. In S. Moscovici and G. Mugny (Eds.), *Psychologie de la Conversion.* Cousset: Del Val.

Petty, R. E., and Cacioppo, J. T. (1986). *Communication and Persuasion.* New York: Springer-Verlag.

Pollis, N. P., Montgomery, R. L., and Smith, T. G. (1975). Autokinetic paradigms: A reply to Alexander, Zucker and Brody. *Sociometry*, 38 (2), 358–373.

Robinson, W. P. (1972). *Language and Social Behavior*. Baltimore and Hardmondsworth: Penguin.

Rule, B. G., and Bisanz, G. L. (1987). Goals and strategies of persuasion: A cognitive schema for understanding social events. In M. P. Zanna, J. M. Olson and C. P. Herman (Eds.), *Social influence: The Ontario Symposium*, vol. 5. Hillsdale, NJ: Erlbaum.

Sperling, H. G. (1952). An experimental study of some psychological factors in judgment. In S. E. Asch (Ed.), *Social Psychology*. Englewood Cliffs, NJ: Prentice-Hall.

Turner, J. C. (1991). *Social Influence*. Buckingham: Open University Press.

Turner, J. C., Hogg, M., Oakes, P. J., Reicher, S. D., and Wetherell, M.S. (1987). *Rediscovering the Social Group: A Self-Categorization Theory*. Oxford: Basil Blackwell.

Turner, J. C., and Oakes, P. (1989). Self-categorization theory and social influence. In P. B. Paulus (Ed.), *The Psychology of Group Influence*, 2nd ed. Hillsdale, NJ: Erlbaum.

Wegner, D. M., Schneider, D. J., Carter, S., III, and White, L. (1987). Paradoxical effects of thought suppression. *Journal of Personality and Social Psychology*, 53, 5–13.

Wilder, D. A. (1977). Perception of groups, size of opposition, and social influence. *Journal of Experimental Social Psychology*, 13, 253,268.

CHAPTER ELEVEN

COLLECTIVE MOVEMENTS AND MINORITY INFLUENCE: THE PROCESSES OF SOCIAL INFLUENCE BEYOND THE CONFINES OF EXPERIMENTAL GROUPS

Giovanna Petrillo

The study of the processes of social influence has received renewed impulse over the last twenty years in the perspective of minority influence towards social change and innovation, through the "genetic perspective" proposed by S. Moscovici (1976). In the present state of things, we have a vast amount of research which, for the most part, supports the hypothesis of a dual model of influence (minority vs. majority). Our body of knowledge, especially in certain particular areas, has now attained a high degree of systematization and enjoys sound support from experimental-type forms of verification.[1]

From a theoretical point of view, this progress has been brought about also by going beyond a prevalently cognitive approach to the study of mental processes involved in social influence and by assuming a socio-cognitive approach. The latter has been developed largely through the contribution made by those studies into minority influence which have illustrated the processes of social categorization and their implications for identity. According to this latter approach, the mental processes operating within both the source and target of influence are considered as expressions of subjects caught up in certain situations of intergroup interaction, in that

they themselves belonged to groups which were holders of certain normative, ideological value and representational systems.

A significant contribution to the advancement towards higher levels of
explanation (Doise, 1982) and to the statement of an approach in a socio-
cognitive key has been made by applying the genetic perspective to the
analysis of concrete processes of influence, actually taking place in historically determined socio-cultural contexts, which have been interpreted as
activated primarily by minority social movements and representatives of
proposals for change regarding specific social objects.

Before dwelling more analytically on some of these studies and
discussing the main findings thereof, we think it expedient to reflect on the
relationships existing between the theory of social minority influence and
certain methodological choices. In our opinion, the implicit assumption of a
"minimal" conception of the group and, more in general, the construction
of laboratory groups, of which frequent use has been made in the study of
processes of minority influences, even though they may have allowed
research to proceed at quite a lively pace and with the rigor of experimental
method, are still responsible for a certain reductionism in the way of
operationalizing the relationship dynamics between minorities and majorities, by diminishing the heuristic relevance of the genetic model of influence. The merit of certain field studies, even amid the fàmiliar difficulties of
not having full control over the variables at play, is that of having adopted
real social groups as protagonists of the processes of influence, contributing
thereby, in a specifically psycho-social sense, to the evolution of research on
the processes of minority influence.

Theoretical and Methodological Questions

If researchers generally agree in stating that more thorough
consideration should be given to the influence exerted by certain methodological choices regarding the understanding of the phenomena under
examination, it appears so much more the case in the area of the processes
of minority influence. In laboratory studies, with ''perceptual'' or ''cognitive''
tasks, the implications associated with the subjects' group membership prior
to experimentation seem, on the whole, to have been less investigated. They
are sometimes called on within the experimental situation through minority
groups, symbolically present as signatories of minorities' messages, by
introducing with this modality dimensions of time and space which, in a
certain sense, transcend the strict limits set by the experimental condition.
Nevertheless, in spite of the efforts to go beyond the here and now actuality
of the laboratory, especially when investigating the deferred and long-term
effects of minority influence (one may well think of the studies on conver-

sion), there evidently exist strong limits to the understanding of the phenomena of influence at the time when they are articulated along the wider dimensions of time and space.

Thus, although the accumulative process of results is really relevant, a strong desire is felt by many for getting over the laboratory or, at any rate, for its integration into the types of research in which minorities and majorities are physically present, within a real dimension of space (within a social context and a situation of "natural" interaction) and time (existence of a group history, evolution and projection of group dynamics and of the members themselves towards the future), going beyond even a "minimal assumption" of the group which is at the basis of all experimental research (Maass and Clark, 1984; Mackie, 1987; Petrillo, 1987). It has been affirmed (Chaiken and Stangor, 1987), in fact, that research that took real groups into account would provide better understanding (at any rate, it is hoped, it would have a greater degree of approximation to reality) of the complexity expressed by the demand for social control and innovation (Allen, 1985; Levine and Moreland, 1985).

Such critical observations seem to us so much more pertinent, especially if referred to minority influence (see also Levine, 1989). In this area, in fact, the definition of minority group refers more particularly to a qualitative criterion rather than to a merely quantitative criterion of differentiation, as has clearly been indicated by S. Moscovici (1976) in the absence of power. On the contrary, the strongly hierarchically stratified character of the relationship between the minority and the majority has been often neglected (see also Apfelbaum, 1979), so that the asymmetrical relationship between the groups has often been operationalized somewhat in terms of a simple difference in the production of responses, overlooking the hierarchically stratified character of this difference. Beyond the theoretical concept of minority, the group which has been assumed in the experimental studies on social influence was composed of minority and majority subjects in function of assignments often prompted by the experimenter through the artificial contrasting of "ingenuous" with confederates of the experimenter, or on the basis of the preferences expressed regarding certain tasks still devised by the experimenter himself.[2] We are, therefore, far from considering group subject memberships as memberships of social groups, that is, groups in which the interpersonal relationships are marked by certain levels of interdependence, activity-sharing, codes and objectives prior to experimental selection and differentation.

Consequently sometimes in minority influence research that "social vacuum"—as I would describe it in the words of Tajfel (1972b), and which is found in so many laboratory studies—is also reproposed. More generally these considerations of a methodological character lead us to pose briefly some more general questions, which affect significant aspects of social minority influence.

First, the high social relevance of the object of influence in the daily lives of the subjects involved in those studies which make use of paradigms we have termed "cognitive" manages only in part, in our view, to bridge this gap. This also involves intrinsic and not purely instrumental attention to the content of influence and the historic consideration of the subjects involved, in that they are individuals or groups not isolated in any way from the social fabric, but are instead immersed in it, starting from their membership.

Secondly, in the experimental research the shared character of certain strategies of influence, even if among subjects belonging to a restricted minority, and of determined forms of resistance to influence on the part of the population, has not been duly considered. To insist on the social sharing of strategies of exertion or of defense against influence means reproposing the centrality of the group in the study of social influence (Turner, 1987; Turner and Oakes, 1989). More specifically, in the minority perspective (Worchel, 1989), the group must not be understood as a simple aggregate (passive minorities or dominated groups), nor as a collection of singular individuals (majorities or dominant groups), but as an organized whole, as a system of interactive individuals with their own history, shared aims and understandings.[3]

Finally a further consequence of the adoption of minimal assumption of the group in the area of minority influence is the parenthesizing of the social character of change, the individual dimension of which is brought to the forefront in terms of acceptance of new responses (whether they be perceptual products of either thought or discourse), putting aside a possibility of minority incidence in terms of petitioning for changes at the level of collective identities and of the creation or modification of social representations, which may act as prelude to innovations in the network of social relationship and even of aspects of a normative order of a given society.

The little available research so far carried out in the field has taken into account highly articulated and complex subjects, such as collective movements set in extremely meaningful processes of change (student questions, the status of women, questions of psychiatry) that have developed along dimensions extending through time and space. The use of research paradigms having certain collective subjects as protagonists, which we might call "paradigms of maximal groups," certainly brings about considerable difficulties, especially in the sphere of field research. If the latter does not offer the same rigor as encountered in experimental research, presenting itself moreover more often as descriptive research, it still affords the exploration of different aspects of social influence as explained above.

Field Research: The Influence of Collective Movements

J. P. Di Giacomo's research (1985) is the first field research that was inspired by minority influence theory. He has focused on social representations (Moscovici, 1981; Farr and Moscovici, 1984), understood as universes of meaning impregnated with evaluation components, typical forms of naif thinking, determined by the system of social memberships and connected with the processes of social categorization and social comparison. The effect of influence is not viewed as a result which reflects mechanically the variation of the stimulus made by the source, but as a result of the re-elaboration of the elements of meaning contained in the minority message, in the light of the nuclei of representations which are owned by the target of influence. The modalities of decoding the minority message and the same image of the source of influence are referred back to the interpretative schemata which are already operative in the subjects, considered as members of definite social categories.

The research into the "Protest Movement against the 10,000" (Di Giacomo, 1985), based on the conflict between the Belgain government and the Belgian student movement that broke out following a tax increase dispute, has shed light on the structures and main contents of social representations that the student population had both of itself, of the power and of the student action organizing committee, and on being exposed to the influence of the student movement. The failure of minority action in trying to promote a general antigovernment strike, which even found student consensus in its objective of contesting the tax increases, is explained in terms of strongly biased and ideologically described attitudes and systems of opinion that are not presented as pure cognitive products all operating within the subjects, but rather as shared products which find a particularly hard and change-resistant element in the representation of one's future identity, in the mental anticipation of the adult self. The subjects were first examined with the free association method, using word-stimulus devised a priori by the researcher, and their subsequent responses underwent multidimensional analysis (Kruskal). The students proved to be close to the student committee in that they were demonstrators, left wing, allies of the workers and powerless, yet nearer the power system in that they represented themselves as future managers, conservative and allied to the power.

However the main motive of interest of this research consists, from a theoretical point of view, in the focusing on the evaluation components of social representations, from the specific social influence point of view its merit is found above all in having shown how influence at the behavioral level can come about and can even be anticipated by keeping an adequate check on the systems of representations of the target subject of influence.

These then, rather than passive receivers of messages, are mutually interacting subjects and active interpreters of the messages to which they are exposed through a well-articulated and operative evaluation system, which acts as filter for one's interpretation of the environment and as a guide to behavior.[4]

Two other pieces of field research have been carried out in Italy that are more directly focused on minority influence. The first interprets the process of confluence of the Italian Women's Union (U.D.I.) within the Women's Movement (Movimento delle Donne) at the end of the seventies as a result of the consistent style adopted by the feminist groups (Crespi and Mucchi-Faina, 1988). The analysis of the interviews with different exponents of the feminist groups and of the party groups, together with the analysis of the documents produced by the different groups taken into examination on the theme of voluntary interruption of pregnancy, has highlighted the importance of consistency in the formal aspects of communication (styles of argument), as well as the importance of superordinate goals for the breaking down of barriers set up by the game of political memberships and for the construction of a new shared social identity (Mucchi-Faina, 1987).

The effect of influence has been also interpreted in terms of conversion. In fact, by subjecting to an analysis of their lexical components the minority and majority documents produced in the various phases of the process of influence, it has been seen that influence is consequent on periods characterized by strong conflictuality and is anticipated by a phase of latent influence, during which the appropriation of the specific nuclei of meaning of the minority message on the part of the target influence takes place through a dissociation at the awareness level between the content and the source of the message (Petrillo, 1988c).

The second piece of research is also presented as a retrospective investigation into the process of influence already taken place. The legislation currently in force in Italy regarding mental illness has been interpreted as a result of a long process of influence which has as leading actors all those who have been inspired by the movement of "alternative psychiatry" (Democratic Psychiatry). By utilizing the historic method, three phases have been distinguished in the ten years prior to the modification of the law, which are considered as various phases of the same process of influence (Petrillo, 1989). The analysis of lexical correspondences has been applied to texts found in the various phases, concentrating particularly on: (1) the image of conflict emerging in the national and local press of both government and opposition; (2) the central nuclei of identity which the movement gives itself at its birth, immediately on being formally constituted with a name and a statute; and (3) the strategy of influence adopted by the main exponents of the movement by using the press, in view of the legislative change. This research has shown that the tendencies towards differentation and convergence are, in fact, present together, even if regulated in function of the interlocutor chosen ad hoc (within or outside the group) and therefore in function of the effect of influence pursued by the minority. The moment in which the minority group ascribes itself its own physiognomy and is set up as an alternative unitary movement, distinguishing itself markedly from the out-group, the articulations within the group are forcefully made clear. While the moment in which the group appeals to the public at large to win its supports in favor of the closure of psychiatric hospitals, it presents itself, albeit composite, tightly knit and coherent. This influence is interpreted in terms of consistency of argumentations, which creates an image of the minority as being determined to reach its objectives, autonomous, coherent and single-minded, altruistic and open to discussion.

Rather than proceed to a more scrupulous illustration of the above-mentioned research (we are compelled for the sake of brevity to refer to the bibliographical references for a deeper insight into the methodology and findings of these research works), we continue by reconsidering some points mentioned above, in order to summarize more effectively the main contributions and suggestions made by these studies for our understanding of minority influence.

The Contents of Social Influence

Experimental research that is inspired by the minority perspective has worked hard in exploring and verifying the formal aspects of influence because of their high explanatory power (Moscovici, 1976; Mugny, 1982). Yet Moscovici himself has suggested that a consistent minority brings about an inference of correctness regarding the source (Moscovici and Nemeth, 1974) from the influence target that has become less sure of its positions (see the same post-experimental interviews in Asch's experiment, 1952, reinterpreted by Moscovici in favor of the effect of synchronic consistency), and that the adoption of a certain style of behavior somehow transmits or, at any rate, is decoded by the majority in term of information about the transmitter and about the object of influence itself. So it transpires that some elements of "content" of the minority position emerge, although overlooked in the interpretation of the results, in various experimental designs, which have operationalized in different manners the behavioral styles[5] or the negotiation styles.[6]

This content, so often rejected as not being a significant factor in social minority influence, seems therefore to be reproposed from time to time under different guises, but appears more explicitly in the research carried out in the field. Here minority behavior is studied in terms of

215

discursive productions during the different phases of the process of influence.

The consistency of the styles of argumentations or of certain key words, demonstrated with textual analysis, is made explicit not only through its quantitative components (in terms of recurrence of the single lexical items and certain combinations of discursive elements) but also in its qualitative ones. In these studies the effect of influence is resubmitted to a thorough examination of speech-form and content, which analyzes not only how the minority message is constructed and presented to the majority, but also what is said, namely, the very content of the communication itself. In fact, by arguing in certain ways, the minority still produces sense (Paicheler, 1987). This production of sense, which is always performed in the processes of social influence, especially if these refer to opinions, attitudes, and evaluations, and which in minority influence is characterized as a product of a new sense, is realized not only through the message formulated by the source, but rather by the integration performed by the target of the message produced here and now: (1) with the other messages produced by the same source on other occasions or by other sources; (2) through the system of social groupings; and (3) with the more general schemes of interpreting the world.

We cannot overlook the extreme care that the minority places not only in its choice of channels and forms of expression, but also in its choice of preferential elements such as "central nuclei of meaning," as irrefutable parts of discourse which typify the message and characterize the very minority identity itself. The formal and content choices form an integrative part of the totality of the minority influence strategy. In research into the question of psychiatry may be seen what role has been played by the press in the process of influence, which may be summed up in having made a positive contribution towards offering, through information regarding contents and source, a positive image of the new growing psychiatry (as being socially involved; competent, professional and altruistic, caught up in processes of modernization, and closely bound to the international drive for innovation, etc.), in contrast with the power represented by the private asylum managers, by operators fixed to medical-type interpretations and reactionary towards their own role, by state and local administrators enticed by private interests and opposed to accepting the stimulus of innovation. Finally it has been seen how in the phase of influence more directly aimed towards reaching the final objective (the new law), this same minority has made use of space in the press to show to the outside world—that is, to the larger public, made up of nonspecialists—the key arguments for rejection of the past and for outlining the alternative. The new representation of the mentally ill and mental illness, as an expression of a status and of a widespread condition throughout a society which produces suffering and sufferer, only later to brand them and ghetto them into places falsely professing to be therapeutic, contains the essential coordinates for recodifying the past as a time of oppression, the present a time for taking a stand, and the future as a time for change.

In the research of the feminist movement, too, the effect of conversion has been demonstrated in terms of appropriation of the minority message. It has been seen that the great themes that through history have marked the condition of women in a negative sense—those of unwanted pregnancies and sexual violence—have been attached to the reflection proposed by the feminist groups temporally consistent among themselves with regard to the female body as an expropriated part of the self and sexuality not necessarily aimed towards reproduction. The more strained the structure of intergroup relationships grew, with contrasts sharpening even regarding the referendum compaign (the referendum on the voluntary interruption of pregnancy at 1978), the longer the influence continued. The dissociation between message and source, a typical mechanism of conversion processes, is evinced from the appropriation of the message by the majority group, which nevertheless, in the course of influence is said to be still outside the feminist movement. Although it is difficult for target subjects to break the strong links with their groups and their ideologized schemes of reference, since they structure not only their representations of reality, but also their identity, it does not mean the influence is not already operative. The dependence on the content in more or less lengthy time periods is susceptible to being translated into a new link and into the sharing of a new common identity. Paradoxically, the more the subjects are desirous of retaining their own independence in the course of interaction with the minority, the more they are setting the foundations for a new form of dependence.

On the whole, these elements induce us to affirm that it cannot be maintained that content represents a completely secondary element of minority influence. Here the classical theme of informative dependence is reproposed in completely new spectrum, by demanding other theoretical elaborations and verifications, of an experimental kind, too. In fact, it is no longer a question of contrasting the truth of one code against the falsity of another, for which information is had or otherwise once and for all, but of accepting the possibility of a pluri-codification of reality at a social level, which at the individual level will be able to lead even to the substitution of the perceptual code, in addition to the discursive one.[7] Access will not therefore be had to an unequivocally correct piece of information, but to a content–type piece of information differing both in lexis and in deeper argumentative structure.

Size, Status, and Social Support in Minority Influence

Other factors rarely examined in the area of minority influence (with a few exceptions: see Clark and Maass, 1990; Nemeth, Wachtler, and Edincott, 1977; and other later-quoted studies) include the size of the minority group, the status of its members, and the social support it receives once the clash with the majority is underway. These elements have however been further considered within the majority spectrum, in which they appear as key factors of influence. Research in the field has shown, in keeping with certain cues which are also found in certain laboratory studies (Mugny and Papastamou, 1980; Papastamou, 1983), the relative importance of these three factors in the perspective of minority influence.

In the works of field research which consider collective movements, the strength of the minority movements depends to a certain degree on its size and on its cohesion. One of the fundamental problems in the history of the setting up and evolution of these movements is represented by the avoidance of fragmentation, that is to say, of the total destruction of minority initiative and realities, which includes the risk of causing loss of strength and therefore one's incisiveness in the social context. The moment in which the single minorities begin a systematic comparison, they give themselves a common organization and common objectives, which moment is not by chance the time when the choice of a name and of a unitary program is made. These elements are accepted by mass media that are more careful of social ferment and are passed on to the general public with more or less positive evaluation connotations, aimed at inducing an interpretation of the new social entity as an element of disaggregation and disturbance, or as an element of innovation.

All this work of interpretation that begins with the quantitative data, aimed at bringing the attention back from the data statistics (how many they are) to the subjects who express them (who they are), leads us to take into consideration the two other above-mentioned factors. If in classical research on persuasive communication and social influence the role played by competence (Hollander, 1960) and by authority and leadership (Milgram, 1974; Haney, Banks, and Zimbardo, 1973; Hollander, 1958, 1964) has been shown, in minority influence research it has been demonstrated that competence and leadership do not play a role of primary importance (Moscovici and Nemeth, 1974; Mugny, 1982; Papastamou, 1985, 1986). Yet, since these experimental results are not definitive, their generalization about and reference to real life and to wider social dynamics are to be made with a certain degree of caution. It is not by chance that the exponents of the alternative psychiatry movement, signatories of articles in the press and members of the executive body of the movement, happen to be psychiatrists, directors of psychiatric hospitals almost always on the fringe of or outside the academic circuit and professional associations. These have obtained credit in their working contexts and among the public of nonspecialists not only for their courage in denunciation, personal exposure to sanctions, altruistic defense of the weaker members of society, but also for their capacity in attacking the academy on the grounds of scientific knowledge, of reexamining the epistemological presuppositions of psychiatric gnosology and of considering the situation of mental illness management within a historical perspective. Although the general public has received this debate only second hand from the press, the big questions of the dangers of the madman, of the therapeutic value of physical and chemical coercion and of the guardian role played by the medical and paramedical personnel, have all been fully reported and discussed. The old science and the new, medical and psycho-relational education, the old/new relationship between the question of psychiatry and various societal institutions are the more recurrent themes expressed by qualified minority sources, set in a debate of international importance. From among the minority some leaders clearly emerge, who not only influence the life of the groups but also exert a particularly significant role in the sense of structuring the minority image that is exposed to the world and who therefore bear a relevant weight in the processes of influence. On the contrary, in the feminist movement individual limelight was reduced in favor of the collective one, so that the documents always bear the group's signature. Thus we may argue that, though the presence of leaders in minority influence seems not essential, the importance of this factor would need further investigation.

Finally, social support (Doms, 1984; Doms and Van Avermaet, 1985; Clark, 1989) seems to play a role not only in majority but also in minority influence, favoring a direct influence. In fact the minority which receives support from some members of the majority can be perceived more easily as not completely different, which may inhibit to some degree the tendency to differentiate itself from the minority. The minority which receives the support of another minority can be perceived as more competent and the process of validation relating to the object of influence will be corroborated. Social support could also be useful to explain the results of experiments on double minority (Maass et al., 1982). Historically, the positive influence of single protest movements has benefited from the concomitant action of other movements, which have all been expressed to the utmost and not for mere chance during the same period of time (1968/78). Of extreme importance was also the support received from cultural, professional, worker, and political organizations.

All these factors propose a more general reflection which has been repeatedly developed in the last decade with reference to the possibility of integrating the models of social influence, which have been conceptualized as opposites (Moscovici, 1976; Maass, West, and Cialdini, 1987; Nemeth, 1985, 1986, 1987), into a unitary model (Latane and Wolf, 1981; Tanford and Penrod, 1984; Wolf, 1987).

Consistency Between Assimilation and Differentiation

Consistency, defined as "a tendency towards reducing variability in responses" (Moscovici, 1976), has often been operationalized in experimental research in such a way (the repetition of responses by one and the same minority or by several minorities) as to supply an implicit presupposition to all the experimental research which considers the minority source of influence as a kind of monolith; that is to say, a social entity always unchanged through time and internally undifferentiated. This is reinforced by the style of negotiation, in which flexibility appears as an expedient purely instrumental to influence.

These considerations lead one to consider more carefully, also in light of the contributions made by research in the field, the relationships existing between intragroup level and intergroups (in keeping with many other scholars, we maintain that social influence is a particularly fertile field of analysis in this sense), considering the studies on comparison processes and social categorization (Tajfel, 1972a, 1972b) and of construction of social identity (Tajfel, 1982; Tajfel and Turner, 1985). The investigation into the processes of conversion has amply shown the difficulty of identifying oneself with the minority (Moscovici and Paicheler, 1978; Moscovici and Mugny, 1987; Petrillo, 1988b), especially if the latter is an out-group. Yet this has brought it about that insistence is made on heterogeneity between source and target (intergroup differentiation) in the processes of social comparison, making this correspond with a high degree of homogeneity within the groups themselves (intragroup assimilation), the more so within the minority group, given its consistency.

Field research on the one hand confirms this tendency towards differentiation of the minority from the majority (and vice versa), especially in the radicalization of intergroup conflict, but does not confirm intragroup homologation, which corresponds to a level and schematized perception that is functional towards intergroup diversification in conflict, but which does not correspond to the real perception which subjects have of their own group and of themselves.

Research into the question of psychiatry has examined the evolution within the minority group more systematically. The password common to the different groups—"Down with the asylum: let's abolish the asylum"—has been the meeting point of an evolutionary journey that has involved the same minority. Being initially convinced that recovery of the asylum structures to their original therapeutic functions was possible (at the end of the sixties the objective of the orthodox minority was that of the "therapeutic community"), it later tried to associate the struggle against the asylum with the struggle outside it (in the first half of the seventies, the objective was that of an "open community," united to the students' and workers' protests on the territory). Finally, the minority aims at taking up an extreme standpoint to give back to society the responsibility for therapy which the same society had delegated—and relegated—to the asylum (heterodox minority).

Not only is this journey clearly distinguishable in a longitudinal perspective of an approach towards minority and the dynamics between the former and the majority. It has also been possible to come across the persistence of certain themes—to be summarized in a new general conception of mental disorder, not expressed in medical jargon but more in socio-relational terms—which however has not led to a total defeat of the minority discourses, at a synchronic level.

It can therefore be concluded that the trend towards differentiation pervades both intergroup relationships and intragroup ones. One can also agree with Tajfel that the greater is convergence towards common positions in the minority, the stronger the contrast with the majority. Yet this does not appear incompatible with a certain degree of intergroup articulation which, in addition to being fundamental for the conservation of an identity for the single individuals, can prove functional for the construction of a flexible image of the minority group, and can in fact contribute to the development of a possible relationship of influence with the majority.

The question of articulation within the minority group complementary to its consistency leads to a theoretical reconsideration of the relationships existing between theories of social influence and theories of social identity, which is translated into a reflection not only on the margins of identification that are possible between target and source of influence, but also between subjects that are part of the same group. These margins of the interindividual differentiation existing at intragroup level can be one of the explanatory elements for the processes of change within the group (also a minority one), and a point on which the minority purposely tries to exert influence in order to set off processes of disassimilation within the target of influence, with the aim of favoring an approach towards its own positions. The results of our research induce us to retain that the consistency of a group and sound development of the social dimension of identity in the subjects who belong to it are perfectly compatible with the development of a personal identity, being expression of the feeling of uniqueness and historic continuity of each subject and of his need to differentiate himself.[8]

This key to interpretation appears to us so much more fruitful in the perspective of social minority influence. If it is true the distinctive element of minority is its difference, why then should this trend toward differentiation (Personnaz, 1984), which the minority charges with positive value, represent a value only in relation to the majority and not also in relation to other minorities? A certain personalization of the innovatory proposal is retained and exploited as an element that does not concur with the emergence of an individual in potential competition with the social aspect (as in the individualization within the majority), but which sees the individual dimension exalted just when the same social dimension best expresses itself.

The Social Context: The Norm of Difference

Moscovici has hypothesized, since the first systematic formulations of the genetic model (1976), that the existence of a certain range of norms within a historically given social context must not necessarily be understood as a product of the processes of influence. On the contrary, the norms existing in a certain social order have a specific weight of influence in that they precede the process of influence and constitute determinants of the outcome of such a process. Change and innovation are made possible in fact by a collection of factors, some of which are not the exclusive property of psychology. Social norms lie at the point of intersection between various disciplines, such as cultural anthropology and sociology. Social psychology, which has for a long time neglected social norms, must still consider them if it wishes to comprehend fully problems of change and innovation.

The more explored norms, on the promptings of Moscovici, have been those of preference, objectivity, and originality. Although Moscovici has stated that it is highly likely that other norms contribute towards structuring the social context in which the dynamics of influence are set, research has not yet been carried out into normative factors except in these directions.

In our view, a norm that has been progressively developing during the last thirty years and that most markedly characterizes post-industrial societies in our historic epoch is the diversity norm, which is accompanied by the value of equal dignity. Without going far back in time to retrace its remote historic roots, we can observe how this new norm of equal dignity in diversity has gradually gone on substituting that of homologating equality, a cover up of every type of diversity. According to this norm all individuals or groups have the same rights, which are then to be recognized and guaranteed to them not in that they are all equal but in that they are all different and equally worthy of social consideration. It is precisely the specificity of their condition that is to be safeguarded and evaluated as a collective as well as individual good. It is a question of a norm now so widespread, following also the influence of minority groups (e. g., defense of civil rights, ecologists), that it extends nowadays even to consider potentially every form of life and every living organism. A consequence of the adoption of this norm is that societies are invested with the responsibility of safeguarding not only those parts of society which are still oppressed and underdeveloped, but also animals and the environment (obviously, with remarkable intercultural and interepoch variations).

This widespread sensitivity towards the rights of the weaker can be understood as an aspect of this normative factor which pervades our societies and which favors the action of those subjects or groups which differentiate themselves in that they are minority, but to which, as a rule, the same respect and attention are to be given which are given to others, being exponents of the majority part of society. And this is so not because one expects them to be in the right or that they have knowledge of the truth, but because the difference assumes a positive value. This norm seemed to us operative in minority influence in real contexts, as an element of Zeitgeist (Paicheler, 1979) that has contributed to bringing about changes in the way hoped for by the minorities considered in this research. Women's rights and the rights of the mentally ill have been affirmed also in that they are supported by a social norm that recognized the legitimacy of the claim by those who are different to receive some social consideration, in the wake of the successful gains of the movements (we may think of the workers and students) that helped to break down the preexisting cultural schemes.

Conclusion

In this chapter we have tried to direct the reader's attention to findings taken from field research that converge with those of some experimental studies. First, these studies show once again the importance of conflict and change considered:

a. not in purely intra-individual and interpersonal terms, but more especially in terms of intragroup and intergroup relationships;
b. as the result of an evolutionary journey, in which the development of influence dynamics is integrated with the development of an individual, social, and collective identity; and
c. directed towards the production of innovation in relation to objects of high social relevance.

These three orders of considerations present problems that are characterized, with regard to majority influence, not so much for the exclusiveness of certain factors or for their greater or lesser recurrence in purely quantitative terms, as for their intrinsic qualitative difference. Thus factors such as behavior style and content of the minority position, size, status and social support of the minority, as well as the same cognitive and motivational processes that the former activates in the target of influence, are referred back to its difference that, once elaborated in positive terms at more or less deep levels, thanks also to a normative context that makes a social norm of the difference, is productive of further differentiations.

Our insistence on a historic approach to social influence has led us to stress (in accordance with Worchel, 1989) the complexity of influence in function of the articulation between multiple social memberships and multiple levels of mediation in the symbolic construction of a reality of representation. The historically recurrent processes on influence of minority groups appear to us as being traceable to a theoretical model in which the genesis of influence, so outlined by S. Moscovici (1976) in his bi-phased model, integrates with the genesis of the identity of the group as active minority, shaping itself in its entirety as a multiphased genetic model of the following type:

> First phase—Beginning of the crises of the majority characterized by widespread microconflictuality and by a continually widening gulf between the level of the institutions and the fabric of the civil society.
>
> Second phase—The extension of conflictuality, which becomes more explicit, frontal, and direct. It is functional for social differentiation and for the construction of a separate minority identity.
>
> Third phase—Consolidation of minority identity. The group gives itself a name and its own forms of organization, expression and action.
>
> Fourth phase—This is a phase of tension to the realization of the alternative, in which the minority tries to translate the ideal clash into a program of struggle with fixed times and places and tries to extend the social importance of the struggle by removing strata of consensus from the dominant power system. It is the operational phase of real influence that often determines the outcome of a latent influence.
>
> Fifth phase—Becoming aware of influence by the target. This can lead to a restructuring of the self and a conscious choice of the change of the social points of reference, bringing about a new definition of identity in relation to new social memberships.
>
> Sixth phase—Crisis of minority group followed by extinction or restructuring on new objectives.

In this model, after a first phase that in a certain way defines the preconditions for influence, a sort of alternation is established between phases of influence development (phases two through four) and phases of minority and majority identity development (phase three through five), closely connected amongst themselves within a cycle that, beginning with a phase of destabilization, closes with a phase of social stabilization, susceptible to being transferred into a new dynamic of influence at a different level.

Numerous questions still remain open, above all, those relating both to the innovatory scope of the processes of influence, which, in the long term, seem destined to bring about changes in the social order and power system, and also to cross-stabilization phases and be translated into new majority orthodoxies (Lemaine, 1974). The original innovatory significance of this can fuse so completely with the most everyday practices and beliefs as to flow off to a place in the collective and individual memory so remote as to seem a far distant echo and as to yield up to attempts of counter-reform.

Notes

1. Further important headway has been made during this past decade in the study of denial (Mugny, 1982; Mugny and Perez, 1986), identification and conversion (Moscovici, 1980; Moscovici and Paicheler, 1978; Moscovici and Mugny, 1987).

2. It is not the case in those studies wherein minorities are such with the regard to the production of minority meaning in the wider social context. One may consider Paicheler's studies on the influence of Zeitgeist of 1976, 1977; or Maass, Clark, and Haberkorn's studies on double minority, 1982.

3. For this typology of experimental groups, see Lorenzi-Cioldi (1988).

4. Another piece of research by the same Di Giacomo (1985) is based on the Walloons as a group susceptible to being influenced by nationalistic movements. However the link with the study of minority influence of this last research is less direct and we find present in it an ambition to predicting the possible outcomes of minority groups initiatives within a social frame in ferment and in presence of a complex system of memberships. Interest in the action of nationalistic groups is also at the center of Orfali's research (1990).

5. Consider consistency as coherence (Nemeth, Swedlund, and Kanki 1974), and extremism as a factor favoring indirect influence, the boomerang effect or polarization (Moscovici, 1985; Paicheler and Bouchet, 1973; Paicheler, 1976, 1977, 1979), accompanied by a perception of minority as being not very pleasant, or dogmatic or strongly intent on influencing (Mugny, 1982; Papastamou, 1983), autonomy (Nemeth and Wachtler, 1973), and involvement as being different from personal interest (Maass et al., 1982). Consider also the research interested in the processes of intragroup communication (Guillon and Personnaz, 1983), which have showed that the conflict between the parts will lead to a taking up of a central position by the minority in the network of communicative exchanges, which will bring the attention to focus on the "new" arguments (see also the studies on originality quoted in Mucchi-Faina, Maass, and Volpato, 1991).

6. Consider also the studies on the forms of resistance to minority influence in

which against the psychologized perception of the minority on the part of the target as inhibiting factor of influence is set the facilitating effect of concentration on the content of the minority message (Papastamou, Mugny, and Kayser, 1980), or perception in a psycho-political key of the minority source (Papastamou, 1983); one may also think of the annulment of the negative effect of rigidity when the minority is not made up of a single individual (Mugny and Papastamou, 1980), interpreted as a result of different cognitive processes (comparison/validation).

7. See Moscovici and Personnaz (1980) and Personnaz (1981) for perceptions of physical characteristics; presumably, this should come about more so in the case of opinions, attitudes, and judgements.

8. Unlike the identity theories of Tajfel and Turner (1985), Turner (1987), and Turner and Oakes (1989) we favor the hypothesis of co-variation (Deschamps, 1984a, 1984b, 1988; Deschamps and Volpato, 1984), according to which the personal and social dimensions of identity develop simultaneously and in parallel, and also research into self-other asymmetry (Codol, 1988), which demonstrates the permanent reference to the self in social comparison (Lemaine, Kastersztein, and Personnaz, 1978).

References

Allen, V. L. (1985). Infra-group, intra-group, and inter-group: Construing levels of organization in social influence: In S. Moscovici, G. Mugny, and E. Van Avermaet (Eds.), *Perspectives on Minority Influence*. Cambridge: Cambridge University Press.

Apfelbaum, E. (1979). Relations of domination and movements for liberation: An analysis of power between groups. In W. G. Austin and S. Worchel (Eds.). *The Social Psychology of Intergroup Relations*, Monterey, CA: Brooks/Cole.

Asch, S. E. (1952). *Social Psychology*. Englewood Cliffs, NJ: Prentice-Hall.

Chaiken, S., and Stangor, C. (1987). Attitudes and attitudes changes. *Annual Reviews of Psychology*, 38,575–630.

Clark, R. D., III. (1989). The role of social support and argument refutation in minority influence. III Workshop on Minority Influence, Perugia, 1989.

Clark, R. D., III, and Maass, A. (1990). The effects of majority size on minority influence. *European Journal of Social Psychology*,20,99–117.

Codol, J. P. (1988). Studies on self-centered assimilation processes. CREPCO European Conference: Cognitive Biases, Aixen-Provence.

Crespi, F., and Mucchi-Faina, A. (1988). *Le Strategie delle Minoranze Attive*. Naples: Liguori.

Deschamps, J. C. (1984a). Categorisation sociale et differentiation interindividuelle. *Bulletin de Psychologie*,37,489–500.

Deschamps, J. C. (1984b). Identite sociale et differentiation categorielle. *Cahiers de Psychologie Cognitive*,4,449–474.

Deschamps, J. C. (1988). L'individuel et le collectif dans la représentation de soi: Analyse de quelques modèles théoriques. CREPCO, Actes du Colloque Européen: Construction et functionnement de l'identité, Aix-en-Provence.

Deschamps, J. C., and Volpato, C. (1984). Identità sociale e identità individuale. *Giornale Italiana di Psicologia*,11(2),275–301.

Di Giacomo, J. P. (1985). *Rappresentazioni Sociali e Movimenti Collettivi*. Naples: Liguori.

Doise, W. (1982). *L'explication en Psychologie Sociale*. Paris: PUF.

Doms, M. (1984). The minority influence effect: An alternative approach. In. W. Doise and S. Moscovici (Eds.), *Current Issues in European Social Psychology*, Vol 1. Cambridge: Cambridge University Press.

Doms, M., and Van Avermaet, E. (1985). Social support and minority influence: The innovation effect reconsidered. In S. Moscovici, G. Mugny, and E. Van Avermaet (Eds.), *Perspectives on Minority Influence*. Cambridge: Cambridge University Press.

Farr, R. M. and Moscovici, S. (1984). *Social Representations*. Cambridge: Cambridge University Press.

Guillon, M., and Personnaz, B. (1983). Analyse des représntations des conflits minoritaires et majoritaires. *Cahiers de Psychologie*,3,1.

Haney, C., Banks, C., and Zimbardo, P. (1973). Interpersonal dynamics in a simulated prison. *International Journal of Penology*,1,69–97.

Hollander, E. P. (1958). Conformity, status and idiosyncrasy credit. *Psychological Review*,65,117–127.

Hollander, E. P. (1960). Competence and conformity in the acceptance of influence. *Journal of Abnormal and Social Psychology*,61,365–369.

Hollander, E. P. (1964). *Leaders, Groups, and Influence*. New York: Oxford.

Latane, B., and Wolf, S. (1981). The social impact of majorities and minorities. *Psychological Review*,88,438–453.

Lemaine, G. (1974). Social differentiation and social originality. *European Journal of Social Psychology*,4,17–52.

Lemaine, G., Kasterzstein, J., and Personnaz, B. (1978). Social differentiation. In H. Tajfel (Ed.), *Differentiation between Social Groups: Studies in Social Psychology of Intergroup Relations*. London: Academic Press.

Levine, J. M. (1989). Reaction to Opinion Deviance in Small Groups. In P. B. Paulus (Ed.), *Psychology of Group Influence*, Hillside, NJ: Erlbaum.

Levine, J. M., and Moreland, R. L. (1985). Innovation and socialization in small groups. In S. Moscovici, G. Mugny, and E. Van Avermaet (Eds.), *Perspectives on Minority Influence*. Cambridge: Cambridge University Press.

Lorenzi-Cioldi, F. (1988). *Individus Dominants et Groupes Dominés: Images Masculines et Féminines*. Grenoble: Presse Universitaire de Grénoble.

Maass, A., and Clark, R. D., III. (1984). Hidden impact of minorities: Fifteen years of minority influence research. *Psychological Bulletin*,95(3), 428–450.

Maass, A., and Clark, R. D., III, and Haberkorn, G. (1982). The effects of differential ascribed category membership and norms on minority influence. *European Journal of Social Psychology*,12,89–104.

Maass, A., West, S. G., and Cialdini, R. B. (1987). Minority influence and conversion. In C. Hendrick (Ed.), *Group Processes: Review of Personality and Social Psychology*, vol. 8. Newbury Park, CA: Sage.

Mackie, D. (1987). Systematic and nonsystematic processing of majority and minority persuasive communications. *Journal of Personality and Social Psychology*,53,41–52.

Milgram, S. (1974). *Soumission à l'Autorité*. Paris: Calman Lévy.

Moscovici, S. (1976). *Social Influence and Social Change*. London: Academic Press.

Moscovici, S. (1980). Toward a theory of conversion behavior. In L. Berkowitz (Ed.), *Advances in Experimental Social Psychology*. New York: Academic Press.

Moscovici, S. (1981). On social representation. In J. P. Forgas (Ed.), *Social Cognition*. London: Academic Press.

Moscovici, S. (1985). Social influence and conformity. In G. Lindzey and E. Aronson (Eds.), *The Handbook of Social Psychology*, vol. 2. New York: Random House.

Moscovici, S., and Mugny, G. (1987). *Psychologie de la Conversion*. Cousset: Del Val.

Moscovici, S., and Nemeth, C. (1974). Social Influence II: Minority influence. In C. Nemeth (Ed.), *Social Psychology: Classic and Contemporary Integrations*. Chicago: Rand-McNally.

Moscovici, S., and Paicheler, G. (1978). Social comparison and social recognition: Two complementary processes of identification. In H. Tajfel (Ed.), *Differentiation between Social Groups*. New York: Academic Press.

Moscovici, S., and Personnaz, P. (1980). Studies in social influence V: Minority influence and conversion behavior in a perceptual task. *Journal of Experimental Social Psychology*,16,270–282.

Mucchi-Faina, A. (1987). Mouvement social et conversion. In S. Moscovici and G. Mugny (Eds.), *Psychologie de la Conversion*. Cousset: Del Val.

Mucchi-Faina, A., Maass, A., and Volpato, C. (1991). Social influence: The role of originality. *European Journal of Social Psychology*, 21(3), 183–198.

Mugny, G. (1982). *The Power of Minorities*. London: Academic Press.

Mugny, G., and Papastamou, S. (1980). When rigidity does not fail: Individualization and psychologization as resistances to the diffusion of minority innovations. *European Journal of Social Psychology*,10,43–61.

Mugny, G., and Perez, J. A. (1986). *Le Déni et la Raison*. Cousset: Del Val.

Nemeth, C. (1985). Dissent, group processes, and creativity: The contribution of minority influence. In E. Lawler (Ed.), *Advances in Group Processes*. Greenwich, CT: JAI Press.

Nemeth, C. (1986). Differential contributions of majority and minority influence. *Psychological Review*,93(1),23–32.

Nemeth, C. (1987). Influence processes, problem solving and creativity. In M. P. Zanna, J. M. Olson, and C. P. Herman (Eds.), *Social Influence: The Ontario Symposium*, vol. 5. Hillsdale, NJ: Erlbaum.

Nemeth, C., Swedlund, H., and Kanki, B. (1974). Patterning of the minority's responses and their influence on the majority. *European Journal of Social Psychology*, 4(1), 53–64.

Nemeth, C., and Wachtler, J. (1973). Consistency and modification of judgment. *Journal of Experimental Social Psychology*,16,270–282.

Nemeth, C., and Wachtler, J. (1983). Creative problem solving as a result of majority vs. minority influence. *European Journal of Social Psychology*, 13(1),45–55.

Nemeth, C., Wachtler, J., and Edincott, B. (1977). Increasing the size of the minority: Some gains and some losses. *European Journal of Social Psychology*,7,15–27.

Orfali, B., (1990). *L'Adhésion au Front National*. Paris: Kimé.

Paicheler, G. (1976). Norms and attitude change I: Polarization and styles of behaviour. *European Journal of Social Psychology*,6,405–427.

Paicheler, G. (1977). Norms and attitude change II: The phenomenon of bipolarization. *European Journal of Social Psychology*,7,5–14.

Paicheler, G. (1979). Polarization and attitudes in homogeneous and heterogeneous groups. *European Journal of Social Psychology*,9(1),85–96.

Paicheler, G. (1987). *Psicologia delle Influence Sociali*. Naples: Liguori.

Paicheler, G., and Bouchet, J. (1973). Attitude polarization, familiarization and group process. *European Journal of Social Psychology*,3(1),83–90.

Papastamou, S. (1983). Strategies of minority influence. In W. Doise and S. Moscovici (Eds.), *Current Issues in European Social Psychology*, vol. 1. Cambridge: Cambridge University Press.

Papastamou, S. (1985). Effets de la psychologisation sur l'influence d'un groupe et d'un "leader" minoritaires. *L'Année Psychologique*,85,361–381.

Papastamou, S. (1986). Psychologization and processes of minority and majority influence. *European Journal of Social Psychology*,16(2),165–181.

Papastamou, S., Mugny, G., and Kayser, C. (1980). Echec à l'influence minoritaire: La psychologization. *Recherches de Psychologie Sociale*,2,41–56.

Personnaz, B. (1981). Study in social influence using the spectrometer method: Dynamics of the phenomena of conversion and covertness in perceptual responses. *European Journal of Social Psychology*,11,431–438.

Personnaz, B. (1984). Perspectives sur les liens entre innovation et différentiation sociale, et réactance psychologique et "libertance." *Bulletin de Psychologie*, 365,501–506.

Petrillo, G. (1987). Questioni aperte nell'ambito dello studio dei processi di influenza sociale. In G. Paicheler, *Psicologia delle Influenze Sociali*. Naples: Liguori.

Petrillo, G. (1988a). Le Nemesiache. Evoluzione di un gruppo minoritario. In F. Crespi and A. Mucchi-Faina (Eds.), *Le Strategie delle Minoranze Attive: Una Ricerca Empirica sul Movimento delle Donne*. Naples: Liguori.

Petrillo, G. (1988b). Influence sociale minoritaire et processus d'identification. CREPCO, Atti del Colloque Européen: Construction et Fonctionnement de l'Identité, Aix-en-Provence, Marzo 1988.

Petrillo, G. (1988c). Movimento femminista e processi di influenza sociale. In A. Quadrio and L. Venini (a cura di), *Strutture e Forme del Rapporto di Potere*. Quaderni di psicologia sociale e politica. Milan: Università Cattolica.

Petrillo, G. (1989). Consistency and intragroup differentiation in social minority influence. III Workshop on minority influence, Perugia, Italy.

Tajfel, H. (1972a). La catégorisation sociale. In S. Moscovici (Ed.), *Introduction à la Psychologie Sociale*. Paris: Larousse.

Tajfel, H. (1972b). Experiments in a vacuum. In J. Israel and H. Tajfel, (Eds.), *The Context of Social Psychology*. London: Academic Press.

Tajfel, H. (1982). *Social Identity and Intergroup Relations*. Cambridge: Cambridge University Press.

Tajfel, H., and Turner, J. C. (1985). The social identity theory of intergroup behaviour. In S. Worchel and W. G. Austin (Eds.), *Psychology of Intergroup Relations*. Chicago: Nelson-Hall.

Tanford, S., and Penrod, S. (1984). Social influence model: A formal integration of research on majority and minority influence processes. *Psychological Bulletin*,95,189–225.

Turner, J. C. (1987). *Rediscovering the Social Group*. Oxford: Basel Blackwell.

Turner, J. C. and Oakes, P. G. (1989). Self-categorization theory and social influence. In P. B. Paulus (Ed.), *Psychology of Group Influence*. Hillsdale, NJ: Erlbaum.

Wolf, S. (1987). Majority and minority influence: A social impact analysis. In M. P. Zanna, J. M. Olson, and C. P. Herman (Eds.), *Social Influence: The Ontario Symposium*, vol. 5. Hillsdale, NJ: Erlbaum.

Worchel, S. (1989). Minority influence in the group context: How group factors affect when the minority will be influential. III Workshop on Minority Influence, Perugia, Italy.

PART FOUR

Final Discussion

CHAPTER TWELVE

THREE CONCEPTS: MINORITY, CONFLICT, AND BEHAVIORAL STYLE

Serge Moscovici

Phenomena of Conformity and Phenomena of Innovation

Obviously, each really new area of research emerges in indifference, then surprises people as a curiosity and rouses acute resistance until it ultimately gains recognition. This book deals with an area of research which did not prove an exception to the rule and it was only lately that the value of its contribution to social psychology began to be acknowledged. What does its novelty consist in and, beyond it, why is it an important area? Because the problem it raises has preoccupied every single human being as well as, generally speaking, the life we lead in common. It emphasizes a dilemma of existence which has been a source of inspiration to poets, novelists, and philosophers since time immemorial. To make you understand this, let it suffice to refer to one of the brightest novels in American fiction. In *The Age of Innocence*, Edith Wharton tells a story of unfulfilled love, the subdued tragedy of a man and a woman born into New York society who have sought each other all through their lives, yet have been prevented by something strong and untangible from uniting their hearts' desire. This something is the web of conventions of their circle, the familiar words and gestures, the refined system of customs and mental habits entangling them so that the man cannot follow his inclinations: "Newland Archer was a quiet and self-controlling young man. Conformity to the discipline of a small society had become almost his second nature. It was deeply distasteful to him to do anything melodramatic and conspicuous, anything that Mr. Van der Luyden would have deprecated and the club box condemned as bad form. But he had become suddenly unconscious of the club box, of Mr. Van der Luyden, of all that had so long enclosed him in the warm shelter of habit'' (Wharton, 1968, p. 32).

Every time the young man tries to escape from conformity and break with his social habits, he is brought back to them as a pendulum which, drawn from the vertical, returns to it. Significantly enough, the woman who has awakened in him the wish to revolt and liberate himself from the spell, Ellen Olenska, is a foreigner (at least by her marriage with a Polish count), who leaves her husband and returns to New York and her family. Her mere presence disturbs the existing social scheme, the conventional relations she had rejected. She questions the unquestioned routine in which everyone is caught. When she asks the man she loves: "Do you suppose that Christopher Columbus would have taken all this trouble just to go to the opera with Selfridge Merrys?" she puts these routines in the right perspective. But not even toward the end of his life will Archer dare settle the dilemma between the necessity of revolting to fulfill his great love and the need to conform to the gentle, yet inexorable pressure of New York society, which induces him to renounce his love. This is what gives a tragic meaning to the destiny of this pair like any other. If we are still moved, even fascinated by Edith Wharton's novel, it is chiefly because we recognize in it a choice dilemma which occurs again and again throughout everyone's life; namely, the familiar dualism between the wish to rebel against shared conventions and the wish to strictly comply with them.

Yet the subjective experience of a couple of individuals can be construed as bearing the mark of a profound dualism of societies themselves. And thinkers, at least Western thinkers, have kept referring to it. Remember first the distinction made by Nietzsche between the Apollinian and the Dionysian sides of man: one based on measure, on balanced forces of life, the other on music, liberty of the instincts, enthusiasm, and excess. Nearer to us, Bergson also stated an opposition between closed sociability and morals grounded on obligation, taboo or tradition, and open sociability and morals roused by a novel emotion and the creative passion of individuals. The most famous theories of society presuppose a similar dualism of contrasting social phenomena. Who does not know the distinction drawn by Max Weber (Moscovici, 1993) between the hierarchical bureaucratic institutions which ensure order in everyday life as well as the stability of collective relationships and the charismatic communities that are gathered together by the revelation of a creed, an ideal, bringing about social mutations, social big bangs?

Again the distinction is found in Durkheim between the routine states of life in common and the states of collective effervescence during which a society is renewed and sometimes changes its foundations after some political or religious revolution. In the same spirit, American sociologists have long ago distinguished between social structures and collective movements. What these descriptions and names make clear is the alternation of phenomena of crystallization and phenomena of expansion in which something new emerges in society. Consequently, people do not behave in the same way or follow the same rules or pursue the same goals in the former type of society as in the latter.

Once again, the dualism is not new. It occurs now and again in the history of societies and everyone has observed it several times in recent years. Therefore it is not surprising if the opposition between system and movement, culture and counterculture, has become a cliché of our common understanding. So there is no need for a long demonstration to make you grasp what is obvious from the point of view of social psychology: the former category of phenomena concerns the necessity of conforming, whereas the latter concerns the desire to change and innovate. Which means to stimulate an upheaval of the state of affairs, giving birth to a new representation of self and society, analogous to the one brought about by religious reforms or scientific discoveries. In general a cognitive turning point has happened. But it also results from a common action that at first binds a small group together, as in philosophical or artistic schools, religious dissent, and so on. These are usually described as displaying remarkable energy and stamina, an outstanding level of courage and a grasp of new and complex realities. Therefore, although the ideas and behavior of these groups are unusual, even bizarre by normal standards, they function exceptionally well in the different conditions of what Max Weber called *in statu nascenti*, in the making.

When you ask: "What is social psychology about?" that is, what is the universal elementary phenomenon in which it is interested, the obvious answer seems to be, social influence. In his fine book, *The Social Animal*, Aronson wrote: "The key phrase in the preceding paragraph is 'social influence.' And this becomes our working definition of social psychology: the influence that people have upon the beliefs or behavior of others" (1992, p. 6). What however seems abnormal to us is that, regarding a phenomenon that defines it, social psychology does not take into account a dualism which is so general and only pays attention to the influence of the group or majority on the individual; in short, to conformity. This bias has shaped most of the theories and empirical researches which put the emphasis on stereotypical thinking and modal behavior. It was only about twenty years ago that the phenomena of innovation began to attract the attention of a growing number of researchers. They did not attempt so much to correct the prevailing "conformity bias" (Moscovici and Faucheux, 1972) as to enlarge the meaning of social influence and the key problems concerning it.

So the nature of social influence can be understood from two standpoints: from the side of change of existing beliefs, relations among people, which is innovation; or from the side of reproduction, stability of these beliefs, relations, which is conformity. Now the best angle from which to approach the study of the phenomena of innovation, even if it is not the easiest, is that of the influence that an individual can exert on a group, or active minorities on the majority. This does not at all imply that minorities alone are capable of innovating; far from it. But the fact remains that, in everyone's mind, minorities are associated with novelty, protest, deviance, or dissent. Even in science, radical alterations have come about through their action. Thus the great physicist Heisenberg wrote that, in order to understand such alterations, we have to ask "how was a seemingly small group of physicists able to constrain the others to these changes in the structure of science and thought? It goes without saying that the others at first resisted the change, and were bound to do so" (1974, p. 157).

In a way, it is Heisenberg's question that we tackle in our studies and to which we propose a general solution. These remarks show what is meant by the phrase *minority influence*. It does not concern any minority or any influence, but only the influence that aims at producing an opportunity for innovating. The least known, it is also the most fascinating. We are naturally prompted to inquire how a handful of individuals or even a single individual dare enter the public stage and gain acceptance for their message from a significant proportion of those it addresses and reaches. In many ways, this seems miraculous and these people sometimes become heroes. But the psychosocial processes are general and easy to grasp. In what follows, I will deal with three concepts which are at the heart of the theory of these processes. I will try to satisfy your curiosity for this kind of remarkable fact. To a certain extent, they condense the ideas which have been stated in a very concrete, fruitful way in the preceding chapters.

The Concept of Minority: The "I" and the "Me" of a Group

In his fine essay *On Liberty*, John Stuart Mill advises us as follows. When two opinions face each other, "if either of the two opinions has a better claim than the other, not merely to be tolerated, but to be encouraged, it is the one which happens at the particular time and place to be in minority. That is the opinion which, for the time being, represents the neglected interests, the side of human well-being that is in danger of obtaining less than its share" (1859, p. 186). There is no shame in acknowledging that this proposition makes a deep feeling of justice vibrate in us. Nevertheless, the question which immediately comes to one's mind is: how is it that we spontaneously understand what he means by minority and how do we recognize the image he proposes of it? This is probably because it corresponds to a powerful idea and emotion that we have experienced in our private lives as well as in the community to which we belong. You can see which experience is meant when reading the admirable description which G. H. Mead gives of the life of the self. Breaking the uniform surface at which one usually stops, he discovers an "I" distinct from the "me," opposing each other. The "I" designates in each of us not only an inner force facing the "me" that tends to comply with the outer norms of the group, but chiefly a force tending to react in a vigorous, reflexive manner—especially in situations where a change is necessary. "The individual," Mead wrote, "not only has rights, but he has duties; he is not only a citizen, a member of the community, but he is one who reacts to this community and his reaction to it, as we have seen in the conversation of gestures, changes it. The 'I' is the response of the individual to the attitude of the community as this appears in his own experience. His response to that organized community changes it" (1972, p. 196).

In fact the values of the "I" and those of the "me" do not overlap, so that in one and the same situation their distinct positions receive distinct meanings. According to G. H. Mead (1972), the values of the "I" are those of the artist, inventor, or scientist, implying a reconstruction of society and consequently of the "me" that is part of this society. With this precision, however: "These values are not peculiar to the artist, inventor and the scientific discoverer, but belong to the experience of all selves where there is an "I" that answers to the "me" (p. 216). Such responses are bearers of new visions and momentous social changes. The individuals who formulate them conceive and inspire the reforms in religion or politics. They are the men whose genial inventions push back the frontiers of knowledge, enlarge the world to which they belong. Or, as Mead says of the change they bring about: "It makes separate individuals stand out as symbolic. They represent, in their personal relationships, a new order, and then become representative of the community as it might exist if it were fully developed along the lines that they had started" (p. 217).

This is clearly another instance of the dualism between the tendency to conform and the tendency to innovate. And above all of the inner tension of the self with which we are so familiar. In many regards the opposition between the "I" and the "me" in each individual offers an image and represents more than an analogy of the opposition in each society between the majority and the minority,[1] between the part that conforms and the part that not only resists conformity but also tries to innovate. This is why we have an immediate experience of the former and spontaneously understand what is meant when the latter is mentioned. For my own part, I am convinced that the first opposition reflects in psychic life the character of the second opposition in social life. And it is quite possible that the individuals with whom the "I" predominates are attracted by a minority to which they correspond, whereas those who have a stronger "me" remain true to the majority to which they belong.

This has nothing whatever to do with a type of personality, as it concerns the inner dynamics of values and attitudes existing at a given time in a particular circle. It is, however, difficult to be sure of it, since our information about what individuals experience in social situations where such a tension between the two aspects of the self is manifest, remain scarce.

Be that as it may, I hope that the attitude of the "I" facing the "me" allows you to see intuitively what is meant by a minority which deviates or dissents from a majority. It is a unit formed by individuals who draw apart or are drawn apart from the usual patterns of life and thinking to the point of separating willingly or unwillingly from the mainstream of society. They seem to obey the imperative that Goethe expressed in these terms: "When you are penetrated by this truth, the only thing that is true and really existing for you is what makes your mind fertile, then observe the general course of the world and, leaving it to follow its own road, associate yourself with the minority." Doing this, individuals condemn themselves, at least for some time, to endure the scorn, lack of comprehension or silence of other people. But it is never easy to picture to oneself what is called a minority. Its most vivid and significant features escape definition, which is generally the case with the definition of every important phenomenon.

Nevertheless, we can ask first: "What is a minority?" and then "Who is a minority?" On one hand it is a question of definition, and on the other hand a question of description. The term itself first denotes an inferiority (the Latin *minor* means lesser) and then a small number which opposes the majority in an assembly. Since the eighteenth century, it has essentially designated the minority in the British Parliament. Everyone is aware however that this entailed that the minority did not possess the same prerogatives as the majority and was therefore in a state of inferiority, being excluded from sharing the power.

Whatever its origin, the term can be understood as designating every group that, for whatever reason, deviates or transgresses from the established rules or norms, or dissents, that is, thinks differently from most members of the community. Truth to tell, such a group can now resist passively, now wish to change actively the state of affairs. But the situation made to it at the origin is practically the same. Considered as marginal, it is not granted much credibility. Above all it is kept apart (Festinger, 1950).

The meaning and purport of this definition will become clearer if we examine who are, concretely, these minorities and how their range has evolved over time. "Over the last four and a half centuries," a historian wrote, "those Welsh and Protestant Christians who have chosen to worship outside the Established Church of England have been known variously by the name 'Anabaptist,' 'Brownist,' 'separatist,' 'sectary,' 'dissenter,' 'Nonconformist,' and 'Free Churchman'" (Watts, 1978, p. 1). So we deal here with small religious groups who were later excluded from the government and universities. A fraction of them emigrated, settled in New England and ultimately fomented the American Revolution. The list can be enriched by adding to it all avant-garde political and artistic movements (the Surrealists, for instance), the protesting currents which emerged in the 1960s (feminists, ecologists, etc.) and dissenters generally speaking. A list that is by no means exhaustive, since different cultures consider other minorities and deal with them in specific ways.

There is however one problem we have to tackle. Most of the time, in fact, minorities are groups of a few people, a small fraction of the community. In this case, numbers acquire symbolic value to the effect that the few stand for the idea of minority just as large numbers stand for the idea of mass. And yet, just as large numbers do not define a mass psychically, the small number does not define a minority. A sect of dissenters or a new scientific school may comprise ten or twenty individuals. What makes them a dissenting sect or a revolutionary school is not the sheer number but the fact that, in the first case, they think differently from the Established Church and, in the second case, differently from the established paradigm. Again, as I emphasized elsewhere (Moscovici, 1976), large groups such as women almost everywhere or the blacks in South Africa happen to be treated as minorities and prevented from assuming normal responsibilities and rights (Crespi and Mucchi-Faina, 1988).

So groups are treated as minorities independently of the number and described or diagnosed in an extraordinary manner. In fact, minorities have been pigeonholed, pathologized, deprecated, stigmatized, and dismissed in countless ways. And that, more than anything else, is a vivid index of their definition in and by society. Let us, however, bear in mind the fact that this definition has evolved over time and space, and the range of groups considered as minorities enlarged in the course of history. At first, traditionally, as long as the Roman Catholic church and religion prevailed, the West distinguished as minorities mostly those who opposed orthodoxy, that is, heretics. "Though 'heresy,'" an historian wrote, "may be used of political and other beliefs, it is primarily a doctrine which is at variance with orthodox religious teaching" (Christie-Murray, 1989, p. 1). No doubt individuals suffering from certain ailments, such as lepra, or having certain occupations, like money lending, provoked the same reactions. But, on closer inspection, you can see that they were treated as heretics and described in analogous ways (Cohn, 1975). Moreover the long, cruel history of heresy reveals one of the most universal and fascinating paradoxes. As a rule, contemporary orthodoxy is regarded as an expression of truth and reality, and contemporary dissent rejected as "crazy," "absurd," and treated with mistrust. Yet the same orthodox people speak with veneration of the "heroes and martyrs of the faith whose self-sacrifice in opposing the majority opinion of their time won for their successors the right to believe the 'truth' " (Christie-Murray, 1989, p. 8). This testifies to a remarkable change in the minds of people and in the fabric of society with far-reaching consequences, and accordingly deserves a profound social psychological inquiry.

During the second stage, there appeared, as I said before, political minorities. Labelled as such, in a democracy they enjoyed their own rights which were recognized and protected. In particular, the declaration of the Rights of Man grants them the right to resist oppression and makes it an obligation for the State to tolerate them. From this point of view, the existence of minorities is the index as well as the warrant of a democracy. They were diversified in it at every level, social, intellectual, and artistic, owing to the same principles and rules which were valid in the society. With good reason one could write that, if a democracy such as the United States is alive, it is precisely "because of the multiple movements of minoritarian type criss-crossing the society" (Soulier, 1989, p.65). Whereas the first concern of totalitarian societies, we have seen it in the course of this century, is to detect and ferociously repress such movements.

The third stage at last, which began a short time ago, is characterized by the recognition of ethnic minorities. For all we know, this is a consequence of the taking consciousness of racial phenomena on one hand, and of the decolonization of Asia and Africa on the other hand. This may seem obvious, but it is amazing to see how quickly people have forgotten that the distinction of out-groups (discriminated groups) is a fairly new one. And it results from the action of the discriminated groups themselves who hitherto accepted rather passively the conditions made to them in society. As a French sociologist wrote: "It is not before the twentieth century that dictionaries record the phrases *national minorities* and *ethnic minorities*. The *Littré* [a famous French dictionary, S.M.] does not know them. . . . Thus in this nineteenth century which is so eventful on the plan of nationalities, the political notion of minority is fully ignored outside the parliamentary context. Neither common language nor legal language know of national minorities. Everything happens as if they did not exist" (Soulier, 1989, p. 41).

It was only later that the difference between "autochthonous" and "ethnic" peoples became relevant and assumed the importance it has today.

All things considered, the broad definition of what minorities are is the same: groups that are more or less restricted and singularized by a way of thinking and different values, outside the norm. But their number and diversity have been growing in the course of their evolution as new issues were embodied by them in society. The focus of attention shifted in accordance with public interest. So we must resist the temptation of reducing them to a single category. And yet, from the point of view of social psychology, they have something in common—that is, their possibility of acting on the majority, influencing it in the direction of innovation. In this sense, the analogy with the "I" is a fruitful one. Everywhere they represent the subjective, energizing part of society, which offers alternatives and stimulates it to change. If it were not the case, we would not understand why minorities have existed since time immemorial and, whether in religion, art, science, politics, or fashion, have been so amazingly successful.

Dissensus and Consensus

One fact strikes us by its universality. To the people in their society, minority groups and individuals appear unwanted, dangerous, eccentric, nonconformist, or irrational and are avoided as such. At the same time, they are seen as figures of awesome power whose action can exemplify the difference between progress and stagnation, knowledge and ignorance, freedom and bondage. Therefore, they stand at the head of a lineage of people who have fought, vanquished, discovered, or created, so that ordinary people look upon them with admiration or envy or both. They are the heroes of mankind—artists, rulers, saints, scientists, and philosophers who inspire and lead, search and enlighten, and whose lives stand out as examples to the unrecognized potentials within each of us. Their lives have been immortalized by stories, legends, and biographies. Everybody has wondered and puzzled about them, venerated and even worshipped them. They have often been thought of as being more than just human, even when they made no such claims. It is useful to remember that Christians were deprecated and denigrated as enemies of mankind before they were seen as its saviors, socialists as enemies of society before they were accepted as its reformers. Socrates was condemned for corrupting youth and fighting religion and only later became the emblematic figure of philosophy. Galileo was judged a heretic, and a long time elapsed before he was recognized as the founder of modern science. Freud was denigrated in every possible manner before a myth began to be built around him.

What I want to suggest through these examples is that minority groups and individuals always rouse these two opposing attitudes, one of attraction, the other of hostility or rejection. In truth, one is inseparable from the other,

241

for what attracts us most of the time, the novelty of ideas or actions, at the same time repels us by the conflict or break of consensus it provokes. In *Moses and Monotheism*, Freud explains very clearly why a scientific theory is not accepted at once. At first,

> the new truth awoke emotional resistances; these found expression in arguments by which the evidence in favour of the unpopular theory could be disputed; the struggle of opinions took up a certain length of time; from the first there were adherents and opponents; the number as well as the weight of the former kept on increasing till at last they gained the upper hand; during the whole time of the struggle the subject with which it was concerned was never forgotten. We are scarcely surprised that the whole course of events took a considerable length of time; and we probably do not sufficiently appreciate that what we are concerned with is a process in group psychology.

Obviously these remarks are of general import and, beyond science, apply wherever change or innovation is at stake. Still more important for us is Freud's assertion that the existence of a conflict and its evolution is a phenomenon of group psychology. Indeed other thinkers have agreed with him, as with Cooley, that "conflict, of some sort, is the life of society, and progress emerges from a struggle in which individual, class, or institution seeks to realize its own idea of good" (1909, p. 199). Among those who agreed we can name Lewin (1948), as long as he took an interest in the situation of minority groups. He stressed the necessity of deliberately creating conflicts in order to ensure the existence and emancipation of the group. But, as the American sociologist Coser remarked, a few years later Lewin's thinking took another turn: "He is still concerned with conflicts, but with avoiding them, rather than fighting them out. In this new context it is taken for granted that social conflicts are dysfunctional and disintegrating and that the social scientist must concern himself with their reduction" (1956, p. 25). Since then, social psychology has attempted to replace the notion of conflict with the notion of tension, inconsistency, disequilibrium, strain, etc. This is why the notion does not play in social science the part it plays in social reality.[2]

Now it goes without saying that the possibility for a minority to have influence depends on its capacity for creating such a conflict among the members of the majority, fueling and handling it skillfully. From its very beginnings, our theory has contended that this is a condition not only of every social influence, but also of every creative reconstruction of life in common.

In an illuminating paper, Levine clearly summed up the meaning of this point of view: "Moscovici takes issue with the traditional view that majorities are sources (but not targets) of influence, whereas minorities are targets (but not sources) of influence. This view dominates research on group influence since the early 1950s when Festinger published his influential paper on informal social communication. It assumes that opinion uniformity is essential to the group welfare, that minorities are troublemakers who threaten this uniformity, and that majorities force minorities to conform to their position or expel them from the group. In contrast, Moscovici argues that both minorities and majorities can be sources as well as targets of influence. He urges social psychologists to pay attention to social change (or minority influence) as well as to social control (or majority influence). His interest in social change is based on the assumption that opinion uniformity is sometimes detrimental to group welfare, that minorities often have valid points of view, and that minorities can prevail if they resist conformity pressure and argue forcefully for their position. Thus, unlike previous theorists, Moscovici asks us to take seriously the possibility that groups can undergo revolutionary change and that minority dissent is an essential catalyst for such change'' (1991, p. 3).

If dissent is essential, so is the ensuing conflict. Why? When a minority emerges, in the ideal case it changes a problem latent in communication into an open issue. To this issue it proposes its own solutions which sometimes entail the necessity of altering the predominant way of thinking and norms. As long as they were predominant, everyone knew what was true or false, allowed or forbidden, good or bad, superior or inferior, and so on. But when the order of these categories is questioned by a minority, as has recently been the case with ecologists or feminists, then the members of the majority are bound to resist and to argue in their favor. Their very resisting and arguing is proof that they recognize the existence of an alternative where none existed before, of a difference in opinions and conceptions in order to attain a certain goal or explain a phenomenon. Where one point of view prevailed, there are now two points of view facing each other, the new one offering an alternative to the old one. If the minority persists in a resolved, coherent way, what at first appeared as a mere disagreement turns into a conflict between two contradictory positions, evaluations, and so on. The sharpening of these contradictions is the condition *sine qua non* for moving from one point of view to another, from an existing social relation to a new one.

This is why we can say that every innovating minority is a creator of conflict, and that the interaction between minority and majority revolves around the emergence of a conflict where none existed before, therefore around the discovery of new solutions regarding the issue at stake. No doubt this conflict can take the shape of a polemics, a debate, a confrontation, even an exclusion. But it can also turn into an intense dialogue in which the majority faces the minority as one individual faces another, an *ego* a real *alter* of whom he becomes conscious. In a sense, this is on the social plan the dialogue between "I" and "Thou" of which Martin Buber wrote: "Here it is certainly no longer just that the *Thou* is ready to receive and disposed to philosophize with the *I*. Rather, and preeminently we have the *Thou* in opposition because truly we have the other who thinks other things in another way. So, too, it is not a matter of a game of draughts in the tower of a castle in the air, but of the binding business of life on the hard earth, in which one is inexorably aware of the otherness of the other but does not at all contest it without realizing it; one takes up its nature into one's own thinking, thinks in relation to it, and addresses it in thought" (1991, p. 227).

Yes indeed, the conflict between the opinions of the majority and those of the minority that is first external tends to become internal to group members. Everyone weighs the pros and cons, tries to assess their degree of truth or falsity, feels attracted by the new point of view at the same time as they refuse it. Without mentioning the attempts to suppress the new opinions and ideas, turn away from them as heretic or unacceptable. A suppression of which one knows that it usually produces the effect contrary to that which is sought. In any case, this type of internal dialogue and struggle obviously conduces to seeing one's own ideas and attitudes in a different light. And, as the event may be, to altering them by accepting the new ideas and perceptions which were hitherto in the minority and peripheral in the individual's field of consciousness.

These are said to be "converted" when a new perception or new ideas become more or less central among their cognitions: "To say that a man is 'converted' means," William James wrote, "that religious ideas, previously peripherial in his consciousness, now take a central place, and that religious aims form the habitual centre of his energy" (1979, p. 196).

The same could be said of any kind of idea, the psychological mainsprings being really very similar. Here it suffices to say that a number of careful studies (Maass et al., 1987; Mugny, 1982; Papastamou, 1987) suggest that such a process is plausible and allows us to discover surprising phenomena. To simply avoid the underlying notion would be an unfortunate bias, preventing us from exploring many unusual aspects of social influence.

Another consideration is that Charlan Nemeth's new and stimulating research (1986, 1987) has shown to what extent pressures towards conformity are detrimental to the creativity of group members. Above all, the mere presence of a minority has a much more liberating effect than was supposed. It provokes divergent thinking which enables them to grasp and propose new solutions to existing problems. And to heuristically alter their previous perceptions and ideas, like a painter inventing a new theme or a scientist a new theory, and so on. This is a very interesting and as yet not fully explored or understood form of change. As if the response of the "I" to the "me" became more energetic and the search of diversity was given as an example and preferred to the search of uniformity which usually prevails. Clearly this form of change deserves more attention and careful research. Then the initial notions of the theory will be seen to have been refined and enriched beyond our present state of the art. This will be the case for the notion of conflict as for the rest, at least we can hope so.

The Semantics of Influence

The time has come, however, to inquire how an active minority can impose its point of view as an alternative different from and even opposed to that shared by the majority. After all, it could simply be ignored and no attention paid to it. Another question is why, things being such, it ultimately exerts influence on the individuals who are compelled to resist, even reject it. Yes, our wonder comes from the fact that it is obvious from the start that such a minority lacks the minimal strength to successfully make its presence felt. It has neither the status that would give it sufficient power to make itself feared, nor the recognized expertise that would invest its evaluations and judgments with some authority. It is not even credible, since people consider it inferior and sometimes judge it irrational as they deny it common understanding.

It is something of a mystery to know what "the power of the powerless"—a phrase coined by the former dissident, now Czech President Havel—consists in and come from. Thus we are again faced with the question: given the initial powerlessness of the minority, why does it exert influence nevertheless? One might answer that truth and the importance of the ideas contained in the message suffice to explain its impact. No doubt, they contribute to it, yet Gibbon has raised an unquestionable objection against such an explanation when he asked the question why the religion of a handful of Christians obtained such remarkable success: "Our curiosity, he wrote, is naturally prompted to inquire by what means Christian faith has obtained so remarkable a victory over the established religions of the earth. To this inquiry an obvious but unsatisfactory answer may be returned: that it was owing to the convincing evidence of the doctrine itself, and to the ruling Providence of its great Author. But as truth and reason seldom find so favorable reception in the world, and as the wisdom of Providence frequently condescends to use the passion of the human heart, and the general circumstances of mankind, as instruments to execute its purpose, we may still be permitted, though with becoming submission, to ask, not indeed what were the first, but what were the second causes of the rapid growth of the Christian church?"

In his splendid prose and learned balancing of arguments, Gibbon firmly suggests that the reason for the influence of a small group cannot be sought in the cognitive value of its doctrine and even less in a supernatural intervention. Consequently, the problem of the ascension of the Christian doctrine on the world stage has to be approached from another side. If firstly the minority is in a disadvantageous situation, and secondly the cognitive value of its ideas and message does not make up for it, then there needs to be a third factor explaining the influence it manifestly exerts on the majority. We have surmised (Moscovici and Faucheux, 1972; Moscovici and Nemeth, 1974) that this factor is what has been termed behavioral style. This is to be understood as deliberate reflexive practices by which groups not only pattern their acts and verbal expressions, but also try to express where they stand, conveying information about what they are. Behavioral style can therefore be defined as a set of elements interconnected by a regularity of expression over time and space, which makes manifest to an audience what an individual or groups intends, or the image they try to create. This is why one has to observe how they express themselves rather than listen to what they say. Style is in fact what reveals their attitude and intention, whereas discourse or "message" can be comparatively common.

Underlying the pattern of expression, where is the tacit hypothesis that everyone is able to understand its message in the frame of a common culture. So that the pattern is designed both to be decoded in a precise way and produce a specific cognitive and emotional effect. Thus a sentence uttered in a quick rhythmical firm voice will be decoded as an order, and the same words in a low interrogative voice deciphered as a prayer. In short, an individual or group must try to produce by its behavioral style a "stimulus" that, when rightly deciphered, will achieve just the intended effect.

This lesson is learned early in life. Just remember how children attract the attention of their parents. When a little girl wants her parents to feel sorry, the best behavioral style is to cry, show her bleeding knee, and desperately claim their help. On the other hand, when persuasion is intended, repetition constitutes the elementary behavioral style to attract and focus the attention of an audience. In the simplest way, it creates an impression of presence and the insistent reiteration of arguments on a given theme elicits the idea of how important it is. In other cases, by repeating various tones one and the same opinion, either by using different yet synonymous words, or by various quotations of one and the same tenor, one creates an impression of urgency of the answer expected by the person who communicates this opinion. To return to the example of children, this is the case for a little boy or girl who tries to persuade his or her parents to buy him or her a toy or take him or her to a play, and so on.

So far we have defined (Moscovici, 1976) several behavioral styles—

consistency, fairness, objectivity, etc. They are like the vehicles which carry the message one wants to communicate. Even more they serve as a context shaping the meaning of the discourse, ideas, etc., which individuals or groups want to share with others. Therefore they tend to express the relationship between ''who says'' and ''what is said,'' between the standpoint one takes and the firmness with which it is held. To be even more explicit, it is not the conflict of opinions or beliefs as such that is heuristic, but the meaning it takes for everyone. Now the behavioral styles of a minority or majority give a certain meaning to the conflict, as they express either their readiness to make concessions or their will to bring matters to a head. A large number of studies have demonstrated that the kind and amount of influence is determined by the behavioral style associated with the message and the clearness with which it is perceived.

Among behavioral styles, consistency chiefly stands out, as it seems to be most often used by the minority and its effects have been best studied (Moscovici, 1980; Mugny, 1982; Maass et al., 1987; Mugny and Perez, 1986; Papastamou, 1987). Whether expressed by the repetition of arguments, a firm position, or coherence between what one says and what one does, it is felt to be an index of deep conviction, courage, or certainty. It makes you understand that the assured tone, trust in ones ideas, or self-confidence do not denote an artificial or provisional attitude. They are dictated by a choice that is neither fluctuating, nor revocable according to circumstances. Luther's famous words, *Here I stand*, illustrate such a behavioral style. People recognize it and can judge him who adopts it either positively (tenacious or single minded) or negatively (rigid, headstrong, or simple minded). But, whatever the judgment, consistency over time makes the minority position visible and compels the majority to pay attention to it and take its point of view into account.

In addition, by expressing a firm commitment of the minority, the consistent behavioral style clearly declares that it will not concede anything about what it believes. Therefore, if people want to agree, if consensus is to be achieved, the concessions must be made by the majority individuals. In fact, the minority cannot make any, for a concession from minority individuals would appear as a lack of conviction, a weakness or defeat. It will make people skeptical about both the value of its ideas and its adhesion to the chosen position. Which creates around it an atmosphere of doubt and contempt. All things considered, by behaving consistently, a minority not only clarifies the difference between its own opinions and the majority's, the conflict between minority and majority also becomes more intense and visible. A kind of tacit negotiation ensues during which it becomes obvious that only a certain amount of yielding from the majority—an index of minority influence—could reduce this conflict. This is a situation which

Schelling described with great precision: "In bargaining, the commitment is a device to leave the last chance to decide the outcome with the other party, in a manner that he fully appreciates; it is to relinquish further initiative, having rigged the incentives so that the other party must choose in one's favor" (Schelling, 1956, p. 294).

In other words, a minority that proposes an alternative, takes a firm stand and shows itself committed to it, compels the majority to accept its proposal or ideas so as to find an outlet. No matter whether conscious or not, the influence effect is unquestionable. A great many experiments have verified the hypothesis according to which consistent behavioral style produces a change of attitudes, perceptions, and judgments. Lately, reading the writings of the great dissenters of Eastern Europe (Solzhenitsyn, Havel, and Sakharov, among others), I was struck by their concern with finding a behavioral style that allowed them to face their common adversary in a regime which ruled out every possibility of existence for minorities. Now the style they had spontaneously discovered is consistency, demonstrating through it their independence, commitment, and zeal in the service of the chosen cause.

Consistency expresses self-control and makes it appear in the eyes of the majority as a calm, resolute force that quite naturally forbids one to obey any other conviction but one's own. At the same time, it commands respect, intimidates, and attracts. For such a degree of self-control is rare and everyone would like to be capable of showing the same. Besides, it is a very old thing. Nearly two thousand years ago, the Christian thinker Tertullian wrote: "The very 'obstinacy' you reproach us with is instructive. Who, in fact, is not shaken at such a sight and does not seek for what lies deep down in the mystery? Who has sought it without joining us? Who has joined us without aspiring to suffer so as to buy divine mercy in its plenitude, obtain from God entire forgiveness at the price of his blood?" (1961, p. 12).

Somehow a minority acts on people and exerts its influence by a skillful handling of symbols, by the semantics of behavior and words, eliciting from its audience specific emotional and intellectual responses. And this is enough to change its handicap into an asset.

I have probably drawn a schematic and perhaps simplistic picture of what a behavioral style is, of its reasons for being and its effects. In a series of original researches, Mugny and his colleagues (Perez and Mugny, 1990; Mugny and Perez, 1990; Personnaz and Personnaz, 1987) have not only explored these reasons and effects but also the diverse styles. We still have to attempt to give more precise descriptions of them and study in more depth their role in persuasion and even in communication in general. Now, after promising preliminaries, we have somewhat neglected the work that is indispensable for clarifying one of the key notions of our theory and even of social psychology. If I have mentioned it, nevertheless, it is to remind you that the semantics of behavioral styles is an answer to the question: "How does a man make another believe something?" An answer that was invented by mankind through ritual, prayer, speech, and the choreography of actions which bind people together owing to this very fact.

This seems an appropriate point to stop at. I have not tried to comment upon the chapters in this book or to sum up their contents. Each author has done it better than I could do and paraphrasing their texts and ideas would be a lack of reverence toward them. In many respects, it would have meant forcing to uniformity a field of research which is rather diverse and fluid. So I judged that there was no fitter conclusion for a book which gathers together so many young talents than stating the tripod of general motions, minority, conflict and behavioral style, on which our work rests. These notions are also unfamiliar and different in social psychology, so that we have both to discuss and make them known. Have I done it clearly and convincingly enough? It is certainly not for me to judge.

I would like to end on a personal memory. My first meeting with Leon Festinger took place at a time when the first ideas about minority influence were sketched and the first experimental findings began to come in. It was normal that we discussed them and I must say that his first reactions were rather critical but very quickly became favorable. During one of our discussions, he said to me firmly what amounted to this: "No doubt you have discovered a new problem in social psychology, but you do not know what it will lead you to." He was right, but it seems to me in retrospect that it has led us toward phenomena which are much more surprising than we thought at the time. This book gives also an idea of the distance we have travelled. I hope it will attract fresh researchers toward what remains, all things considered, a scientific adventure.

Notes

1. Undoubtedly the analogy I propose between the division of the self and the division between minority and majority may seem conventional. It is not completely so, however, when one takes into account their historical association. According to some indications, the notion of "Ich," which we translate "I," would have been coined among the sects and religious dissenters, so as to express the quest for individual liberty, individual consciousness, and the possibility of communicating directly with God. Thus the notions of the Moravian brethren, the Puritan the Wesleyans allowed the formulation of an equation between self and consciousness (cf. Mauss, 1950).

2. In fact, a deeper question would be, Why has social psychology, especially in the United States, managed not to pay any attention to such groups? Not only because this country was founded by dissenters, but also because religious innovation

and political dissent are endemic in American culture. To be sure, they were studied as "objects" of stereotypes, discrimination, and so on. They have however very seldom been studied as "subjects" in this process. The answer, one can suppose, is the same in social psychology as in history. "Religious outsiders," Robbins wrote, "have continually played a key role in American religious history, but the importance of their contribution has been obscured by a tradition of 'consensus' history" (1988, p. 10).

References

Aronson, E. (1992). *The Social Animal*. 6th ed. New York: Freeman.

Buber, M. (1991). *Between Man and Man*. New York: Collier.

Christie-Murray, D. (1989). *A History of Heresy*. Oxford: University Press.

Cohn, N. (1975). *Europe's Inner Demons: An Enquiry Inspired by the Great Witch-Hunt*. London: Chatto and Heinemann.

Cooley, Ch.H. (1909). *Social Organization*. New York: Scribner's Sons.

Coser, L. (1956). *The Functions of Social Conflict*. New York: Free Press.

Crespi, F., and Mucchi-Faina, A. (Eds.). (1988). *Le strategie delle minsranze attive*. Naples: Liguori.

Festinger, L. (1950). Informal social communication. *Psychological Review*, 57, 271–282.

Freud, S. (1937–1939). *Moses and Monotheism*. Standard Edition. Vol. 23. London: Hogarth and the Institute of Psychoanalysis.

Heisenberg, W. (1974). *Across the Frontiers*. New York: Harper.

James, W. (1979). *The Varieties of Religious Experience*. London: Penguin.

Levine, J. (1991). Symposium on Majorities, Minorities and Persuasion. Mimeo. Columbus (Ohio), Society of Experimental Social Psychology.

Lewin, K. (1948). *Resolving Social Conflicts*. New York: Harper.

Maass, A., West, S. G., and Cialdini. R. B. (1987). Minority influence and conversion. In C. Hendrick (Ed.), *Group Processes*. Newbury Park, CA: Sage Pubns.

Mauss, M. (1950). *Sociologie et Anthropologie*. Paris: P.U.F.

Mead, G. H. (1972). *Mind, Self and Society*. Chicago: University of Chicago Press.

Mill, J. S. (1859). *On Liberty*. London: J. W. Parker.

Moscovici, S. (1976). *Social Influence and Social Change*. New York: Academic Press.

Moscovici, S. (1980). Toward a theory of conversion behavior. In L. Berkowitz (Ed.), *Advances in Experimental Social Psychology*, Vol. 13, New York: Academic Press.

Moscovici, S. (1993). *The Invention of Society*. London: Politeia.

Moscovici, S., and Faucheux, C. (1972). Social influence, conformity bias and the study of active minorities. In L. Berkowitz (Ed.), *Advances in Experimental Social Psychology*, Vol. 6. New York: Academic Press.

Moscovici, S., and Mugny, G. (1983). Minority influence. In P. B. Paulus (Ed.), *Basic Group Processes*. New York: Springer Verlag.

Moscovici, S., Mugny, G., and Van Avermaet, E. (Eds.). (1985). *Perspectives on Minority Influence*. Cambridge: University Press.

Moscovici, S., and Nemeth, C. (1974). Social influence II: Minority influence. In C. Nemeth (Ed.), *Social Psychology: Classic and Contemporary Integrations*. Chicago: Rand McNally.

Mugny, G. (1982). *The Power of Minorities*. London: Academic Press.

Mugny, G., and Papastamou, S. (1984). Les styles de comportement et leur représentation sociale. In S. Moscovici (Ed.), *Psychologie Sociale*. Paris: P.U.F.

Mugny, G., and Perez, J. A. (1986). Le déni et la raison. *Psychologie de l'Impact Social des Minorités*. Cousset: Delval.

Mugny, G., and Perez, J. A. (1989). L'influence sociale comme processus de changement. *Hermès*, 5/6, 227–236.

Mugny, G., and Perez, J. A. (1990). Les routes de la persuasion: vers une intégration théorique. *Bulletin Suisse des Psychologues*, 8, 21–27.

Nemeth, C. (1986). Differential contributions of majority and minority influence. *Psychological Review*, 93, 23–32.

Nemeth, C. (1987). Influence processes, problem solving, and creativity. In M. P. Zanna, J. M. Olson, and C. P. Herman (Eds.), *Social Influence*: The Ontario Symposium, vol. 5. Hillsdale, NJ: Erlbaum.

Nemeth, C. and Kwan, J. (1987). Minority influence, divergent thinking and detection of correct solutions. *Journal of Applied Social Psychology*, 9, 788–799.

Papastamou, S. (1987). Psychologisation et résistance à la conversion. In S. Moscovici and G. Mugny (Eds.), *Psychologie de la Conversion*. Cousset: Delval.

Perez, J. A., and Mugny, G. (1990). Minority influence, manifest discrimination and latent influence. In D. Abrams and M. A. Hogg (Eds.), *Social Identity Theory, Constructive and Critical Advances*. New York: Harvester.

Personnaz, B., and Personnaz, M. (1987). Un paradigme pour l'étude expérimentale de la conversion. In S. Moscovici and G. Mugny (Eds.), *Psychologie de la Conversion*. Cousset: Delval.

Robbins, T. (1988). Cults, Converts and Charisma. London: Sage.

Schelling, T. C. (1956). An essay on bargaining. *American Economic Review*, 46, 281–306.

Soulier, G., (1989). Minorités, etat et société. In A. Ferrier and G. Soulin (Eds.), *Les Minorités et Leurs Droits depuis 1784*. Paris: L'Harmattan.

Tertullien, S. F. (1961). *Apologétique*. Paris: Belles-Lettres.

Watts, M. R. (1978). *The Dissenters from the Reformation to the French Revolution*. Oxford: Clarendon Press.

Wharton, E. (1968). *The Age of Innocence*. New York: Scribner's.

INDEX

Abortion opinions, 28, 50, 117
Activators of minority influence, 173–78
"Advocatus diaboli," 75
Afrikaaner, as a minority, 24
Afterimage, 28, 167–68
The Age of Innocence, 233–35
Aggregates, 105–6
Alternative psychiatry, 214, 220, 223
Ambiguity, 192, 197
Anagram experiment, 105–6
Anticonformity, 123
Apollian side of man, 234
Argument quality, 151, 155–58
Argumentation, 78
Aronson, E., 235
Asch-like tasks, 201
Assimilation, 115, 116–19, 220–22
   and personal autonomy, 117
   and time delay, 117
Asymmetrical relationships, 211
Asymmetry effect, 49, 50–51. *See also*
   Symmetric vs. asymmetric position
Attitude change, 12, 63
Attitudinal judgments, 70
Attraction feelings, 126, 177–78
Attribution, principles of, 68
Attributional accounts, 71
Augmenting principle, 72
Autokinetic effect, 67, 166, 191
Automatic information processes, 125, 126
Autonomy. *See* Personal autonomy
Aversion feelings, 126
Awareness of theory, 76

Behaviorial style, 246–50

Biased thinking, 151
Bipolarization phenomenon, 119. *See also* Group polarization
Birth control opinions, 28, 117
"Black box approach," 48
Blacks, 50. *See also* South Africa
Blue-green paradigm. *See* Color slide experiment
Blue-green studies. *See* Color slide experiment
Boomerang effect, 119–20, 127
Bredes, Nora, 149
Buber, Martin, 244

Camouflage strategy, 118
Carmichael, Stokeley, 21
Categorization. *See also* Social categorization
   and influence, 197
   of majority, 197
Category width scale, 38
Central route processes, 125
Change. *See also* Influence
   direct vs. indirect, 5, 28–30, 64, 116
   majority vs. minority sources, 62–64
   nature of, 63
   stages of, 170–71
Cheese experiment, xi, 190–93
Choice
   dilemma, 77, 107, 234
   individual behavior in group situations, 79
Choice-Dilemmas Instrument, 49
Churchill, Winston, 55
Clandestine reference system, 169, 172
Cognition, need for, 143–44

CONTRIBUTORS

Fabrizio Butera has a doctorate in psychology and is currently research assistant at the University of Geneva, Switzerland.

Russell D. Clark, III, is professor of psychology at the University of North Texas, Denton. His primary research interest is social influence, with a particular emphasis on minority influence.

Dawna Coutant is a Ph.D. candidate, Department of Psychology, Texas A&M University, College Station, Texas. Her main research interests are interpersonal relations and power.

William D. Crano is professor of communication and psychology, Department of Communication, University of Arizona in Tucson. His main research interests are social influence and attitude change, cross-cultural psychology, and research methods.

Michele Grossman is a Ph.D. candidate, Department of Psychology, Texas A&M University, College Station, Texas. Her main research interests are interpersonal conflict and human psychophysiology.

Claude Kaiser has a doctorate in psychology and is currently a researcher at the Psychopedagogical Research Center (CRPP) in Geneva, Switzerland.

Douglas T. Kenrick is professor of psychology at Arizona State University, Tempe. His main research interests are mate selection and an evolutionary perspective of social-psychological processes.

Anne Maass is associate professor at the University of Padua, Italy. Her main research interests are minority influence and stereotyping, particularly the role of language in sterotype maintenance.

Serge Moscovici is professor of social psychology at the Ecole des Hautes Etudes en Sciences Sociale, Paris, France, and at the New School for Social Research in New York City. His main research interests are minority influence, social representations, and cultural psychology.

Angelica Mucchi-Faina is researcher and temporary professor (*professore affidatario*) of social psychology at the University of Perugia, Italy. Her main research interests are social influence and intercultural relations.

Gabriel Mugny is professor of social psychology at the University of Geneva, Switzerland.

Charlan Jeanne Nemeth is professor of psychology at the University of California at Berkeley. Her primary research interests are creativity, quality of decision making, social and numerical minorities as agents of change and creativity, and social influence.

Juan A. Pérez is professor of social psychology at the University of Valencia, Spain.

Bernard Personnaz is Directeur de Recherche (CNRS) at the Ecole des Hautes Etudes en Sciences Sociale, Paris, France. His main research interests are minority influence and dynamics of change processes, intergroup context and social influence, and differentiation, social identity, and unequal intergroup relations.

Marie Personnaz is teacher of social psychology at the Paris X Nanterre University, France. Her main research interests are social influence and attitude change, and self-image and social identity in influence context.

Giovanna Petrillo is a researcher in social psychology and temporary professor (*professore affidatario*) in psychology of language and communication at the University of Naples, Italy. Her main research interests are minority influence, persuasion, social representations, and communication processes, as well as the feminist movement and the psychiatric movement in Italy, particularly the discursive strategies of influence.

Patricia Roux has a Ph.D. in sociology and currently is a researcher at the Swiss Foundation for Scientific Research (FNRS), University of Lausanne, Switzerland.

Melanie R. Trost is assistant professor of communication at Arizona State University, Tempe. Her primary research interests are minority influence strategies and relationship communication (attraction, flirtation, and jealousy).

Chiara Volpato has a Ph.D. in social psychology and is currently at the University of Padua, Italy. Her main research interests are intergroup relation, minority influence, and the social psychology of literature.

Erich H. Witte is professor of psychology at the University of Hamburg, Germany. His main research interests are small groups, intimate relationships, technology transfer, and technology assessment.

Stephen Worchel is Ella C. McFadden Professor of Liberal Arts, Department of Psychology, Texas A&M University, College Station, Texas. His primary research interests are group dynamics, intergroup relations, and conflict resolution.